Garland of Visions
(DARŚANAMĀLĀ)

Garland of Visions

(Darśanamālā of Narayana Guru)

With an Extensive Commentary by
Swami Muni Narayana Prasad

D.K. Printworld (P) Ltd.
New Delhi

Cataloging in Publication Data — DK
[Courtesy: D.K. Agencies (P) Ltd. <docinfo@dkagencies.com>]

Narayana Prasad, *Muni*, 1938-
Garland of visions = Darśanamālā of Narayana Guru / with an extensive commentary by Swami Muni Narayana Prasad.
ix, 326 p., 23 cm.
Text of Darśanamālā in Sanskrit (Devanagari and roman); translation and commentary in English.
Includes index.
ISBN 812460391X

1. Narayana Guru, 1856-1928. Darśanamālā. 2. Advaita. 3. Philosophy, Hindu. I. Narayana Guru, 1856-1928. Darśanamālā. English & Sanskrit. II. Title.

DDC 181.4 22

ISBN 81-246-0391-X
First published in India in 2007

Published and printed by:
D.K. Printworld (P) Ltd.
Regd. Office: 'Sri Kunj', F-52, Bali Nagar
Ramesh Nagar Metro Station
New Delhi-110 015
Phones: (011) 2545-3975; 2546-6019; *Fax*: (011) 2546-5926
E-mail: dkprintworld@vsnl.net
Website: www.dkprintworld.com

Preface

VEDĀNTA's ultimate teaching is that there is one Reality alone. As there is but one single Reality, each person is inseparably one with the whole, with the one changeless Reality underlying all that is changeful. Directly realizing this oneness requires no teaching or learning; it only has to be experienced, like a wave finding its oneness with the ocean. But conveying this apparent secret to someone else, in a systematic manner, taking into account everything we know about ourselves as individuals, about the total universe, and about the one all-underlying Reality, makes a science of it. That science is what we now call Vedānta.

The most authentic source of Vedānta is the Upaniṣads, authored by some ancient *ṛṣi*s of India, who preferred their names remain unknown while their teachings remaining ever known. Narayana Guru, a *ṛṣi* of the Age of Science, restored the essential content of the Upaniṣadic wisdom, and restated it in terms quite understandable to the mindset of the modern age. This he accomplished with as many as fifty-two original works spread out in three languages — Malayalam, Tamil and Sanskrit.

In the *Darśanamālā*, his most important Sanskrit work, the Guru adopts a hitherto unattempted method, to systematically expound what he intends to teach. The method is that of visualizing the one and one-dual Reality — *Brahman*, the Absolute — that beginninglessly and endlessly assumes the form of all the worlds of endless variety, from ten different philosophical vantage points. In doing so he leaves the seeker-student to intuitively perceive or realize within oneself, or as oneself, that one Reality. These ten visions together form a garland, so to say, to be worn by the seeker on his or her own.

The Guru's three consecutive disciple-successors, strangely enough, happened to write three separate commentaries on this unique text. Nataraja Guru's commentary, in reality is more than a commentary. He re-introduces the work as forming the nucleus of a Science of sciences. *Brahman* being the one Absolute Reality that assumes the form of everything perceivable and conceivable in all the worlds, which form the object matter of all the sciences, a science that expounds that *Brahman* has, has necessarily to be the one Science that could find expression as all the sciences. Such is the perception with which Nataraja Guru, the first disciple of Narayana Guru, interpreted *Darśanamālā* in his *An Integrated Science of the Absolute.* His disciple-successor, Nitya Chaitanya Yati, in his *Psychology of Darśanamālā*, approached the text from a rather psychological point of view, that means, treating the theme of the work as a science that deals with consciousness and its functions, for *Brahman* in essence is pure Consciousness. The present commentary written by another disciple of Nataraja Guru and next in succession to Nitya Chaitanya Yati as the Head of Narayana Gurukula, tries to look at the text to find out how it revisualizes and condenses the core-teaching of the Upaniṣads in a way comprehensible to the modern mind, while fully acknowledging the tradition. These three commentaries, thus, are mutually complementary. Each supplements and derives inspiration from the previous one.

It is the mysterious Will of *Brahman* that makes Itself creatively unfold as all the apparent knowable objects as well as subjects, the writing and publishing of books not excluded. It may look strange that the same Will worked in this case in such a way that these three commentaries happened to be published in succession by one and the same publishing firm, namely, Messers D.K. Printworld. All of us, associated with Narayana Gurukula, are very grateful to them for bringing out these commentaries and our other publications with the quality these books deserve, thereby bringing Narayana Guru to the attention of the world at large.

In fact, the ideas contained in this commentary are not my own. The first ever commentary on the text by Swami Vidyananda, a direct disciple of Narayana Guru, who happened to be the compelling force behind the Guru writing this text, was also of great help. Similarly, helpful was the daily discussion I had with a group of Gurukula students at our evening prayer sessions. The commentary on each verse is an outcome of such discussions, and the dictation of it was given then and there. My gratitude to these students, whose names I do not mention here, is measureless. Dr Peter Oppenheimer, a long time friend and disciple of Narayana Gurukala, took great pains to go through the entire commentary, editing it and very often giving clarity to certain points after discussing it with me.

Finally, I remember with great love, all the friends of Narayana Gurukula, who had always encouraged me in my writing career, particularly on Narayana Guru and his philosophy.

I am sure this commentary of *Darśanamālā* will help to a great extent to look at Vedānta as *brahmavidyā* in its broadest sense, as the Science of sciences, as the Upaniṣads claim themselves to be *sarvavidyā-pratiṣṭhā* (the firm foundation of all sciences). Of course, more elucidations in the future would be necessitated, and it is our sincere hope that competent followers in the future will take up this responsibility, to the full satisfaction of the inquisitive seekers of those days. It is with such a hope that this commentary is offered as an altar-flower at the feet of my direct *guru*s as well as all the *guru*s of the past, to be made use of by all those who are interested in enlightenment on the oneness of Reality, and thus the oneness of mankind.

Swami Muni Narayana Prasad

Narayana Gurukula
Srinivasapuram, P.O.
Varkala – 695 145, Kerala
23rd October, 2006

Contents

Introduction

WHAT is the meaning of life? Who am I? Whence this world? Such fundamental problems get cleared in the intuitive vision of certain exceptional individuals. Their vision, when systematized, is known as *darśana*. This vision implies a high degree of unfaltering certitude.

The problems that well up in the minds of inquisitive seekers may be many. The nature of the problems depends mostly on the life-interest of the seeker and the point of view he or she chooses. When all such possible problems find resolution in the wake of such a transparent vision of Reality, it is considered a comprehensive school of thought. Such schools of thought, in India, are known as *darśana sampradāya*s. Of many such Indian schools, the one that dominates others in respect of clarity, comprehensiveness and integrity is Advaita Vedānta, also known as Advaita Darśana.

Vedānta is the one school of thought well-remembered by those who are interested in Indian philosophy. But many other schools of thought also have their legitimate place in the history of Indian philosophy. The Nyāya system given shape to by the sage Gautama, the Vaiśeṣika system conceived by the sage Kaṇāda, the Sāṁkhya system of the sage Kapila, the Yoga system of Patañjali, the Pūrva Mīmāṁsā system of Jaimini and the Uttara Mīmāṁsā system formulated by the sage Bādarāyaṇa are the six schools that admit the Vedas, the most ancient scriptures of India, as authoritative. These schools together are known as *āstika darśanas*, meaning "orthodox systems." What is called Vedānta is none other than the Uttara Mīmāṁsā system.

The basic texts of Vedānta are three — the Upaniṣads, *Brahma-Sūtras* and *Bhagavad-Gītā* — together known as *prasthāna-trayī*. The masters (*ācāryas*) who commented on them differed in their interpretations, often one going against that of another. This resulted in the emerging of different schools within Vedānta itself. Śaṅkara's Advaita (non-dualism), Rāmānuja's Viśiṣṭādvaita (qualified non-dualism), Madhva's Dvaita (dualism) or Tattva-vāda (basic philosophy), Nimbārka's Dvaita-advaita (dualistic non-dualism), Vallabha's Śuddhādvaita (pure non-dualism), Caitanya's school of devotion to Kṛṣṇa — these are some important Vedāntic systems. The *Vedānta-Sūtras* of Bādarāyaṇa being the one text that all these *ācāryas* commented on, they differed on the essential content of Vedānta mainly based on this one text. Each commentator claimed that his was the real intention of the original author Bādarāyaṇa.

Schools of thought that do not accept the authority of the Vedas also exist in India. Such schools generally are known as *nāstika darśanas* (heterodox schools). The most important of them are Cārvāka (Indian materialism), Jainism and Buddhism. Buddhism itself has within its four sub-schools, known as Sautrāntika, Vaibhāṣika, Yogācāra and Mādhyamika. Both the orthodox and heterodox lines of thought thus have their own separate six schools or *ṣaḍ-darśanas*. Yet the name *ṣaḍ-darśanas* is commonly used referring only to the orthodox schools.

All these schools of thought were formulated millennia ago. The long flow of time since then effected many changes in the way of man's thinking, and the Age of Science emerged. Narayana Guru appeared as a world-teacher at this juncture.

He, as a true representative of the Upaniṣadic seers, reformulated and restated their vision of Reality, with a clarity and methodological cogency that strictly is in line with that of the Age of Science. Moreover, he lived as wisdom-incarnate, showing through his own personal life how wisdom could enlighten man's day-to-day life, making it worth living and of high value.

Narayana Guru was an Advaitin (non-dualist) as he has openly declared himself. This in no way means that he was simply repeating what Śaṅkara said. What Śaṅkara did basically through his commentaries was to prove that the philosophy of the *prasthāna-trayī* was non-dualism and nothing else. Śaṅkara systematized that philosophy by strictly adhering to the sense of scientificity that prevailed then. He claimed that all other schools, whether orthodox or heterodox, were defective in one respect or another, and that Advaita alone was the one faultless philosophy acceptable to any reasoning mind. For this reason, his presentation of philosophy was rather argumentative in style, and hence the name Advaita-vāda given to his philosophy, *vāda* meaning "argument."

Narayana Guru, on the other hand, never tried to prove how superior is non-dualism to other schools. Instead, the Guru perceived how non-dualistic vision encompasses within it all lines of thought, philosophical, religious or even scientific. He simply made his own the finality of the transparent vision of Reality of the Upaniṣadic ṛṣis, and in his own style he restated it in a way understandable and appreciable to a modern mind. He, in short, was not an Advaita-vādin, but was an Advaitin pure and simple.

It was through Śaṅkara's commentaries on the *prasthāna-trayī* that he made Advaita a systematic school of thought. The method he relied on in those commentaries was always that of arguing for his stand and arguing against those of others. Narayana Guru's method was entirely different. He wrote no commentary on any text. He, on the other hand, made clear what he visualized directly in his own words, as his original works, adopting a unique style of his own in each case. Such works embody the pristine clarity of an Upaniṣadic *ṛṣi*, while being saturated by the spirit and preciseness of a modern scientific thinker. Śaṅkara was a commentator, of olden days, of the Upaniṣads. Narayana Guru, on the other hand, was an Upaniṣadic *ṛṣi* of the modern age. This difference is quite evident both in the context and style of presentation of their philosophies. Śaṅkara's arguments for non-dualism apparently gave room for later opponents to pinpoint many weak points and thus to argue against it. The non-dualism represented by Narayana Guru, on the other hand, is so comprehensive that none of the arguments raised against Śaṅkara would be relevant.

Śaṅkara brought in many technical terms and original concepts that have no place either in the Upaniṣads or the *Bhagavad-Gītā*, in order to systematize the thought he developed. The concepts of *jīvātmā* (individuated self) and *paramātmā* (supreme self), perceiving what is real as pertaining to the realms of *vyāvahārika* (transactional), *pāramārthika* (ultimate) and *prātibhāsika* (illusory), the notions of *para-Brahman* (the higher Absolute) and *apara-Brahman* (the lower Absolute), classifying bodily existence into *sthūla śarīra* (gross body), *sūkṣma-śarīra* (subtle body), and *kāraṇa-śarīra* (causal body), the idea of *pañca-koṣa*s (five sheaths) are some such. Whether deliberately or not, such accretions did not find place in the works of Narayana Guru.

The Guru expresses himself in his own unique way in his *Ātmopadeśa Śatakam* (One Hundred Verses of Self-Instruction), *Advaita Dīpikā* (Lamp of Non-duality), *Arivu* (Consciousness),

Brahmavidyā Pañcakam (The Science of the Absolute in Five Verses), *Darśanamālā* (Garland of Visions), and *Vedānta-Sūtras*. The first three are in the Malayalam language, and the rest in Sanskrit. Since Bādarāyaṇa wrote his *Brahma-Sūtras*, which might have happened at least 2500 years ago, no master, except Narayana Guru, in the very long history of Indian philosophy, dared to put in efforts to codify the essence of Vedānta in *sūtra* style. Narayana Guru did it by writing his original *Vedānta-Sūtras*, consisting merely of twenty-four *sūtra*s. What the *ācārya*s, who commented on the *sūtra*s of Bādarāyaṇa, did in effect was creating confusion in the minds of impartial seekers as to the real intention of Bādarāyaṇa. The water in the pool of Vedānta that remained muddy for a very long time as a result of this confusion created by the contending schools of Vedānta, was for the first time made clear again by Narayana Guru's new *Vedānta-Sūtras* text. But the Guru did not follow the argumentative style adopted by Bādarāyaṇa and continued by Śaṅkara. Instead, he simply restated the essential content of the Vedānta philosophy as an original vision, adopting a strictly scientific methodology.

In his Malayalam work *Ātmopadeśa Śatakam* (One Hundred Verses of Self-Instruction) the Guru presents his philosophy in a comprehensive way. His Advaita philosophy is dominated by one basic notion: the non-dual ultimate Reality, called *ātmā*, is Consciousness in essence; all the world emerge in that one Reality as do waves in the ocean. And this happens because of the creative urge for self-unfoldment inherent in *ātmā*. *Ātmā* cannot remain without manifesting as the world; and this world cannot exist without *Ātmā* underlying it as its causal substance. How the one Consciousness remains the substratum of all that appears to be and how it assumes the apparent form of the phenomenal world, both subjective and objective, is the theme dealt with in the work *Arivu* (Consciousness).

After Śaṅkara's systematization of Advaita and its elaboration by his later followers, a sort of rigidity crept into the precincts of Vedānta, making it more like a mechanistically conceived science. This style became so well-rooted in Vedānta that anyone who preferred to be off its beaten track would be treated as a heretic. Re-energizing Vedānta from this state of inertia by imbuing it with a new life of scientificity is what Narayana Guru accomplished through his philosophical poems. Most of such earlier works, except *Brahmavidyā Pañcakam*, were in the Malayalam language, and hence inaccessible to the orthodox Vedantins familiar only with the Sanskrit background. *Brahmavidyā Pañcakam* was the only earlier work of the Guru in Sanskrit, and in it he followed Śaṅkara's line of thought, though his originality peeps out through its lines here and there. Still, it was not a comprehensive work.

Some senior disciples of the Guru, Swami Vidyananda among them, realized that the Guru had already made sufficiently clear what he intended to say as a wisdom-teacher. They felt that those who were familiar only with the traditional Vedānta would never have the opportunity to appreciate the originality of the Guru's philosophical vision. Hence Swami Vidyananda made an appeal to the Guru to write a Sanskrit work expounding his philosophy in a comprehensive way. The Guru asked him to be always beside him with a notebook and pencil and to take down the verses as and when they slipped out of his mouth. *Darśanamālā* was its outcome.

Darśanamālā is a *mālā* (garland), a garland of visions of Reality. Sāyaṇa Mādhava, a disciple of Śaṅkara, wrote *Sarva-darśana-saṁgraham*, a compendium of the essentials of all the schools of Indian philosophy existing then. Eighteen systems are included in it, which include some systems, like Pāṇini's grammar, that normally are not counted as of any philosophical import. Some historians of literature happened to evaluate Narayana Guru's *Darśanamālā* also as a similar compendium. Actually, *Darśanamālā* is not such a garland.

Reality, ultimately, is one alone. It could be visualized from various perspectives. It is similar to enjoying the beauty of a monument built with perfect architectural taste, by viewing it from different angles. Each point of view gives a different picture of the beauty of the structure, whereas the structure remains differenceless. The observer formulates an idea of the overall beauty of the monument with the help of the various pictures he gets from the different perspectives. Similarly in the *Darśanamālā,* the one Absolute Reality — *Brahman* — is visualized from ten different perspectives, each vision constituting one chapter. Each chapter depicts how the one Reality looks when viewed from the particular point of view it chooses. None of such visions is meant to be treated as more important or true than another. All are equally important, as are the beads in a garland. Certain specifics perceived in a particular chapter may be relevant only as related to the particular perspective of the chapter. The non-dual ultimate Reality is to be intuitively perceived by the seeker-student as that which gives room for all such varying visions. It, in other words, remains invisible and unstated in this work, like the invisible thread that strings all the beads together. The job of the reader or rather of the seeker-student is seeking out this invisible thread, and stringing together all the visions into a garland to be worn around his own neck. Real *jñānins,* the enlightened ones, on the other hand, are those who are already having this garland around their neck.

Paving the way for a new avenue in the methodology of Vedāntic speculation is what the Guru accomplishes in this work. The previously existing method was that of putting forth all philosophical problems one by one, answering them by holding fast to the basic stand of the school of thought, and thus expounding the overall picture of the school. The Guru here, taking an entirely different path, adopts the method of viewing the non-dual Reality from different philosophical angles, describing how the vision appears from each point, and then leaving to the student or seeker the task of making use of these visions to arrive at a comprehensive experiential awareness of the otherwise ineffable Reality. It seems, none of the earlier philosophers, either in the East or the West, has tried his hand at this novel method. The one that comes very near is of Henry Bergson.

Adhyāropa (superimposition), *apavāda* (negating what is superimposed), *asatya* (the unreal), *māyā* (illusion), *bhāna* (self-manifestation of consciousness), *karma* (action), *jñāna* (knowledge), *bhakti* (contemplation on the adorable), *yoga* (union), *nirvāṇa* (final absorption) — these are the ten chosen points from which what is ultimately Real is examined systematically in the work. These ten visions are the beads strung into a garland. Any garland naturally should have a well-conceived structural arrangement of its own, and the two ends have to be tied together. The positioning of the beads in between the ends also has to be perfect. And after all, a pendant should beautify it at its middle. All such details are evident in this garland of visions also.

The first *darśana* (vision) is from the point of view of an inquisitive ordinary man. He sees the world as existing as it appears to be. Then he asks himself, "From where and how was this world originated?," "Who created it?," "Why was it created?" Answering such questions in a way understandable to the ordinary man, the first chapter ends with the statement that one *Parameśvara* (Supreme God) is the causal Substance and Creator of all these worlds. If at all a Creator (Brahmā), a

Sustainer (Viṣṇu), a Destroyer (Maheśvara) are to be conceived, such deities are nothing but the same Parameśvara conceived as pertaining to specific functional contexts and He alone is everything. The final chapter (*Nirvāṇa-darśana*), on the other hand, ends by asserting that one and non-dual *Brahman* alone exists, and that one who realizes that *Brahman* as the Reality in the being of oneself, realizes complete absorption with *Brahman*, a state beyond all dualities. In other words, the individual originated as a specific manifest form of the Absolute, finally realizes his or her self-absorption with the same Absolute. Perceived thus, the final verse of the first chapter and the final verse of the final chapter look like two sides of a single coin. These are the two ends of the garland tied together.

Relating systematically the observing individual, the observed world and the all-underlying Reality is the major task of all philosophising. Here, in this work, the first five chapters are devoted to relate the world with the ultimate Reality in different ways. This part begins with the idea that the world is a created one, and ends with the subtlest perception that the world is nothing more than the functional manifestation of one Consciousness. The second half concentrates on how the observing individual and the Reality are one in essence. This part begins with examining the most phenomenal aspect of the external activities (*karma*s) of individuals, and ends with the individual experiencing his or her final absorption in *Brahman*. The beads of the garland, thuswise, could be seen as gradually increasing in size in respect of subtlety in the first half, and gradually decreasing in size in respect of grossness of experience, in the second half. *Darśanamālā* thus is a perfectly and beautifully shaped garland.

An Overview of the Chapters

ADHYĀROPA DARŚANAM (VISION BY SUPERIMPOSITION)

That the world really exists as it is perceived with our senses, is a common notion. A question arises out of it: how did this world originate? The first chapter is in the form of answering this question.

The Advaita school teaches that the world is an appearance superimposed on *Brahman*. The present chapter is named Adhyāropa Darśana in the sense that it makes an enquiry as to how the superimposed appearance of creation, sustenance and dissolution emerges. This emerging of the apparent world is compared in this chapter to dreams seen while asleep, to magic shows, to seeds sprouting, to a talented artist's painting, to the yogic attainments of *siddha*s, to a devilish city, to the experience of the sudden emergence of the world felt by a person who wakes up from sleep, and to the growth of a giant banyan tree from a tiny seed. The creator of this world is first conceived as *Parameśvara* (the Supreme God), and finally this *Parameśvara* is equated to everything created (*sarva eva saḥ*). The creation of the world, in other words, if at all it happens, takes place within the being of *Parameśvara*. It is not a creation that takes place gradually, but is an instantaneous creation, comparable to the sudden emergence of the world felt by a man who wakes up from sleep. In Vedānta such a concept of creation is known as *yugapat sṛṣṭi* (instantaneous creation). It is the same *Parameśvara*, the Causal Reality, that is named Brahmā (causal to creation), Viṣṇu (causing the sustenance of created beings), and Śiva (effecting dissolution). Really *Parameśvara* alone exists. What is thought of as creation in this context is nothing more than superimposing the apparent form of the world on that one *Parameśvara*, and the vanishing of such appearances is what is called dissolution or *laya*.

APAVĀDA DARŚANAM (VISION BY NEGATION)

We are accustomed to taking to be real the apparent world-form superimposed on *Brahman*. An earnest seeker should, therefore, perceive only the real as being real. A seeker of Truth should search for the substance that underlies all evanescent apparent forms. The unreal appearance is called *pratīti*, the whole world thus is a *pratīti*. The reality that causes this *pratīti* is what is to be searched for. If appearance is considered as effect (*kārya*), then the underlying reality is cause (*kāraṇa*). The search in this context, therefore, is for the cause of all effects. Visualizing this cause as *Brahman*, *sat*, *cit*, *ānanda* (existence, consciousness, value-experience) in essence, forms the core of the teaching of this chapter.

Apavāda means "refutation" or "negation." What the chapter negates in order to assert the irrefutable is the unreal effect. Negating effect and asserting cause, in other words, is the methodology of this chapter. No effect is substantially real. Effects have no being apart from the causal substance, just as a pot has no existence apart from clay. This stand of Vedānta is known as *sat-kāraṇa-vāda* (the theory that cause alone is real). Śaṅkara was its chief proponent. The causal substance, *Brahman*, alone thus has real existence; all that appears as the world is nothing but various apparent forms superimposed on *Brahman*. Unless and until we realize this Truth, life remains full of problems and sufferings, the worst of such being that of death. Ignorance of the Real is what pushes us into the mire of having to undergo repeated births and deaths.

ASATYA DARŚANAM (VISION BY NON-EXISTENCE)

It was seen in the previous chapter that the world is merely an effect manifesting in the causal Reality. The superimposed effect's real being is rather in the mind of the observer than in the causal Substance, and in that sense, the effect is unreal. What is real is *sat-cit-ānanda* alone. Everything specific is projected onto this Real. All such projecting functions take place in the mind, and to that extent, the entire world could be thought of as mind-made or mind in essence (*mano-mayam-idam sarvam*). The mind projecting the world-experience onto *Brahman* happens only because of the *avidyā* (ignorance) inherent in it. Though unreal like a dream, the world imagined by mind causes fear to itself. *Avidyā* vanishes only at the dawning of *vidyā* (knowledge of the Real), and the unreal world also disappears then. What then remains as real would be one Substance onto which previously everything was projected. This Substance appearing as the world remains throughout without undergoing any intrinsic change to itself. An effect emerging as a result of the material causal substance undergoing substantial change, as in the case of milk curdling into yogurt, is called *pariṇāma* (evolution). According to the Guru, there is no place for such an evolution in the creation of the world. Instead, the world emerges as a *vivarta* (illusory appearance). This implies that the appearance of the unreal world is assumed by the mind while the cause itself remains unchanged, as in the case of a piece of rope appearing as a snake, or water appearing as waves. This *vivarta* is caused by *māyā*, and freeing oneself from the grip of it results in the emerging of *Ātmā* as the one and only Reality. One then realizes: *Ātmā* alone is what appears as the world, just as it is nothing but stone that appears as a *śivaliṅga*.

The one all-underlying causal Reality, in the last chapter, was seen as *Brahman*. On the other hand, *māyā* is what is stated in the present chapter as the primal cause. Are there two such different causes for the world? It cannot be so. The causal Reality perceived in the last chapter was the ontological substance. *Māyā* has no such ontological status. *Māyā*'s causality, on the other hand, is of an epistemological order. To clarify it: our mind malfunctions resulting in perceiving the real as the unreal world, just as in the case of seeing a piece of stone as a *śivaliṅga*. This malfunction of mind, common to all, is the domain of *māyā*. And because of it the real remains unseen and the unreal seen. It is in this particular sense that *māyā* becomes causal to the world-appearance. Resulting in a delusion and the consequent appearance of the world, this cause is not the material one, but is of an epistemological order. That is to say, it is related to something that happens within knowledge.

In short, *Brahman* and *māyā* being causes of the world, are notions that pertain to two different contexts or frames of reference within philosophy. Many frames of reference, different in nature, would have to be relied upon in a systematized philosophy. The difference between the two frames of reference we are concerned with here, could well be clarified thus: *Brahman* is the real substance or *sat* that underlies the unreal world-appearance. Knowing is one of the functions of *cit*, like *sat*, another defining factor of *Brahman*. This knowing function could go wrong sometimes; it is then that the unreal world is thought of as real. How does this happen? The answer is, "It is because of *māyā*."

MĀYĀ DARŚANAM (VISION BY MĀYĀ)

It was stated in the last chapter that *māyā* causes the wrong notion that the world has its own existence. What is this *māyā*? It is a mysterious factor that has no existence of its own, yet is inherent in *Brahman*. The present chapter sheds light on the various aspects of this *māyā*'s effects. The chapter begins with the enigmatic definition of *māyā*: "That which has no existence is called *māyā*" (*na vidyate yā sā māyā*). Its effects appear as dualities like *vidyā* and *avidyā* (science and nescience), *parā* and *aparā* (the transcendental and the non-transcendental), and *tamas* (darkness), *pradhāna* (potential), *prakṛti* (nature or creative self-unfoldment) and the like. *Māyā* being non-existent, its effects, though seemingly existent, are also to be understood as really non-existent.

Māyā, as a methodological device to explain the mysteriousness of what is ultimately Real, was first formulated by Śaṅkara. According to him, *māyā* and *avidyā* are almost synonymous, the only difference being that *māyā* is related to total beingness and *avidyā* to individuated beingness. The vision of *māyā* represented by Narayana Guru, on the other hand, conceives both *vidyā* and *avidyā* as dualities that become manifest as the effects of *māyā.* Knowledge can become right or wrong, *vidyā* or *avidyā,* only when Consciousness functionally unfolds itself in the form of knowing. Both *vidyā* and *avidyā,* as two different functional modes of one and the same Consciousness-Reality, are unreal, and thus the effects of *māyā.*

Śaṅkara conceived *māyā* as having two powers, namely, *āvaraṇa* (putting a veil on what really exists) and *vikṣepa* (projecting something unreal on the real). This differentiation is not made by Narayana Guru. He simply conceives the entire power of *māyā* as *āvaraṇa.* Unveiling the *āvaraṇa* and directly perceiving what is hidden behind, is part and parcel of the spiritual discipline a seeker has to undergo. *Māyā,* in the present chapter of the *Darśanamālā* too, is conceived as having *vidyā-avidyā, parā-aparā* and all such factors as the veil put on the Reality. The serious student must remove them on his or her own in order to see Reality directly.

For this reason, a peculiarity is noticeable in the case of this chapter. The vision conceived in each chapter is put in a nutshell in the concluding verse in each case. This chapter alone is an exception. Being *māyā-darśanam,* it is left to the student or seeker to remove the *māyā*-veil and perceive what is covered over by it. What precisely is that ultimately perceived Reality is not directly stated at the end of the chapter. The subtlety implied in visualizing the non-dual Reality in this context is explicated by the Guru himself in his *Ātmopadeśa Śatakam*, Verse 72, as follows:

> Activity, on the one side, constitutes *avidyā*. On the other side comes *vidyā*, *cit* in essence. Though remaining constantly bifurcated thus because of *māyā*, the metadual intuitive perception yields *turīya* experience.

BHĀNA DARŚANAM (VISION BY MANIFEST FORMS OF CONSCIOUSNESS)

The ultimate Reality is unconditioned *sat-cit-ānanda*. Of these three, when the *cit* aspect is separated out conceptually, the apparent world would have to be seen as the functional modes of that *cit* or unconditioned consciousness, and such functional modes are known as *bhāna*s. Such is the way the Reality is perceived in this chapter.

Conscious experience (*bhāna*) could either be subjective or objective. Such *bhāna*s are classifiable as *sthūla* (gross), subtle (*sūkṣma*), causal (*kāraṇa*) and the fourth (*turīya*). The Guru in this chapter takes care to clarify how even the seemingly external gross objects are also simply specific functional modes of the one unconditioned Consciousness or *cit*. Each such *bhāna*-context has involved in it a generic and a specific conditioning factor. So too the *bhāna* and *bhānāśraya* sides (functional modes and the bases of functional modes) are to be distinguished. Even *turīya*, traditionally equated in Vedānta to the transcendental state of yogic merger, is also treated by the Guru here as a *bhāna*, yet another deviation from the line of thought of Śaṅkara. It is to be explained thus: *turīya* too, when conceptualized, becomes conditioned, and to that extent it is one of the *bhānas*, and cannot be counted as the transcendental state of merger, where no conceptualization has any role.

Whatever finds expression as a functional mode is conditioned, and that which is unconditioned, is the pure and ineffable Consciousness or *cit* alone. The only verbal expression possible concerning that unconditioned *cit* is this much: *sat* alone is That (*sad eva tat*).

In the Śaṅkara School *sthūla*, *sūkṣma* and *kāraṇa* are the names given to the bodies (*śarīras*) the self assumes in its waking, dreaming and deep sleep states. The self abiding in these bodies is known as Vaiśvānara, Taijasa and Prājña respectively. The Guru here perceives everything, bodies included, as merely manifest forms of Consciousness or as *bhānas*. For this reason, the names *sthūla*, *sūkṣma* and *kāraṇa* are given by the Guru to different levels of *bhāna* rather than to bodies. And *turīya* also gains a status equal to these three.

These five visions, as already stated, show how the world-appearance and one underlying Reality could be seen as one and inseparable, from five different perspectives. The first chapter perceives the world as an emanation from, and inseparable from, Parameśvara, the one Reality. The second chapter conceives the world as effect and *Brahman* as cause, from which this effect is inseparable. The third one sees the world as unreal. If so, what is real? This question is answered. The fourth chapter pre-conceives the world as an illusion effected by the non-existent *māyā*. How then the real is to be attained by the seeker by freeing himself from the grip of *māyā*, is stated in an indirect way by delineating various effects of *māyā*. The fifth chapter perceives the entire world, both subjective and objective, as an aggregate of the functional modes of one Consciousness, which in itself is unconditioned. The world, in other words, is the conditioned form of Consciousness.

The remaining five chapters, in a similar manner, show five facets of the individual seeker's attaining oneness with the Absolute Reality or *Brahman*.

KARMA DARŚANAM (VISION THROUGH ACTION)

The previous chapter as well as the first half of the work terminated with the word *tat*, meaning "That," signifying *Brahman*. It is the very same *Brahman* that manifests itself as every individuated self or *ātmā*. The next half of the work as well as *Karma Darśanam*, therefore, meaningfully begins with the word *ātmā*.

It was clearly seen in the *Bhāna Darśanam* that the entire world, both subjective and objective, both subtle and gross, is nothing but the aggregate of the conditioned manifestations of the one unconditioned Reality or Consciousness. This Consciousness, called *Ātmā* also, is creative because of the *māyā* inherent in it. And this creativity, become manifest, appears as all the activities everywhere in the world. Every individual performs *karma*s (actions) both internal and external, both voluntary and involuntary. Such *karma*s find expression either bodily, verbally or mentally. All such *karma*s have no being other than as part of the overall *karma* of *Ātmā* or *Brahman*. Similarly, *karma*s like wind blowing, water flowing, fire burning, rain pouring down take place externally in the cosmos. Within each being also occur involuntary actions like breathing, blood circulating, heart beating and so on. All really take place in one *Ātmā* alone. All such *karma*s are seen in *ātmā* because of the non-existent *māyā*. *Ātmā*, on its own has no *karma*. All *karma*s, in other words, are merely superimposed on the one *Ātmā*, the one underlying, actionless Substance.

JÑĀNA DARŚANAM (VISION BY KNOWLEDGE)

One's own beingness becomes apparent to oneself in the grossest way in the activities (*karma*s) one is engaged in. All such *karma*s were seen in the last chapter as really taking place in the Self, in the Ultimate Reality. Subtler and more interior than *karma*s are the knowing functions peculiar to each. And this function too takes place nowhere else other than in the one Consciousness-Substance or *Ātmā*. The present chapter perceives all the various kinds of knowledge as arising in one Consciousness.

This chapter is named *Jñāna Darśanam*. The word *jñāna* in it does not connote the final wisdom Vedānta aims at. It, on the other hand, signifies the knowing function normal with each individuated consciousness. Such knowing could either be unconditioned or conditioned in form. The former is one alone, and that is the *ātma-jñāna* Vedānta ultimately aims at. The same, in a different way, is termed *para-jñāna* as the chapter ends. All others are conditioned knowledges. *Anātma-jñāna* (knowledge of the non-self), *yathārtha-jñāna* (knowledge of actualities), *ayathārtha-jñāna* (knowledge of that which is not actual), *pratyakṣa-jñāna* (perceptual knowledge), *anumiti-jñāna* (inferential knowledge), *upamiti-jñāna* (knowledge by comparison) *jīva-jñāna* (knowing oneself as an individual), *indriya-jñāna* (sense knowledge) — these are some discernible conditioned knowledges.

The one non-dual Self-Reality, according to the perception of this chapter is to be intuitively visualized as the Consciousness-Substance that unfolds itself as both conditioned and unconditioned knowledges.

BHAKTI DARŚANAM (VISION BY BHAKTI)

Different levels of certainty attained in knowledge were delineated in the *jñāna-darśana* as the conditioned forms of one *jñāna*. The present chapter, going one step deeper, shows *bhakti* as more subjective and intimate than knowing. *Bhakti* means, developing a sort of intimacy through contemplative adoration, with that which one finds to be of the highest value. And this most valuable object is nothing but *ātman*. *Bhakti*, therefore, is defined as *ātmānusandhāna* (constant contemplative adoration of *ātmā*). And this *ātmā* is nothing but *Brahman* in essence. *Bhakti*, then, could also be defined as *Brahmānusandhāna* (constant contemplative adoration of *Brahman*). *Ātmā* or *Brahman* is sought by a seeker aiming at unconditioned Happiness (*ānanda*). No one contemplates on anything that gives unhappiness. Therefore, *bhakti* could be defined also as meditation on *ānanda*. A real *bhakta* is one who is fully convinced of the oneness of *ātmā*, *Brahman* and *ānanda*. He always remains filled with the feeling "I am *ātmā*," "I am *Brahman*," "I am *ānanda*." *Bhakti*, when seen as meditation on *ānanda*, does not exclude from its scope the adoration a husband has for his wife and vice versa, one's love for God, for one's *guru*, father, mother, king and the like.

Bhakti, particularly as understood in the religious context, suggests a sort of emotional attachment towards God or deities. So is *bhakti* defined in the *Nārada Bhakti-Sūtra* also, as, *bhaktiḥ parama-prema-rūpā* (*bhakti* comprises supreme love). But much different is the rather philosophical *bhakti* conceived here. Still it is not to be concluded that the ordinary *bhakti* was not also favoured by the Guru. His earlier works, particularly the hymns, are soaked in such a *bhakti*.

The ultimate Reality, according to the *Bhakti Darśana*, is to be visualized intuitively through meditation. This meditation could be *ātmā*-based, *Brahman*-based or *ānanda*-based. Such a philosophical *bhakti* culminates in the supplicant experiencing identity with that which he adores contemplatively. This experience of identity is called *yoga*.

YOGA DARŚANAM (VISION BY YOGA)

Ātmā, the absolute Reality, is consciousness (*cit*) in essence; and so it is called *cidātmā*. The seeker deliberately uniting himself with this *cidātmā*, and remaining fully united with it, constitutes the essence of *yoga* conceived by the Guru here. This experience of self-identity, of course, involves restraining the mind (*mano-nirodha*). What is called mind (*manas*) here is really nothing but the very same *cit* finding expression as the functions of imagining, fancying and thinking. *Manas*, in other words, in essence is the very same *cidātmā*. Such is the mind that is now in search of *ātmā* or *cidātmā*.

The searching *manas*, to attain this goal, does not have to do anything other than looking inwardly at itself and perceiving itself in essence as *ātmā* or *cidātmā*. Then it realizes: "I am but a tiny spark of the great bon-fire of *ātmā*." With this realization it becomes natural for the *manas* to become uninterested in the external petty affairs of the world. Adding the positive effort to withdraw the mind from worldly interests, completes the picture of *mano-nirodha* (restraint of mind) as understood by the Guru here.

To make oneself unified with *cidātmā* (*yojayati*), to remain united with *cidātmā* (*yunakti*) — both these are involved in the *yoga* conceived here. If the former stands for means (*sādhanā*), the latter represents ends or attainment (*siddhi*). The unity of ends and means is also implicit in *yoga*.

The seeker (*sādhaka*), in the usual course, is the subject (*dṛk*) and the end attained pertains to the objective side (*dṛśya*). The object attained here being what is real in one's own being, the subject-object duality is also subtly transcended in this *yoga*-concept.

The ultimate Reality, according to this chapter, is visualized in the form of the pure *yoga* experience where the experiencer and the experienced merge together non-dually.

Many are those who practise various yogic postures by straining the body in different ways. Of such practices, one of the most difficult is *khecarī-mudrā*. A reference to it is made by the Guru, but the status given to it is that it helps reduce sleepiness and sluggishness. The Guru's biographers have put in record the event of the Guru making a general remark about practising yogic postures, that they are good in helping easy removal of phlegm from the body. More than all such bodily exercises, *yoga* is conceived by the Guru in a more philosophical sense to be experienced intuitively.

Many schools or cults have grown up in India and abroad as well, all centred around one *yoga*-principle. Some new ones shoot up also. Rājā-yoga, Laya-yoga, Mantra-yoga, Nāda-yoga, Haṭha-yoga, Jñāna-yoga, Bhakti-yoga, Karma-yoga, Dhyāna-yoga, Sudarśana-yoga Atīndriya-yoga, Kuṇḍalinī-yoga, Kriyā-yoga are some such. But the Guru, when concluding the chapter, categorically says, all *yoga*s can summarily be brought under either *karma-yoga* or *jñāna-yoga*. It is to be noticed that the *Bhagavad-Gītā* in Verse III.3 also takes the same stand.

Mind (*manas*) finding its identity with *cidātmā*, in effect, means, *manas* losing its identity as *manas*, a state known as *amanībhāva*. Similarly, each individual, on realizing his or her being *Ātmā* or *Brahman* alone in essence, loses his or her identity in the total beingness. This self-absorption is what is termed *nirvāṇa*, and therefore, the next and the final chapter is named *Nirvāṇa Darśanam* (Vision through Absorption).

NIRVĀṆA DARŚANAM (VISION BY ABSORPTION)

The word *nirvāṇa* means "to burn out." It implies the individual burning himself or herself out in the beingness of the Absolute or *Brahman*, an experience, even subtler than the yogic unity seen in the last chapter. Perceiving the object as subject in essence, in another sense, comprises *yoga*. *Nirvāṇa* then is the event of the subject burning itself out, a wordless experience.

Though *nirvāṇa* signifies the attainment of the final goal, each individual seeker may think of that goal in his own way. This makes it possible to classify *nirvāṇa* also.

First, the Guru categorizes *nirvāṇa* into two: *śuddha* and *aśuddha* (pure and impure). And then *śuddha nirvāṇa* itself is classified as *śuddha* and *ati-śuddha* (pure and greatly pure). Those of the former class are called *brahmavit*s. Among those of the *ati-śuddhas-nirvāṇa* are discernible three types: *brahmavid-vara* (better knower of *Brahman*), *brahmavid-varīyān* (excellent knower of *Brahman*) and *brahmavid-variṣṭha* (the most excellent knower of *Brahman*).

The impure *nirvāṇa* is also classified as *aśuddha-śuddha* and *aśuddha-aśuddha* (impure pure and impure impure). There are those who aim at gaining *siddhi*s (unworldly attainments) as the desirable goal of spiritual practices; such are counted amongst the impure impure by the Guru.

As the work ends, attaining the functionless state (*vṛtti-śūnya*) from where there is no return, is depicted as the best of all desirable goals of an aspirant.

The purpose served by experiments in modern science, is fulfilled by analogies in Vedānta. Though many such are there popular in the Vedāntic tradition, the present commentator feels, almost all subtle points intended to be clarified could well be laid bare with the help of two of these — the gold and ornament analogy, and the wave and ocean analogy. Hence the repeated using of the same analogies almost all through the present commentary despite the monotony it seemingly results in. Each time an analogy is repeated, it is a different subtle philosophical point that is attempted to be clarified. Noticing that particular point wipes out the apparent monotony of repeating the same analogy, making it more appreciable.

Let us with this much in our mind proceed to examine the verses and chapters of the *Darśanamālā*, and see how do they make our life more meaningful.

1

Adhyāropa Darśanam
(Vision by Superimposition)

Verse 1

आसीदग्रेऽसदेवेदं भुवनं स्वप्नवत्पुनः ।
ससर्ज सर्वं संकल्पमात्रेण परमेश्वरः ॥१॥

āsīd agre 'sad evedaṁ bhuvanaṁ svapnavat punaḥ ।
sasarja sarvaṁ saṁkalpamātreṇa Parameśvaraḥ ॥1॥

All these worlds, in the beginning, were non-existent, indeed. The Supreme Controller (*Parameśvaraḥ*), thereafter caused the emanation of it (from Himself), by virtue of the willful urge inherent in Him, as though dreaming.

Darśanamālā begins with the perception common to all — that we and the world we perceive exist as they appear to be. Then arises a question: how was this originated? The first chapter answers this question.

Adhyāropa Darśanam is the name given to this chapter. *Adhyāropa* is a technical term in Vedānta. It denotes that the world-form is superimposed (*āropa*) on something that basically exists (*adhiṣṭhāna*). For example, we see waves. They are merely forms projected onto the reality of water that alone has existence. Likewise, the world-form is superimposed on the one all-underlying substance. Though that substance alone is real, and the apparent world-form is unreal, the common person does not treat the world either as unreal or as superimposed, but simply takes it as real. The questions that may arise in such a person's mind are answered in this chapter without deviating from the basic tenets of Advaita Vedānta. As implicit in each verse can be seen by a keen student, that although the entire chapter apparently deals with the problem of creation, basically only the existence of a single Reality, here called *Parameśvara*, is admitted.

A convention prevails in India that a serious literary work should begin with an invocation. It could be to God, to one's own *guru* or in some other form preferred by the author. Some like to express the invocation in a direct way, while some others do it indirectly. Narayana Guru preferred the latter way. The invocation in all his major works is done in a suggestive way, and the *Darśanamālā* is no exception. *Śivaśatakam* is the only work in which the Guru fulfils this convention in a direct way.

Āsīt is the word with which the work begins; and the word means "was," or "it was so." Though the word is used to denote things of the past, it is not used in common literature. Its use is only in Vedic literature and refers to the state of existence of the world before creation.

A is thus the letter with which the work begins. In India this letter, is considered to signify the Absolute. In the *Bhagavad-Gītā* the Lord Kṛṣṇa says, "Among the letters of the alphabet I am *A*" (*akṣarāṇām akārosmi* X.33). This work thus begins with an indirect reference to the Absolute, serving the purpose of an invocation.

What existed previous to creation, being unoriginated, cannot cease to exist. It will continue to exist forever. The word *āsīt*, therefore, suggests also the eternality of the causal

Reality. Beginning thus with an indication of the eternal Reality also stands for an invocation.

Moreover, the word *parameśvara* (*parama* + *īśvara*) or Supreme God, directly finds a place in this very first verse. *Īśa* means "one who controls" and *vara* "of a high order." *Īśvara* thus means, "controller of a high order." The prefix *parama* means "Supreme."

That the world as we see it, was created by God, is a notion common to almost all religions. Who then created God? If a God is thought of as the creator of the creator, then the question arises, "Who created that God?" This leads to the logical fallacy known as infinite regression, known in Indian logic as *anavasthā doṣa*. The prefix *parama* to *Īśvara,* meaning the Supreme or Transcendental, signifies that one should not go further behind in search of this cause. Asking for the cause of *Parameśvara* is like asking for the time of the bus before the first bus. This reference to *Parameśvara* (the Supreme Controller) also serves the purpose of invocation.

Seemingly the world exists. Who created it? Why was it created? How was it created? In addition to these philosophical questions, scientists even ask, "When was it created?" These questions are but normal, for the reason that what seems to exist does not continue to exist for ever. All that appears to be, ceases to be as well. Suppose they do not cease to be; then the above questions would become irrelevant. But the case here is different. Every apparent entity ceases to be, and therefore the questions are also relevant. It is to be admitted, then, that there was creation. This first verse tells us, who created it, and how it was created.

If the world is a created one, then it was not existent before the event of creation. In that sense it is stated here, *"āsīd agre asat eva idam bhuvanam"* (this entire world, in the beginning, was non-existent). What is stated here as "non-existent" is "the world," and not the "Causal Reality." It signifies only that the world that appears to exist now, did not exist before creation. A sentence very similar to this appears in the *Taittirīya Upaniṣad*: *asad vā idam agra āsīt, tato vai sad ajāyata* (II.6.1). It means, "In the beginning this world was non-existent. Therefrom indeed was this existent (world) born."

This statement apparently contradicts the basic stand of Vedānta that there was *sat* (Existence) in the beginning. That existence is *ātmā* or *Brahman* (the Self or the Absolute) in essence. From this perspective the *Aitareya Upaniṣad* (I.1.1) says, "*ātmā vā idam eka evāgra āsīt*" (the Self alone verily existed in the beginning). The *Chāndogya Upaniṣad* (VI.2.1) also says, "*sad eva somya idam agra āsīt*" (O my dear, Existence alone was there in the beginning). Grammatic rules allow us also to interpret the present words of the Guru, as meaning, "All these worlds, in the beginning, were Existence (*sat*) alone." But such an interpretation does not befit the philosophical perspective adopted in this chapter. Here the existence of the visible world is taken for granted. Then the question arises, "Who created it, and how?" That the world is a created one is also admitted. What is explored here in this chapter is not the nature of the Ultimate Reality, but the origin of the world that appears to exist. The statement, therefore, only means, this world did not exist before creation. The non-existence (*asat*) in this statement is that of the world, and the Existence (*sat*) of the *Chāndogya Upaniṣad* is that of *Ātmā* or the Ultimate Reality.

The focus in this chapter, as we have seen, is on *bhuvanam* (the world), literally "that in which everything happens or takes place." "Who causes these happenings?" is, therefore, a pertinent question in this context. The direct answer given is, "It is caused by *Parameśvara*." That this *Parameśvara* is neither a personal God nor a deity will become clear as the chapter ends. *Parameśvara,* is a name, befitting the frame of reference of this chapter, given to the one primordial causal Substance signified by *sat.*

How did *Parameśvara* create this world? As if in a dream. All that one dreams appears to one from within the being of one's own mind. Dream has no existence apart from the being of the dreamer, or rather from the dreaming mind. And more, a dream has existence only till the dreamer wakes up. The world is a dream dreamt by *Parameśvara,* and its existence is only in His mind.

As the dreamer wakes up, all that was seen in dream disappears in one's being. *Parameśvara* waking up from the present dream results in the disapperance of all the worlds in His own being. He alone remains as existing. The dream-like-creation-concept thus leads us back to the basic stand of Vedānta that the Causal Reality alone really exists.

When will *Parameśvara* wake up? A seeker becoming enlightened means, one visualizes the entire world as disappearing in one's own being, or in the Ultimate Reality one visualizes. That Reality is what is portrayed here as *Parameśvara* so as to fit in with the creation context. Everything disappearing in the being of *Parameśvara* becomes a realized experience when the seeker attains his or her goal. It could therefore as well be said, a seeker realizing one's goal and *Parameśvara* waking up mean the same thing. Who then wakes up, *Parameśvara* or the seeker? Both, for the two really are not two.

Sasarja is the Sanskrit word used here to mean "created." Unlike the creation-concept of Western theology, *sasarja* signifies the actualization of potentials hidden in something already existing, resulting in the emanation of new forms from within itself. What is the Reality that existed before, in the present case? *Parameśvara* alone. The creation of the world is thus merely an actualization of the potentials hidden in *Parameśvara*, as if in a dream. The ordinary dreams we experience are similar in nature. Thuswise is the question "How was the world created?" answered.

The original word *agre*, means "in the beginning." If an actual creation had taken place at all, the word could be taken to signify the state before the taking place of such a creation-process. Closely looked at, it is evident, no actual creation took place, other than *Parameśvara* having a dream experience. Then, *agre* could be understood as meaning the state before the emerging of the dream. Actually this dream had no beginning, nor will it cease to be; it will continue for ever. Seen from that perspective, *agre* stands for the infinite potential inherent in *Parameśvara* or the ultimate Reality, for this dream-experience. The word thus loses its temporal dimension.

How did this world remain concealed in *Parameśvara* before this conceptual creation? This question is answered in the next verse.

The first chapter of the *Darśanamālā*, it would be noticed, abounds in references to the ultimate Causal Reality in the masculine gender, as though that Reality is a "he," by using words such as *Parameśvaraḥ*, *Prabhuḥ*, *Bhagavān*, *Jagatpatiḥ*, *Vibhuḥ*, *Saḥ* (he). The philosophical significance of these words, made sufficiently clear in the comments, shows how that Reality is beyond all gender concepts and anthropomorphization. In Sanskrit Grammar, it is to be noticed, using a masculine gender word does not mean that what it signifies is necessarily a male being, because the gender, according to that grammar, is related only to the word concerned, and not to what it denotes. Yet such an anthropomorphized concept is unavoidable in this chapter as its philosophical perspective is based on acknowledging the Ultimate Reality as the "Creator" of the world.

Verse 2

वासनामयमेवादावासीदिदमथ प्रभुः ।
असृजन्मायया स्वस्य मायावीवाखिलं जगत् ॥२॥

vāsanāmayam evādāvāsīdidam atha prabhuḥ ।
asṛjan māyayā svasya māyāvīvā khilaṁ jagat ॥2 ॥

The entire world, in the beginning, remained in the Lord (*Prabhuḥ*), as pure *vāsanā* in essence. He, then, by His power to create illusory visions (*māyā*) brought it forth as is done by a magician.

Being directly experienced, this world has existence as it appears to be; then how did it originate? This, we know, is the central problem around which thought revolves in the present chapter. The Perceived changeful world must have underlying it a causal Substance or Reality remaining unperceived. A search for this Reality is the most fundamental task modern science undertakes. The same remains the most important problem in philosophy as well.

Modern Science considers energy-particles as constituting this most fundamental reality. As energy, they are not material; and as particles, they have necessarily to be material in nature. In other words, what appears here as the world consisting of minerals, vegetables and animals, is all an invisible energy that is neither material nor non-material. How can something invisible and non-material assume a visible, material form? Though not logically tenable, that it so happens is the confirmed stand of modern science. In essence this implies, a latent potential in the invisible and non-material energy to assume the form of the visible and material world.

Though energy is one, endless is the manner in which it assumes apparent forms. Energy is the underlying reality even in the most inert entities such as rocks. It is also the substance that seems to be iron and steel appearing as the moving and non-moving parts of all the machineries everywhere in the world. Both the priceless stone diamond and the filthy muck and mire equally have energy for their essential content. The human body, inclusive of the brain which serves as the seat of mind, is also nothing but energy become concrete. The world conceived by the human mind as a result of the working of the brain, is as wide as, or even wider than, the external physical world. From the internally existing conceptual world, to the externally existing physical world, inclusive of the ideas conceivable about them, all have one energy alone for their underlying substance. All this is mysterious indeed! The one energy-reality, in short, has latent in it the mysterious potential to assume the form of all these worlds. In Sanskrit this potential, is known as *vāsanā*.

Those who seek reality philosophically also conclude that the Ultimate Reality is one alone. That one is what the word *Parameśvara* (Supreme God) of Verse one signifies, and here the same God is called *Prabhuḥ* or Lord. Both words admittedly have a touch of anthropomorphism implied in them, which is but natural with the point of view adopted in the present chapter. The subject dealt with here is, how the world was created by a Creator. Scientists admit this creator as the infinite potential hidden in energy. The only way *Darśanamālā* differs in this respect is in its perceiving of the same Creator in the *Prabhuḥ* or Lord. Whether called energy or *Prabhuḥ*, it is a mysterious reality; it is beyond the grasping power of human mind. Whatever name is given, the unthinkable remains unthinkable untouched by the name.

The *vāsanā* for emanating everything from it is already hidden in itself. How is it that something too subtle and unknowable appears as all these knowable gross objects? Modern science apparently does not answer this question. It treats this as a problem outside the field of scientific enquiry.

A prejudice against the conclusion that the Ultimate Reality could be a mystery, seems to have gripped the minds of scientists. But philosophy, particularly Eastern Philosophy, and more specifically Vedānta, has no such prejudiced view. What Vedānta actually does is not to help the seeker attain a "clear knowledge" of the Ultimate Reality. It, on the other hand, enables you to realize that the Ultimate Reality is a Great Mystery, you forming part of it. The best outlook of life Vedānta recommends is, for you to experience the Blissful Freedom of your short span of life as being part of a Great Mystery.

How did everything physical and mental, everything internal and external, both mind and matter, emanate from this one Mysterious Reality? The one blanket answer Vedānta gives to this question is this: it is because of *māyā*.

We, for the present, are not going into a detailed study of this *māyā*, reserving it for Chapters 3 and 4. Here *māyā* is compared to magic shows, also called *māyā*, played by magicians (*māyāvin*). The enjoying spectators are ignorant of the tricks played by the magician; but they are fully known to him. Likewise, the secret of the emanation of the mysterious magic-like world from the magician-like *Prabhu* (Lord) is unknown to us the spectators; but the *Prabhu* knows it well. This ignorance of ours is called *ajñāna* in Vedānta. In fact, we spectators too are nothing but part of the magic-show of the *Prabhu*. How can we, being such, know the secret of this *māyā*? Almost the same is the vision seen in the *Śvetaśvatara Upaniṣad* when it says, *māyām tu prakṛtim viddhi māyinam tu maheśvaram* (IV.10)

(Know that *prakṛti* is *māyā*, and the Great Lord (*Maheśvara*) to be the wielder of *māyā*.)

It is people like us who enjoy the magic-show of ordinary magicians. Who, then, are the spectators of the *Prabhu*'s magic-show? It is none other than Himself. Little children could be seen playing with whatever is available at hand, making many forms out of them and destroying them before long. They enjoy doing so. Its purpose is nothing but giving vent to the *vāsanā*s latent in the children. Similar is the case of the *Prabhu*, when He emanates the world from Himself. Countless *vāsanā*s are there latent in the *Prabhu* too. As they find expression, there appears the world. The process of new forms emerging and the old ones disappearing goes on endlessly as part of it. The *Prabhu* enjoys doing so — the sheer joy or *ānanda* of self-expression (*ātmāviṣkāra*), or the joy of actually visualizing what Himself really is (*ātmā-svarūpa-darśana*). The same *Prabhu* is what the Guru calls *arivu* (pure unconditioned Consciousness) in his *Ātmopadeśa Śatakam* (One hundred Verses of Self-Instruction). Why this *arivu* emanates the world from itself is described by the Guru in its verse 33.

Verse 3

प्रागुत्पत्तेरिदं स्वस्मिन् विलीनमथ वै स्वतः ।
बीजादङ्कुरवत्स्वस्य शक्तिरेवाऽसृजत्स्वयम् ॥३॥

prāg utpatter idaṁ svasmin vilīnam atha vai svataḥ ।
bījād aṅkuravat svasya śaktir evā'sṛjat svayam ॥3॥

Before creation, this world remained latent in Himself; His own self-activating power, then, brought it forth from Himself, as is a sprout from its seed.

Each of the verses of the present chapter uses a separate simile, each helping further the seeker-student's clarity of insight as to how this world of infinite variety emerged from one Reality or God. The creation of the world, in fact, is an inexplicable mystery, and hence great *ṛṣis* resort to the practice of using more than one analogy to give an utmost possible clarity to the picture. No analogy in itself would be complete and sufficient in depicting the picture clearly. Using many analogies gives the freedom of one supplementing another, the insufficiency of one being compensated by another, and the defects in one made good by another.

The analogy in the first verse was that of dreaming. What is seen in a dream has no substantial existence. Nor can one decide in advance which dream is to be seen. The remainder of a dream we saw yesterday cannot be brought to view today either. Dream is only a vision that arises and merges back in the mind in its unconscious or rather semi-conscious state. The visions seen in it are substantially not real; they are simply unreal. But the unrealness of the world, even as a dream of *Parameśvara*, is of a different order. The world continues to be perceptible to sense-organs even after realizing its dream-like unrealness. It can also be seen as existing continuous to what was being experienced so far. It will never vanish from our vision, like a dream. The analogy of dream alone will not, therefore, suffice to give clarity to the creation-picture presented here.

A magician showing his skills is the analogy resorted to in Verse 2. That all magical shows are substantially unreal is a fact well known. What a magician does is to entertain his audience by creating an illusory impression that something interesting happened. That illusory vision disappears the very next moment. But the appearance of the world is not merely such an evanescent illusory vision; it is more substantial.

The impression given by the first two analogies is that the world has no existence other than as an illusory vision. This shortcoming is made good by adopting yet another analogy, according to which something emerges out of something already existing — a sprout emerges from an already existing seed. The seed has existence; so too does the sprout. The substantiality of the sprout is as undeniable as that of the seed. The sprout, and subsequently the tree as well, grows out of the seed. Yet breaking the seed and examining its inside will never help you find out where the tree hides within it. The tree's existence in the seed is simply as a potential. As circumstances become favourable, this potential gets actualized and emerges as the sprout, and then as the tree. It is the existence of the seed that becomes transformed into the existence of the tree. Likewise, the potential hidden in the Causal Reality, God or *Ātman*, unfolds itself and manifests (*vyākṛta*) as the world. This God, as the unmanifested seed-like Reality, is then termed *avyākṛta*.

A seed, having become unfolded, manifests as the tree; so too, *Ātman* or *Parameśvara*, having become self-unfolded, appears as the world. Stated otherwise, the world is the divine apparent concrete form assumed by the otherwise abstract God. The Guru himself, therefore, says in his *Ātmopadeśa Śatakam* (One Hundred Verses of Self-Instruction):

> Mental faculties, sense-organs,
> Physical body, and also the many worlds.
> That we have contact with —
> When cogitated on, all this is
> But the divine form of the one Sun
> That shines up in the transcendental sky;
> It should be known searchingly.
>
> — Verse 2

This process of the one Causal Reality self-manifesting as this world is called *sarjana* in Sanskrit, a word much different in connotation from the supposedly English equivalent "creation." Suppose a potter takes a lump of clay and gives it a pot's shape. The potter here is the creater and the pot the creation. But suppose the clay on its own assumes the form of pot without the help of a potter; then this process is to be called *sarjana* — the way a latent effect becomes actualized from the material cause without a different efficient cause. This process thus requires no "creator" or *sraṣṭā* as such. An inner indomitable urge for this self-unfoldment is already latent in the Causal Reality. The Guru describes this urge, in his *Ātmopadeśa Śatakam,* as "this primeval potential is the original seed that gives birth to everything" (Verse 53). The potential to produce the sprout is inherent in the seed, and the sprout thus produced does not exist separately from the seed. It is simply a new form attained by the seed. Likewise, the potential to produce all the worlds from Himself is latent in God. The world thus produced does not have an existence separate from God. The Guru, concisely conceiving the whole of this creation-picture, tells God in his universal prayer *Daivadaśakam*, thus:

> You are the act of creation,
> You are the creator,
> You are also the myriads of created beings;
> O God, you are also the Substance for creation.
>
> — Verse 5

The emerging of a sprout from a seed happens on its own; only that a favourable circumstance has to be prevailing there; no influence of an external agency is needed. Similar is the way the world emerges from God. At least some helpful external circumstance is a must in the case of seeds sprouting.

Even such a conditioning factor is not there in the case of God self-manifesting as the world. Therefore, no moment in which God remains unmanifest is actually there. The sprouting of the world from God happens from Himself, because of Himself, both denoted by the word *svataḥ*.

Though compared here to the sprouting of seeds, the emerging of the world from God is not to be treated as if having happened at any particular point of time, it really being a process that goes on beginninglessly and endlessly. There is no actual existence of God without its assuming the form of the phenomenal world. Though, as a Causal Reality, God is "conceivable" by human mind as different from the created world, God "has" no actual existence separate or separable from the phenomenal world of which the human mind is a part. This is like water having no existence separate from waves and ocean, or gold having no existence separate from ornaments.

Without appearing as the world, God has no existence; without God the apparent world has no existence either. The usage *atha vai asr̥jat* (was created then) in the verse might give the impression that the creation took place at some particular point of time, and such a usage is unavoidable here as forming part of the frame of reference of this chapter where creation is an admitted fact. But this impression will be found to be corrected in the ensuing chapters. The same fundamental fact is put in the *Bhagavad-Gītā* as "no *sat* (being) exists without *bhāva* (becoming), and no *bhāva* is there without *sat* existing." (Verse II.16).

The potential to assume the form of ornaments is latent in gold. The potential to sprout is latent in seeds. Likewise, the potential to unfold as the world is inherent in God. This latent potential is called *śakti* here. The next verse examines *śakti* in detail.

Verse 4

शक्तिस्तु द्विविधा ज्ञेया तैजसी तामसीति च।
सहवासोऽनयोर्नास्ति तेजस्तिमिरयोरिव ॥४॥

śaktis tu dvividhā jñeyā taijasī tāmasīti ca ।
sahavāso 'nayor nāsti tejas timirayor iva ॥4॥

This self-activating power, in its turn, is known to be of two kinds: the bright and the dark. These two never exist together as is the case with light and darkness together.

Speculation in the present chapter is centred around the stand that the world exists as it appears to be. Nothing in this perceptual world — including ourselves, the perceivers — exists as changeless. A constant flow of changes is seen everywhere. Day breaks as the sun rises, and night falls as the sun sets. The rising and setting of the sun and the alternation of day and night are beginningless and endless phenomena. As day breaks, most living beings, gain vitality and become engaged in activities. As night falls this vitality also subsides and they fall asleep until day-break.

It is thus evident that the external alternating states get reflected in the internal states as well. New life sprouts on the one side, and the old ones decline on the other. Growth on the one side is marked by decay on the other. Thus, the perceptual world is such that everywhere in life are there two constantly alternating phases — one bright and the other dark.

Just now we have seen how the emergence of the world from God can be likened to that of sprouts from seeds. The immense vitality for this self-unfoldment is inherent in God. This vitality admittedly has latent in it the capability to produce the above-mentioned twin phases. Hence the capability of God to produce the world from Himself has to be thought of as having inherent in it these two faces, one bright and the other dark. The bright face is called here *taijasī*, meaning (the bright) and the dark face is called *tāmasī* (the dark). The two being opposite in nature, there can be no darkness in the perceptual world where there is brightness, and vice versa. Where the bright aspect of God's creative capability is predominant, the other goes dormant, and the other way round as well. Logically speaking, the two existing together is an impossibility, but factually the two remain inherent in God, only that where one finds expression the other does not, or when one appears the other does not.

The non-co-existence of darkness and brightness means only that their togetherness is not in the world. The seed-sprout analogy of the previous verse also has implicit in it the very same principle of togetherness. In a sprouted seed, its upper part goes up towards light, and the lower part goes down to the darkness beneath the surface of the earth. On both sides, by branching out at both ends many times, it creates a cluster of branches and roots. The immense power to bring both these sides out is latent in the seed. The root does not grow towards where the trunk grows, and vice versa, yet the two growing simultaneously alone ensures the emergence of the tree. Similarly, this world, as well as the phenomenon of life in it, always has inherent in it the bright and dark faces, like the two sides of a single coin. God, as understood here, is the source-Reality that causes the emergence of such a world.

Verse 5

मनोमात्रमिदं चित्रमिवाग्रे सर्वमीदृशम् ।
प्रापयामास वैचित्र्यं भगवांश्चित्रकारवत् ॥५॥

manomātram idaṁ citramivāgre sarvam īdṛśam ।
prāpayāmāsa vaicitryaṁ bhagavāṁścitrakāravat ॥5॥

> As in the case of a painting, this world in the beginning was merely imaginative mind in essence. All these perceptible marvels were then achieved by *Bhagavān* like an artist of high talents.

Given that the world was created by God, how did it exist in God before creation, and in what state did it exist? This is the point given stress to in the present verse. It was stated earlier in Verse 2 that the world existed in God in the form of *vāsanā* or latent potential. *Vāsanā* as such has no specificity; on gaining specificity it is called *bhāvanā* or creative imagination. It is in the form of this *bhāvanā* that the world existed in God before creation. God gave expression to this *bhāvanā* in all its details from Himself, and thus emerged the world. How this *bhāvanā* existed in God and how it found expression, is something indescribable. Therefore, instead of describing it, the Guru gives clarity to it by bringing in yet another analogy — the analogy of a talented artist.

An artist, before creating a work of art remains for a while in a contemplative mood. A meaningful imagery then gets formulated in his mind. This imagery is called *bhāvanā*. On gaining some clarity of such an imagery in all its details, he finds himself restless with the indomitable inner urge to give expression to it on a canvas or paper. Immediately he starts the effort towards this end. His attention goes nowhere else until he is fully satisfied of having brought out the imagery completely. On completion, he makes an overall inspection of it to check whether all that he perceived mentally is in the painting or drawing perceivably. A final touch is given if any imperfection comes to his notice. Thus he completes the picture. As far as he is concerned, what he conceived in his mind and what he perceivably painted or drew are in essential content not two; one simply being the replica of the other. An art-lover's admiration becomes complete as he, with the external painting as a means, gains for himself the inner vision the artist had as he was painting. The art work, in the present case, is this world of endless variety, and the admirer is the seeker.

In the endless variety of phenomenal appearance, he perceives how mysterious the *bhāvanā* of God is, his own ability to admire it being part of the very same *bhāvanā* . It is this perception that reveals to him the intrinsic oneness of the greatness of God's *bhāvanā* and his own existence.

God, in this context, is like an artist. The construct of the world, in all its details, first gets formulated in the *bhāvanā* of God. It is in the creative imagination of God the artist that an ordinary artist, his creative imagination and urge for creation also get framed. Then how great must be the creative imagination of God, that systematizes even the creative imagination of artists! A creative imagination never subsides until it is given expression, God's creative imagination no exception. On finding expression, God's creative imagination appears as all the worlds, as all the countless living beings and even as the creative minds of artists. The nature and content of the visible world and the creative imagination of God, in essence, are not two. An almost similar picture is seen depicted in the *Īśa Upaniṣad* when it says:

> The wise, the omniscient, the over-ruling, the self-existent one distributed existentially the functions of the substance as they were already existing virtually in himself.

An art work is merely the replica of the imagination of the artist. Of the two, which has real existence? This question is very difficult to answer. As the world is the expression of the creative imagination of God, which of these two is the real? Really, the inseparability of the two, like the two sides of a single coin, is what has real existence.

God, in the present verse, is termed *Bhagavān*, meaning, the one in possession of *bhaga*s. What the word *bhaga* means varies according to contexts. Greatness (*māhātmya*), firmness (*dhairya*), fame (*kīrti*), wealth (*sampat*), wisdom (*jñāna*) and sense of detachment (*vairāgya*) form the six *bhaga*s in one context. All these are positive qualities evident in those who yearn to know Reality and live as embodiments of Reality. This Reality, in the perception of the realized person, is God Himself, and therefore he perceives all these *bhaga*s as pertaining to God also; he then calls God, *bhagavān*.

A seeker's case is different. For him or her the auspicious qualities driving him or her forward in the spiritual quest consist of discriminating the pairs such as creation and dissolution (*utpatti-vipatti*), coming and going (*āgati-gati*), and knowledge and ignorance (*vidyā-avidyā*). All such pairs pertain always to the cosmic system which is nothing but God embodied. Therefore, God, in a seekers' perception, is endowed with these qualities, and is called *bhagavān* in this sense.

The non-duality of Gods' mind and the visible world resounds all through this verse of the *Darśanamālā*, transforming even a context in which the creator-creation duality dominates, into a setting to teach non-dual wisdom (*advaita*).

Verse 6

आसीत् प्रकृतिरेवेदं यथाऽदौ योगवैभवः ।
व्यतनोदथ योगीव सिद्धिजालं जगत्पतिः ॥६ ॥

āsīt prakṛtir evedaṁ yathā 'dau yogavaibhavaḥ ।
vyatanod atha yogīva siddhijālaṁ jagatpatiḥ ॥6 ॥

As *prakṛti* indeed was this world existing in the beginning; comparable is it to the psychic powers attained through

> yoga. The Lord of this changeful world (*Jagatpatiḥ*) thereafter unfolded it from Himself like a *yogī* who unfolds his multitudinous psychic powers.

The specific point stressed in this verse is that the world, before creation, existed as *prakṛti*. What is *prakṛti*? Translating it as "nature" may create the impression that some definiteness is given to the meaning of the word, but it really is not so. We will find a clear definition of the term in the present work only in the last verse of the fourth chapter. It will be defined there as "that which properly makes specific the three *guṇa*s" — *sattva*, *rajas* and *tamas*. *Prakṛti*, thus, is of the essence of three *guṇa*s.

The word *prakṛti* has another word *kṛti* forming part of it. *Kṛti* means action or *karma*. Nature is constantly active. *Kṛti* is inherent in it. The activities going on everywhere in nature is *karma* in the cosmological context. The same in the Vedic context refers to the rituals performed as enjoined in the Vedas. The *karma* inherent in nature results naturally in the constant emerging of apparent manifest forms.

An indomitable urge for this self-manifestation exists. Where does it exist? In *jagatpati*, the *pati* of the *jagat*. *Pati* means "Lord" and *jagat*, the changeful world, and *Jagatpati* is yet another word for God. The *kṛti* that forms part of the word *prakṛti* is the activity that causes the changefulness of the world. This indomitable urge for activity, in another context, is called *viśva-vīrya* by the Guru himself, the word meaning "cosmic vital urge," a notion almost equal to the concept of "elan vital" of Henry Bergson.

As *kṛti* is eternally a part of it, it is but normal that manifest forms ceaselessly emerge from *prakṛti* and that such manifestations together form the cosmos.

How does it emerge? Just like the *siddhis* (unworldly attainments) of *yogīs*. Where do the *siddhis* exist in a *yogī*, and how do they exist? They exist in himself as the potential for specific manifestations (*vaibhava*). This cosmic *vaibhava* is no ordinary *vaibhava*; it is *yoga-vaibhava*, meaning a *vaibhava* always united with what exists basically as substance. *Vaibhava* stands for both the urge for manifestation, and the creative process (*bhava*) because of which something specific (*viśeṣa*, *vi* standing for it) emanates. This *vaibhava* exists as inseparably one with God and hence is a *yoga-vaibhava*. In the case of a *yogī*, what appears as *siddhis* has no existence apart from him. They are simply his *prakṛti* finding self-expression. Yet, those who are ignorant of the *yogī*'s inherent nature, think of such self-expressions as unworldly attainments; and even claim that such phenomena are spiritual attainments. Even when all these misconceptions happen, the *yogī* simply remains himself with his *prakṛti* functioning in all its specificity. It is others, because of their ignorance, who see unworldly attainments.

Entirely different are the *yogī*'s self-awareness and that of the non-*yogīs*. A *yogī* being an enlightened person, his normal state of existence is never understood by a non-*yogī*. Therefore, the normal behaviour of a *yogī* is perceived by a non-*yogī* as unworldly. It is here we have to notice the difference between the magic show of the magician of Verse 2 and the *siddhis* of a *yogī*.

The magic shown by a magician, though existing within as *vāsanās*, is not part of his or her normal life. These skills are displayed merely to entertain others. On the other hand, the *siddhis* seen by others in a *yogī*, are not demonstrated simply to show others. They are just part of the *yogī*'s normal behaviour in life. A real *yogī* perceives everything within himself and himself in everything, and this perception is the ultimate *siddhi*.

The world was created by God not from a void or from some other substance already existing, but He expanded Himself through His own imagination and assumed the form of the world. The world, though thought of as created by God, thus is not essentially different from God. We who stand amazed at the mysteriousness of this creation, also do not exist apart from God. This world, we, and the mysteriousness we feel are all not different from God. This world will last as long as God and His mysterious *prakṛti* lasts. An illusory magic is not of that kind.

We thus are essentially not different from our own creator. Why, then, do we treat God as different and make life miserable? This aspect is clarified in the next verse with the help of yet another analogy.

Verse 7

यदाऽऽत्मविद्या संकोचस्तदाऽविद्या भयङ्करम्।
नामरूपात्मनाऽत्यर्थं विभातीह पिशाचवत् ॥७॥

yadā 'tmavidyā saṁkocas tadā 'vidyā bhayaṁkaram ।
nāma-rūpātmanā 'tyarthaṁ vibhātīha piśācavat ॥7॥

As knowledge of oneself shrinks so nescience (*avidyā*) becomes prevalent. It, assuming names and forms, in a most terrible fashion, looms here ghost-like.

Only when the world is considered real as it appears, does living in it arouse fear. If considered unreal, the world would give no cause for fear. How can something unreal be fearful? Therefore, the enquiry for the cause of fear and sufferings in life also comes within the range of the study of *adhyāropa* or superimposition.

Human beings naturally are afraid of ghosts. When do we see them? They are never seen at day-time. They are seen only at night. At night, you may see a ghost standing there in darkness. Almost similar is what happens in the absence of wisdom-light. There too is a darkness — the darkness of ignorance or *avidyā*. A clear definition of this *avidyā* is reserved for Chapter 4. Here it is simply portrayed as the state in which self-knowledge (*ātma-vidyā*) is lacking.

What is *ātma-vidyā*? It is knowing the self or knowing oneself properly. It is the clarity of awareness you get as an answer to the question you ask yourself, "Who am I?" According to what we have learnt so far from this study, this world — each one of us forming an integral part of it — is nothing but Him self-emanated because of the *prakṛti* inherent in Him. I should then become fully aware, "I am but a minute particle of God-become-self-unfolded." Then I realize, "My existence and Gods' existence are inseparably one."

No one is afraid of oneself. Fear is always of someone or something else. That which arouses fear is also really only a speck of God become manifest. That means, oneself and the fearful object are merely two different facets of one God. This much awareness having been attained, all fears seem to vanish. This disappearance of fear is caused by self-knowledge or *ātma-vidyā* — the knowledge that I am part of God's beingness.

Though everything in the world is part of the manifest form of God, we somehow remain ignorant of this basic fact. Why is it so? Because each entity has its own specific form (*rūpa*), and these forms, when seen, are taken to be the real, forgetting the substance that assumed these forms. One apparent form is different from another, and such forms are countless in the manifestation of God. As a result, the world is taken to be the aggregate of these forms. One form is not only differentiated from another, a different idea is also conceived about each form. In order to separate out these ideas and also to communicate to others what such conceived ideas are, we formulate words or names (*nāma*s). Such names are merely linguistic signs. Still we find ourselves incapable of perceiving this world without the aid of these signs and the ideas they signify. In short, it is almost impossible to say definitely whether the world is the aggregate of external visible forms or the aggregate of conceived ideas. The world-experience, as far as humans are concerned, would be there only in the presence of both. It is taken for granted that the conceptual world is a replica of the perceptual world, but no evidence is available to prove it; so it remains a belief — so to say a blind belief. Our world-experience, in short, is one in which both names and forms (*nāma*s and *rūpa*s) fuse together in an undefinable way. And such is the world that arouses fear.

Everything, perceptual as well as conceptual, being part of the self-manifestation of God, human minds, the ideas conceived by them and the names given are also so. We are thus part of the becoming of God, so are the names and forms as well. It is the ignorance of this basic oneness that arouses in us fear of the world of names and forms.

Given that everything is part of God's self-manifestation, fear too is to be considered so. God Himself then, would have to be thought of as the cause of fear. Why did God make such a world, is the point contemplated on in the next verse.

Verse 8

भयंकरमिदं शून्यं वेतालनगरं यथा।
तथैव विश्वमखिलं व्यकरोदद्भुतं विभुः॥८॥

bhayaṁkaram idaṁ śūnyaṁ vetālanagaraṁ yathā ।
tathaiva viśvam akhilaṁ vyakarod adbhutaṁ vibhuḥ ॥8॥

> This world, non-existent on its own, is terrible like an infernal city. Such is the way the all-pervading Lord (*vibhuḥ*) mysteriously did make appear (from Himself) the whole of the universe.

The present context takes for granted that this world was created by God. *Vibhuḥ*, the word used here to signify God, suggests God's all-pervasiveness and omnipotence. Such a God who becomes self-expanded as the world, indicates that He is not to be conceived as a personal God, but as the Substance underlying the being of all the worlds. Each individual, therefore, has to perceive the presence of God as the Substance that has assumed his or her own form. Such a perception is what the word *ātma-vidyā* of the previous verse denotes. Not seeing thus indicates *ātma-vidyā* is absent. In that case one sees the world as ghost-like and fearful.

Admitting all this arouses another question: why did God create the world like this, where *ātma-vidyā* naturally remains shrunken, leaving living beings fearful?

One question remains a riddle in all the religions. Particularly in prophetic religions: why is there evil in this world created by God, the planitude of goodness? Theologians have always been trying to resolve this riddle, but it eludes any satisfactory final answer. The fact is that it has no such an answer. The reason is this: the question arises from the preconceived notion, "God is the plenitude of goodness." No evidence to testify the correctness of this notion is available. Really, good and evil are human ideations, and are not God-related. It is happenings that are evaluated as good or bad; happenings on their own are neither good nor bad; they just arise from God. They become so only when we humans appraise them. Such appraisals have our own likes and dislikes and value notions for criteria. What is thought of as good by some is seen as evil by some others; for one and the same person, what is felt good in one context may, turn out bad at another.

All happenings, it is admitted, take place as one Reality's or God's creative self-unfoldment. Even human beings who habitually evaluate events as good or bad, are merely part of that creative unfoldment of God. It is such humans that differentiate happenings emerging from God as good or bad. Happenings, as they emerge from God, are neither good nor bad. Such creative self-unfoldment of God was heedlessly classed as "good" by man with his own likes and dislikes as criteria, and this basically wrong notion is from where the above-mentioned question arose, and it is the reason for it having no satisfactory answer.

In India, the Upaniṣads have always remained the one sturdy support of all philosophic speculation. In them *Brahman* replaces God. They have never thought of *Brahman* as the plenitude of goodness alone. On the other hand, *Brahman* in them is conceived as the basic source of everything we classify as good or bad, righteous or unrighteous (*dharma* and *adharma*). For instance, the *Bṛhadāraṇyaka Upaniṣad* stanza, of which the famous dictum *ayam ātmā brahma* (This Self is the Absolute) forms part, reads as follows:

> This same self, indeed, is *Brahman*, consisting of (or identified with) understanding, mind, life, sight, hearing, earth, water, air, ether, light and no-light, desire and absence of desire, anger and absence of anger, righteousness and absence of righteousness and all things. This is what is meant by saying (it) consists of this (what is perceived), consists of that (what is inferred). According as one acts, according as one behaves, so does he become. The doer of good becomes good, the doer of evil becomes evil. . . . (II. 19)

The Upaniṣad apparently asserts here that, what we humans treat as good and evil, merit and sin, all emanated from the one all-underlying Substance called *Brahman* or *ātman*. It is we humans who classified actions (*karmas*) as good and evil and their doers as meritorious and sinful. Actions, as they take place in nature's eternal flow, are neither good nor evil. In short, Vedānta does not consider *Brahman* or God, the ultimate causal Substance, as the plenitude of goodness, and therefore the above question does not pose itself in Vedānta. If at all the good and the evil are admitted as intrinsic with the world order, they are to be treated only as having emerged from God or *Brahman*. The problem becomes relevant only when the apparent world is considered real.

How did such dichotomies emerge from the one God? Why did God create the world in such a way that it arouses fear in the minds of His own creations? Such possible questions are many. No logically convincing answer to these is available. One possible overall answer is this: all this is a great mystery; the world is a mystery; the phenomena of life and mind are mysteries; and God Himself is a mystery!

Indian philosophy, particularly Advaita Vedānta, though it considers itself as a systematically conceived school of thought, does not claim that it answers all the logical questions possible about the world and Reality. On the contrary, Vedānta ultimately concludes that the ultimate Reality is an unthinkable and ineffable mystery. In this respect, Vedāntic speculation departs from the way of thinking of the West, where defining Reality as a mystery is never considered as philosophically sound, though mystics may approve of it. Mystics are never considered philosophers; they are rather treated as related to religion. Religion and Philosophy, in India, have never become divorced.

Why the world and life cause fear was made clear in the last verse: absence of self-knowledge or of knowing oneself is the cause. It is when, through self-knowledge, the Reality is revealed that it becomes evident how It is a great mystery; and till then one may think all problems could be solved through logical reasoning.

The word *śūnya*, rendered here as "non-existent on its own" is not to be understood as it is meant by the *śūnya-vādins* (Nihilists) of Buddhism. It is rather the valuelessness that some feel sometimes about life that is implied. Incessant miseries and fear sometimes make people think of life as valueless. This sense of vacuity, like an infernal city (*vetāla-nagaram*), is fancied by them because of their ignorance (*avidyā*). It is not a state of utter non-existence; the existence of the Consciousness that finds expression as ignorance is there. Knowing this Consciousness-Reality results in realizing that It is nothing but God, and that everything phenomenal is fancied by that God. Then alone does one realize how mysterious all this is!

Verse 9

अर्काद्यथाक्रमं विश्वं तथा नैवेदमात्मनः ।
सुप्तेरिव प्रादुरासीद्युगपत्स्वस्य वीक्षया ॥९॥

arkād yathākramaṁ viśvaṁ tathā naivedam ātmanaḥ I
supter iva prādur āsīd yugapad svasya vīkṣayā II9 II

The coming into being of this world happened not in gradual steps as from the Sun. Instantaneously from the Self, owing to Its own wilful perception, was its emergence, just as it appears on waking up from sleep.

Given that the world was created by God, a question arises from this notion: how did God create the world? Was it a gradual creation, or was it an instantaneous one? The emergence and growth of all physical phenomena in nature, as we see it, is a gradual one, and each stage of its evolution is visible. God, being a mystical Reality, could perhaps be an exception to this rule.

There already exists a creation theory acceptable to modern physics. According to it, parts of the Sun, when molten, splintered away and began to revolve around it, forming its planets, the earth being one of them. The chemical permutations and combinations going on ceaselessly in it resulted in the emergence of particles capable of giving rise to life. These particles, evolving further constantly for millions of years, caused the coming into being of objects (brains) that can reflect or emit consciousness. Further evolved, the same process gave rise to brains (human brains) that can even reflect on the function of the very same consciousness. Yet, the concept that consciousness is an after-effect of material evolution is not a finally established truth. It remains a mere hypothesis.

The process of sense-perception, according to this hypothesis, is as follows: contact with an object stimulates the concerned sense-organ; the stimulation gets transformed as electrical waves, which travelling through the nervous system, reach the brain and cause certain chemical changes in its neurons; and the emergence of consciousness is the end-result of these chemical changes. In short, sense-perception, according to this stand, is the event of the world existing unquestionably outside, getting reflected in the interior brain.

New hypotheses questioning this theory also have emerged among scientists. One of them is the "San Diego Theory" which claims, "Cognition, then, is not a representation of an independently existing world, but rather a continual bringing forth of a world through the process of living."[1]

---

1. Fritjof Capra, *The Web of Life*, Harper Collins Publishers, London 1996, p. 260.

This San Diego Theory comes very close to the instantaneous creation theory (*yugapat-sṛṣṭi-vāda*) the Guru supports in this verse. According to both, the world and consciousness emerge together.

Creation theories could generally be classified into the gradual creation theory (*krama-sṛṣṭi-vāda*) and the instantaneous creation theory (*yugapat-sṛṣṭi-vāda*). The former is the stand, as is the case with modern science, that creation took place step by step through evolution. *Yugapat-sṛṣṭi-vāda*, on the other hand, holds that creation took place instantaneously, *yugapat* meaning "simultaneous." This is often compared to one's feeling upon waking up from sleep, that the world emerges altogether all at once. The world, as far as a man asleep is concerned, is non-existent. How did the world, so far non-existent, emerge to view? It emerged instantaneously along with one's waking up. Likewise, the ideation or willing of God or *ātman* resulted in the instantaneous appearance of the world, in Itself. Such is the essential content of the theory known as *yugapat-sṛṣṭi-vāda*, popular with the Śaṅkara School of Vedānta.

There are also evolution theories which are meaningful in limited fields of study. For example, the Darwinian Theory of Evolution is pertinent to Biology. The modern science of Genetics was unknown when Darwin conceived the idea of evolution, the former's inception being from the time of Mendel only. The Evolution Theory has evolved to accommodate into it the ideas of Genetics. This new brand of evolution theory is known as Neo-Darwinism, which now continues to be the sturdy basis for biological research, in spite of the fact that it remains an idea yet to be proved scientifically. Darwinian Evolution and Neo-Darwinism are all meaningful only within the limited domain of Biology.

The overall evolution, or the gradual change that takes place in the cosmos beginninglessly and endlessly does not come within the purview of these theories. On the other hand, the evolution and gradual creation we are concerned with here is all-inclusive, it does not exclude from its scope anything or any field of enquiry — organic or inorganic, mental or physical, subtle or gross. We are concerned with the creation of the entire cosmos, from which mind is not excluded.

Some Upaniṣads describe the creation with a picture that resembles evolution. For example, according to the *Taittirīya Upaniṣad,* in the beginning there was *Ātman* alone existing; from *ātman* emerged pure space (*ākāśa*); from space air (*vāyu*); from air fire (*agni*); from fire water (*ap*); from water earth (*pṛthivī*); from earth vegetation (*oṣadhi*); from vegetation food (*annam*); from food semen (*reta*s); and from semen human (*puruṣa*). (*Taittirīya Upaniṣad* II.1.2).

A different picture of creation is portrayed in the *Aitareya Upaniṣad* as follows:

> The Self verily was all this, one only, in the beginning. Nothing else whatsoever winked. He thought, "Let me now create the worlds."
>
> He created these worlds, water, light-rays, death and waters. This water is above the heaven. The heaven is its support. The light-rays are the atmosphere. Death is earth. What are beneath, they are the waters. He thought, "Here then are the worlds. Let me now create the guardians of the worlds." From the waters themselves, he drew forth the person and gave him a shape.
>
> He brooded over him. Of him who has thus been brooded over, the mouth was separated out, like an egg. From the mouth speech, from speech fire. The nostrils were separated out: from the nostrils breath, from breath air. The eyes were

> separated out: from the eyes sight, from sight the sun. The ears were separated out: from the ears hearing, and from hearing the quarters of space. The skin was separated out: from the skin the hairs, from the hairs plants and trees. The heart was separated out: from the heart the mind, and from the mind the moon. The navel was separated out: from the navel the outbreath, from the outbreath death. The generative organ was separated out: from it semen, from semen water.

Who created the world? How was it created? Where and how did it exist before creation? What was the impelling force behind creation? Given that the will of the Creator was the cause of creation, then how are the mind of the Creator and the world related? All these questions arise when we agree that the world as we see it exists, as is assumed in the present chapter. It was also clarified that the world is perceived as world only when Self-knowledge is in a fully shrunken state. Such a state of ignorance renders life full of fears, accompanied by a sense of evil. If such a world is thought of as having emerged as the result of a creation process, then that creation has to be instantaneous, the point cleared in the present verse.

Now the chapter ends by pointing out in the next verse that nothing really exists apart from the transcendental and causal Substance. This verse clears the path to the next chapter.

Verse 10

धानादिव वटो यस्मात् प्रादुरासीदिदं जगत्।
स ब्रह्मा स शिवो विष्णुः स परः सर्व एव सः ॥१०॥

dhānād iva vaṭo yasmāt prādur āsīd idaṁ jagat ।
sa brahmā sa śivo viṣṇuḥ sa paraḥ sarva eva saḥ ॥10॥

The One from whom this changeful world came out like a banyan-tree from its seed, He is Brahmā, He is Śiva and Viṣṇu, He is the Transcendental, He is indeed everything.

So far we were trying to sort out some of the main problems that arise when it is taken for granted that the world as we perceive through the senses, exists. Given that the world was created, its sustenance and dissolution also have to be taken into account. Some Reality, whatever the name it is known by, must have been existing before creation. It is natural to suppose that the same Reality causes the sustenance and dissolution of the world. To assume that creation, sustenance and dissolution entails the existence of more than one reality is an idea that goes against the integrity of the world order. For these reasons, before concluding the *Adhyāropa Darśanam*, the Guru asserts that Brahmā the creator, Viṣṇu the sustainer and Śiva the destroyer are essentially no other than the one Reality variously named in various contexts.

The presiding deity of creation, according to Indian Mythology, is Brahmā; of sustenance Viṣṇu; and of dissolution Śiva. Though the gods (*deva*s) are conceived as many in the Purāṇas (Mythological Legends) some Purāṇas admit that the substance underlying the appearance of all the gods, all the demons (*asura*s), all the humans, all the beings, all the worlds, is one alone, only that each Purāṇa gives a different name to this one Reality. For example, the Purāṇas of the Śiva tradition call It Śiva; of Viṣṇu tradition Viṣṇu; of the Śakti cult Devī; and so on. How the phenomena of creation, sustenance and dissolution are to be perceived in relation to the one all-underlying Reality is clarified by Narayana Guru himself as follows:

> Individual forms, like waves in the ocean emerge in sequence and so do they merge. Alas! when will this process come to an end! O, this is nothing but the action of creative self-unfoldment happening within the ocean of primeval Source-Consciousness! — Verse 56, *Ātmopadeśa Śatakam*

Saṁvit is the original word used by the Guru to mean "Source-Consciousness." It literally means "unconditioned consciousness," and the same will be called *caitanya,* meaning the same, in the next verse. This *saṁvit* or *caitanya* is compared to a boundless ocean. The ocean always has inherent in it the urge to produce waves from within itself. This creative urge finding expression is called *karma* (action). The waves that emerge as a result roll on for a while and then disappear.

Similarly in the *saṁvit*-ocean there is an inherent and indomitable *karma*-urge. Its unfoldment results in the emergence of individual beings such as each of us. Each such individual entity, while having particular traits, remains for a while as if having its own existence, and finally merges in the very same *saṁvit*-ocean. The emergence of wave-like individuals is what we call birth, and the aspect of the creative urge that causes birth is allegorically called Brahmā. The duration of the existence of each wave-like formation is called our life span, and the totality of all the waves constitutes the existence of the world. The inner urge that ensures this is called Viṣṇu. The merging of the wave-like entity back into the ocean is called death, and the aspect of the creative urge that ensures this merger is called Śiva.

The words *Brahmā* and *Brahman* are both derived from the same verb-root *bṛh,* meaning "to grow" (*bṛhi vṛddhau*). *Brahmā* means "the Creator" and *Brahman,* "the Absolute." Though the ordinary ocean does not grow in size, the waves emerging in it do. The emerging of waves could itself be treated as a process of growth. Similar is the case of the *saṁvit*-ocean. It also does not grow in size, but the waves that we are, grow in it ceaselessly, each finally to merge back into it. Every emerging process, every growing process, should have underlying it a knowledge as to what should emerge, how they emerge, and when should they emerge. This knowledge, functioning variously while remaining one, was poetically called *Brahmā* the Creator, by the ancient *ṛṣi*s of Indian Mythology.

Viṣṇu, the presiding deity of sustenance, literally means, "that which pervades everywhere." No wave that emerges in the ocean remains inactive; so too are the waves emerging in the *saṁvit*-ocean. Each being passes through six distinct stages known in Vedānta as *ṣadbhāva*s. They are existence (*asti*), birth (*janmam*), growth (*vṛddhi*), evolution (*pariṇāma*), decline (*apakṣaya*), and dissolution (*vināśa*), and this continuous phenomenon is what we call life. The being of all the waves is pervaded by one Substance — water. So too one Substance fills the being of each and every individual entity in this cosmic system ensuring the continuance of the phenomenon called life. That Substance, which is no other than Consciousness in essence, is called Viṣṇu.

Śiva, according to Indian Mythology, is the god of dissolution, but the word literally means "that which brings about auspiciousness." Śiva is the god that keeps the life system auspicious by the constant process of dissolving individual wave-like beings, to let the new ones emerge. This dissolution phenomenon is what we call death, an event which is not at all thought of as auspicious by human beings. No one likes to die either. Suppose the phenomenon of death ceases to be. We can then imagine how inauspicious life would be. The novelty of life is ensured though the never-ending process of old beings disappearing and new ones emerging. Really, one entity emerging means another getting destroyed, like a chick emerging means an egg dying. If birth could be considered as one side of the coin called life, then its other side is death. The god who ensures this kind of auspiciousness in life is called Śiva.

It is the one God or Reality that could be variously called Brahmā, Viṣṇu or Śiva, that was called *Parameśvara* (the Supreme Controller) in the first verse. That God here is compared to a seed (*dhāna*), the original word meaning "that which conceals within." A tiny seed hides within itself the potential to grow as a giant banyan-tree that can sometimes live for millennia. Likewise, the extremely subtle Reality, called *Parameśvara* here, unfolds itself as all the worlds, including the birth, sustenance and dissolution of all the beings in them. *Parameśvara*, for this reason, has to be beyond the Brahmā-Viṣṇu-Śiva-multiplicity, beyond creation, sustenance and dissolution.

For the reason that it is one Reality that is variously called Brahmā, Viṣṇu and Śiva as their various functions, namely creation, sustenance and dissolution, the same Reality could well be equated to everything (*sarvam*). So it is said "He indeed is everything" (*sarva eva saḥ*). These words re-echoe the *sarvam hy etad brahmā* (Everything here indeed is *Brahman*) of the *Māṇḍūkya Upaniṣad*. (2) and *Sarvam khalvidam brahma* (Every thing here indeed is *Brahman*) of the *Chāndogya Upaniṣad* (III. xiv.1).

What we saw in the present chapter as beyond everything is conceived as *caitanya* (pure and unconditioned Consciousness) in the next chapter.

2

Apavāda Darśanam
(Vision by Negation)

ATTEMPTS to know the Ultimate Reality were made in the last Chapter from the perspective of admitting the existence of the apparent world. Superimposed appearance (*adhyāropa*), in other words, was the springboard for our efforts there. *Adhyāropa* causes the mistake of not seeing what really exists, and treating the external apparent form as real. That this wrong perception is caused by *avidyā* (ignorance) which occurs when self-knowledge (*ātmavidyā*) remains shrunken, was mentioned earlier in Verse 1.7.

Adhyāropa is traditionally defined as *vastuni avastu āropam* (projecting the unreal on the real). In the Vedāntic context it refers to projecting the unreal world on the real *Brahman* and thus becoming deluded by the resulting wrong vision. The only way for a seeker to get out of this trap-like situation is through discrimination. One must negate what is superimposed or projected, and perceive intuitively what really exists underlying the appearance, that is, what really assumes the forms we apparently see. This way of negation is the chief methodological tool of Vedānta, and is known as *apavāda* (*apa* + *vāda*), *apa* meaning "negatively," and *vāda* "to argue," the word *apavāda* thus meaning "to argue out," or to affirm the real through negating the unreal.

The apparent world, for the sake of argument, was treated as real in the last Chapter, and then we had to answer questions like, "Who was its creator?," "How was it created?" and so on. Such a search finally landed us in the vision of non-dual Reality. What we see at the end of the present Chapter, after negating everything superimposed, as the causal Reality, is *sat-cit-ānanda* (Existence-Consciousness-Value Experience) alone. *Sat-cit-ānanda* alone being Real does not mean that the existence and value of the apparent world is totally denied. On the other hand, it reveals that the apparent world is the manifest form of *sat-cit-ānanda*. What the word *sat* signifies is clarified in the first six verses. Verses 7 and 8 show what *cit* is — (i.e. it is nothing but the essential content of *sat*). The next verse shows that the one Reality that is *sat* and *cit* at the same time, is *ānanda* as well. The Chapter ends by categorically asserting that everything is one *sat-cit-ānanda* alone, that those who perceive many in it go from death to death. This assertion signifies that those who realize themselves as *sat-cit-ānanda*, attain immortality. We thus finally again reach the non-dualistic vision, although this time from a different direction.

Verse 1

चैतन्यादागतं स्थूलसूक्ष्मात्मकमिदं जगत् ।
अस्ति चेत् सद्घनं सर्वं नास्ति चेदस्ति चिद्घनम् ॥१॥

caitanyād āgataṁ sthūla sūkṣmātmakam idaṁ jagat ।
asti cet sad ghanaṁ sarvaṁ nāsti ced asti cid ghanam ॥1॥

From pure and unconditioned Consciousness was the coming into being of this changeful world, gross as well as subtle in form. Everything, if considered existent, is simply *sat* in essence; if counted as non-existent, then everything is *cit* in essence.

The present Chapter begins at the point where the last Chapter ended. It was seen there that one Transcendental Reality (*paraḥ*) alone was causal to the phenomena of creation, sustenance and dissolution. At the beginning of the Chapter, that Transcendental Substance was called *Parameśvara* (the Supreme Controller). Here, the same is called *caitanya* (pure and unconditioned Consciousness). What is signified by the terms such as *Ātman, Brahman, Paramātman* and *Prabhu,* is none other than this *caitanya.*

The world that emerged from the one *caitanya* appears here as having two facets: the gross (*sthūla*) and the subtle (*sūkṣma*). Traditionally in Vedānta, worldly existence is classified as having different grades of bodies (*śarīras*), namely *sthūla śarīra* (gross body), *sūkṣma śarīra* (subtle body), and *kāraṇa śarīra* (causal body). Apparently these bodies are not under reference here. Verse 7 of the last Chapter portrayed the world as constituted of names and forms (*nāma* and *rūpa*). The gross world referred to here is akin to *rūpa,* and the subtle to *nāma.* The *sthūla* could also be considered as the physical or concrete aspect of existence, and the *sūkṣma* to the abstract or mental aspect. The former is the objective world and the latter the subjective. This perception is more in line with the outlook of modern science.

The object of every sense-organ exists externally. But its existence becomes an experienced actuality and thus of any value, only when perceiving it or knowing it. To say that something that has never been known and will never be known, exists or does not exist mean the same. In fact, no assertion or negation of something completely unknown is possible, for both are possible only with respect to something known. Therefore, along with the assertion of the existence of the gross world comes the knowledge — that is subtle —

about the world thus asserted. This knowledge is not an external event or phenomenon, but it is an internal experience. This conceptual counterpart of existence is what is called *pratibhā* by the Guru in the opening verse of his *Advaita Dīpikā* (Lamp of Non-duality).

The modern science uses the word "world" only to denote the external gross aspect of existence. Consciousness and the knowing function that takes place in it are never counted as realities. Science relegates mind simply as a side-effect of some chemical action taking place in the physical object, that is the brain. The reason for maintaining such an attitude is the fact that all scientific search has for its basis one fundamental stand, or rather a prejudice, that matter is the cause of everything in the universe. This is a hypothesis never provable scientifically. No such pre-conceived ideas condition Vedāntic speculation; it is a search for the all-underlying Reality with an open mind, taking into account all aspects of our experience comprehensively and integrally.

That the gross world exists outside is our direct experience. Equally real is the internal and the subtle ideas that get formulated in our mind. This latter world of internal experience — the world of ideas — is what the word *sūkṣma* in this verse signifies. Both the worlds — of the external objects and of the internal ideas — are experienced by us, and all experiences take place in one Consciousness or *cit*. This neutral all-underlying Consciousness-Substance is termed *caitanya* in this verse. It is in this one *caitanya* that both the objective and subjective worlds get formulated as experiences. Signifying all these, it is stated, "From pure and unconditioned Consciousness was the coming into being of this changeful world, gross as well as subtle in form."

The word used here to denote "the world" is *jagat*. Derived from the verb root "*gam*" 1 (to go), it means "that which always changes." The external world is in a constant state of change. Equally changing is our inner experience of it. The external world and the world of ideas, in fact, are not to be perceived as two different worlds. On the other hand, what we call *jagat* here signifies both, as inseparably co-existing. The world (*jagat*) seen by a Vedāntin is thus much different from the physicist's world. It is the unitive reality in which the external objective appearance and the internal subjective appearance are like two sides of a single coin.

Is the world, being such, real or unreal? Certain thinkers conceive the idea that the perceptible material world alone has existence. They are called materialists. Some others think, what is perceptible is not the real. According to them, the realness of the world is in the perceiving mind, and that mind alone is real. They are called idealists. There are some scholars who think Vedānta is a sort of idealism; but it is not so. One Absolute Reality alone exists; It manifests on the one side as the materialistic world and on the other as the idealistic world. That one Reality is what Vedānta calls *Brahman* or *Ātman*. The very same Reality is denoted here by the word *caitanya*.

Let us assume that the world exists; then the experience of it also exists. A common factor — existence — is there in both these. Existence of what? In attempting to answer this question, what the Vedāntin arrives at is this: it is the existence of *cit* or pure, unconditioned Consciousness, and that existence is undeniable. Undeniable existence is called *sat* in Vedānta. It is this *sat*, that is *cit* in essence, that assumes the form of both the gross material world and the subtle idealistic world. The substance that underlies the being of both the worlds is one *sat* alone, and the being of everything is *sat* in essence, just as we can say, the being of all ornaments is gold in essence.

Suppose the argument is that the apparent world, the gross and subtle aspects together, has no real existence; then also there is one thing undeniable: the awareness that the world has no real existence. That means, awareness, consciousness or *cit* has indisputable existence. It is in this *cit* that the world-experiences emerge. Therefore, asserting that the world has no real existence virtually means agreeing that the world is *cit* in essence.

How are *sat* and *cit* related? They are not relatable entities; only that the essential content of *sat* is *cit*. This Substance that is *sat* and *cit* at the same time is the material-cum-efficient cause of the world that could be proved logically as both existing and not existing. Such a world then is to be treated as an effect, of which the cause is *sat-cit*.

How are cause and effect related? This point is clarified in the next verse.

Verse 2

अन्यन्न कारणात् कार्यं असदेतदतोऽखिलम् ।
असतः कथमुत्पत्तिरनुत्पन्नस्य को लयः ॥२॥

anyan na kāraṇāt kāryaṁ asad etad ato 'khilam ।
asataḥ katham utpattir anutpannasya ko layaḥ ॥2॥

Apart from cause, effect has no existence. For this reason, everything here is simply unreal. How can the unreal have any origin at all? And how can the unoriginated have dissolution either?

This Chapter is named *Apavāda Darśana* or vision by Negation or Refutation. What is it that is refuted or argued out? It is the non-existing and illusory world-appearance imputed on something Real. Anything can be imputed only on some substratum that really exists. The world form is attributed on a Substance, as are ornament-forms attributed on the gold-substance. On finding out that substratum, one realizes the appearance of the world is illusory and transitory, and what really exists is that substratum alone. Ascertaining the non-existence of the world-appearance on the Substratum-Reality is called *apavāda*.

What then is that Substratum? The world, if "real," should have everlasting existence. Our experience is otherwise; everything apparent has a transitory existence only. That means, what appears to be is not "the real." What then is "the real?" That was the *sad-ghana* (essential Existence) cited in the last verse. Suppose the world has no existence; even then the existence of the knowledge of a non-existing world, exists. It was in that causal knowledge, or rather Consciousness, that the impression that the world exists, occurs. That Consciousness-Substance was called *cid-ghana*. Whether called *sad-ghana* or *cid-ghana*, the causal Substance necessarily exists. Now our attempt is to ascertain the nature and content of this causal Reality.

Relying on cause-effect relationship is a method preferred equally by philosophers and scientists all over the world. The way of the method is to enquire of the cause of something that could be thought of as an effect. Though accepted universally, this method has hidden in it a mystery apparently not noticed by many. What is the scientific basis for the acceptability of the theory of causality? How is effect related to cause? Though many philosophers have tried their best to resolve this conundrum, no logically convincing definite answer has been arrived at. A perplexing paradox hides in it — that the logic we make use of to explain causality has the very same causality for its basis. Scientists simply believe in causality, just as religious adherents believe in God; one belief is no more scientific than the other.

A clear understanding of what cause is and what effect is, is necessary to perceive clearly what the Guru tries to convey here. It is easier to clarify with the help of an example. Pots, plates and many such utensils are made of clay. Clay here is to be understood as cause, and pots and plates as effects. Clay on its own does not assume the form of utensils; a potter's effort is also needed. Potter then is yet another cause. The former cause (clay) is called material cause (*upādāna kāraṇa*), and the latter (potter) efficient cause (*nimitta kāraṇa*). In the place of the utensils is to be seen the world. The problem is, "What is its cause?" In the present case, the world's material cause and efficient causes cannot be different, for one God or *sat* alone is there to serve as both the causes. God or *Brahman*, for this reason, in Vedānta, is considered the material-cum-efficient cause (*abhinna-nimitta-upādāna-kāraṇa*) of the world.

Vedānta too relies on the law of causality in the search for Reality. Effect, here, is the apparent world, and the cause is what we are in search of. This cause is none other than the *caitanya* already referred to. The philosophical position Śaṅkara prefers on this particular point is *sat-kāraṇa-vāda* or the theory that cause alone is real and that effects are unreal. What appears as pot is clay alone; what appears as effect is the causal substance alone. Śaṅkara was an *advaitin* (non-dualist), but Rāmānuja's interpretation of Vedānta is as a *viśiṣṭādvaitin* (qualified non-dualist). According to him, both cause and effect are real, the effect being the qualified mode of expression of the cause.

Narayana Guru here sides with Śaṅkara. The pot has no existence apart from clay; likewise, the world has no existence apart from the Causal Reality, *caitanya*. The pot is *asat* (unreal); clay alone is *sat* (real). Likewise the world is *asat*; *caitanya* alone is *sat*. The pot being treated as unreal means only that it does not have its own existence. What we have here in the place of the pot is ourselves and the world. Like clay in pots, there should be a substance that underlies the apparent being of ourselves. Apart from that causal substance we have no existence. It is in this particular sense that Advaita Vedānta claims the world is unreal (*asat*). We, the perceivers of the world too, in that sense, are unreal. In short, everything visible is unreal.

It is senseless to say that the unreal had an origin. Equally meaningless is to state that the unoriginated will get dissolved. In short, the world was never originated and it will never get destroyed either. In the same sense, we, the individuals were never born and will never die. One Causal Reality alone exists, beginningless and endless, assuming the constantly changing form of the world as well as of us. In essence we are really that one Substance, just as, a pot in essence, is really clay.

Visualized thuswise, creation and dissolution, birth and death, and all such become unreal and without content. Therefore, *sat-kāraṇa-vāda*, in effect, is *ajāta-vāda* (no-creation theory) as well. This theory means, nothing new is created, and nothing existing is destroyed. It is not the total denial of the visible world that this theory leads us to, but it is to the assertion that *Brahman* alone has real existence. This point is clarified further in the next verse.

Verse 3

यस्योत्पत्तिर्लयो नास्ति तत्परं ब्रह्म नेतरत् ।
उत्पत्तिश्च लयोऽस्तीति भ्रमत्यात्मनि मायया ॥३॥

yasyotpattir layo nāsti tat paraṁ brahma netarat ।
utpattiśca layo 'stīti bhramaty ātmani māyayā ॥3॥

> That which has no origin and dissolution is the Transcendental *Brahman* alone, nothing else. That there is origin and dissolution is a delusion that arises in the self because of *māyā*.

Here our search for Reality is based on the law of causality. The phenomena of creation, sustenance and dissolution are apparent in the world that simply is an effect. The search for the one cause underlying all effects resulted in the realization that the effect as such is unreal. This means, it has no existence of its own. How can something unreal be thought of as having birth as well as death? Creation-dissolution, birth-death, all such phenomena, in other words, are also unreal. Based on this we arrive here at the conclusion that what really exists can have no birth and death, and the only Reality that is birthless and deathless is *Brahman*. Everything except *Brahman* has birth and death. Let us set aside the birth-death phenomenon as related to the effect and thus as unreal; then what remains would be the realness of *Brahman*.

That which is ultimately real and that which is ultimately unreal, both cannot be subject to creation and dissolution. The former has no beginning and will never cease to exist. It was neither created nor subjected to dissolution. To say that the latter (that which is ultimately unreal) was born is meaningless. Equally meaningless is the dissolution of something unreal. The unreal (*asat*) also thus has no creation or dissolution. From these facts we arrive at two basic conclusions: that *Brahman* alone can have real existence, because That alone is birthless and deathless, and that the phenomena of creation, sustenance and dissolution appear to be real only because of the delusion caused by *māyā*.

The Causal Reality is termed here *param brahma* (the Supreme Absolute or *Brahman*), and the same Reality, when subject to individuation due to *māyā*, is termed *ātman* (the self), which also means oneself. Does the Supreme Reality become something else as an effect of *māyā*? Or, is it only an illusory appearance? The latter is the case. Therefore, the apparent world and the phenomena of its creation, sustenance and dissolution are all illusory impressions each of us has in ourselves (*ātmani*). Even the idea that we individuals, who have birth, life-span and death, exist, is simply part of that delusion.

We treat this individual phenomenon as a criterion and project it onto the world as a whole and then say it has creation, sustenance and dissolution. All these are experiences or ideas getting formulated in our mind or consciousness. We assume also that a replica of the world internally experienced exists externally as the actual world, but it has no proof other than our own experiences and conclusions, which again are internal phenomena. The proof of the existence of the objective world, in other words, is subjective events alone. All these phenomena, the Guru points out here, are nothing more than illusory appearances happening within the being of oneself (*ātmani*). This delusion, in Vedānta, is known as *māyā*, a concept to be studied in detail later in Chapter 4. The subject or the self in which all such delusions take place, in essence, is *Brahman*, and has no existence apart from It.

Verse 4

कारणाव्यतिरिक्तत्वात् कार्यस्य कथमस्तिता ।
भवत्यतः कारणस्य कथमस्ति च नास्तिता ? ॥४॥

kāraṇāvyatiriktatvāt kāryasya katham astitā? ।
bhavaty ataḥ kāraṇasya katham asti ca nāstitā? ॥4॥

> Being not different from cause, how could effects have their own existence? For the same reason, how could the cause become non-existent either?

We arrive at two important conclusions here, based on the law of causality: that the apparent world has no real existence, and that *Brahman*, the causal Reality, cannot be non-existent. In other words, the existence of the world is negated, and the existence of *Brahman* asserted.

It is not that the world has no being of any sort. Only its existence as an entity existing different from *Brahman* is denied. The real substance in the ocean is water, and wave-forms get formulated in that essential content, and continue appearing and disappearing. Waves have no being apart from that of water; that is to say, it is the water-substance that is the essential content of waves as well. Waves have no being of their own. Likewise the world has no being of its own; it is *Brahman* that assumes the form of the appearing and disapearing world. The real content of the apparent world is *Brahman* alone.

That the world exists is our perceptual experience. We find that it has no real existence only when subjected to examination in the light of the law of causality. Even when so ascertained as unreal, its continued appearance as existing cannot be ruled out. If something unreal appears as real, then there should be something existing causal to that appearance. That causal reality thus can never be non-existent. No appearance would be possible in the absence of a causal substratum. What really exists is cause alone; manifesting itself it appears as the world. Such manifest forms always appear and disappear one after another, like in the case of waves. As is water immutable in the waves, so is Causal Reality immutable in the apparent world.

The next verse asserts that the Causal Reality must exist, and that It is nothing but *Brahman*.

Verse 5

कार्यत्वादसतोऽस्यास्ति कारणं नह्यतो जगत् ।
ब्रह्मैव तर्हि सदसदिति मुह्यति मन्दधीः ॥५॥

kāryatvād asato 'syāsti kāraṇaṁ nahy ato jagat ।
brahmaiva tarhi sad asad iti muhyati mandadhīḥ ॥5 ॥

The unreal world, being an effect, necessarily has an existing cause. And for the same reason, the world does not really exist. On the contrary, *Brahman* alone does exist. It simply is thought of as the world by those of little understanding, because they are in delusion.

The fact that the effect is unreal was given emphasis in the last verse. Here the stress given is to the cause as necessarily real. This causal reality is nothing other than *Brahman*.

How does *Brahman* attain such a high status? The word literally means, "that which is on the constant process of growth." It also signifies "that which is all-inclusive." The causal Reality conceived here, includes within it all the apparent effects, like one water remaining the cause of all the waves. *Brahman* is to be seen in the place of water here. Having no form of its own, It assumes the form of everything. It is the one abstract Reality that manifests as all the concrete forms.

Really, *Brahman* is simply a word. Which arouses within our meditative mind, the idea of the formless Reality that assumes all the forms. That Reality alone existed in the past, That alone exists in the present, That alone will exist in future. As the contrasting other side of it comes the unreality of the world in the past, present and future.

A question arises then: how can the world, which is constantly being perceived with the senses, be unreal? What we really see in the form of waves is water alone. But while seeing it, we do not think of the water-reality but of the wave-form alone, and say, "I see the waves." Waves are merely transitory apparent forms arising in water. Similarly, even when directly seeing *Brahman,* we think we are seeing the world, completely oblivious of the reality that we are seeing *Brahman*. The world, including the perceiver, is merely the ever-changing apparent form *Brahman* assumes.

Only the dull-witted, incapable of undertaking a search for reality and not being in the habit of contemplative thinking, will hold what appears and disappears moment after moment as real, unmindful of the everlasting substance in those apparent forms.

In fact, the senses and mind are responsible for this misconception. What these faculties are capable of grasping is only the evanescent apparent forms, and never their underlying substance. It could well be said, in this particular sense, that our own sense-organs and mental faculties constantly keep us dull-witted. We are merely tiny ripples emerging and re-merging constantly in the *Brahman*-ocean.

Our above-mentioned faculties form merely part of the qualities that specify those ripples, and their being too is simply as part of the *Brahman*-ocean. How, then, will those faculties ever be capable of grasping *Brahman* as thier objects? This is the reason why realized *ṛṣis* have always warned that knowing *Brahman* is no ordinary knowledge, that it is beyond the bounds of such knowledges.

This world is in a state of constant change. We too constantly change. Our mind and sense-organs also do not remain changeless. The entire world, thus, is an eternal flow of events or of actions (*karmas*). One knowing another is simply one among such *karmas*. Mind, a part of the world, becomes aware of some object, yet another part of the world. This event is what we call knowing. This knowing function cannot help taking place, for what is real in both the knowing mind and the known object is *Brahman* alone, which is *cit* or pure Consciousness in essence, as will be made clear later in Verses 7 and 8. Knowing is a function which is normal and natural with consciousness. Both the knowing mind and the known object being changeful, the knowing experience has also necessarily to be changeful.

Some of these experiences cause pleasure, and some others pain, but both are events taking place in *Brahman*. Realizing this *Brahman* as one's own essential substance — each wave becoming aware of being water in essence — renders pain no-pain, and pleasure no-pleasure. Such is the state of ultimate release or freedom (*mukti*) from delusion.

Verse 6

एकस्यैवास्ति सत्ता चेदन्यस्याऽसौ क्व विद्यते ।
सत्यस्त्यात्माश्रयो यद्यप्यसति स्यादसंभवः ॥६॥

ekasyaivāsti sattā ced anyasyā 'sau kva vidyate ।
saty asty ātmāśrayo yady apy asati syād asaṁbhavaḥ ॥6॥

If one alone has existence, then how could something else have being? If it be said that the being (of that something else) is in what already exists, then it is wrong by the fallacy of tautology; if it be said that the being (of that something else) is in what does not exist then it is wrong by contradiction.

Sat-kāraṇa-vāda (the doctrine that cause is what is real) is the basic stand relied on in the present Chapter. *Brahman* is the reality causal to all that appears as the world. This multiple world, thus, is the effect of the one causal *Brahman*. The world has no existence apart from this cause just as pots have no being apart from clay.

The enquiry based on the law of causality, for the one causal reality, ends with this verse. It was concluded in the last verse that *Brahman* alone has real existence. It follows naturally that the world, as an entity existing on its own, has no reality. If it be argued that it is not so, and that the world also has existence, then such a stand would be logically wrong. The two logical fallacies by which such a stand would be vitiated, are also pointed out in this verse. The Guru's argument is: if one Substance (*Brahman*) alone has being, then how can another (the world) also have being. The scientific fact underlying this argument is that two entities cannot occupy the same space at the same time.

If it be said that the being of the world is in the being of *Brahman*; it is equal to say, "Being is in being," a logical fallacy known as tautology in the West and *ātmāśraya* in the East. This fallacy means, the proof depends for its validity on that which is to be proved. Suppose someone says, "These are the words of God, so everyone is bound to accept these." When asked, "How can you prove that these words are God's?," his answer would be, "It is so stated in those words themselves." This statement is logically wrong. The same fallacy (tautology) could be there in the case of defining something. When asked "What is beauty?," suppose one says, "What makes something beautiful is beauty." This is a tautological definition. Equally wrong is to say that what exists has its being in existence. In other words, it is logically wrong to think that the world has existence after admitting that *Brahman* alone exists.

Suppose the world's existence is seen not in *Brahman* but in itself. Having already proved that the world has no existence of its own, the above statement means, existence has non-existence for its basis, a logical impossibility known as contradiction in the West and *asambhava* in the East. Stating something impossible as a reason or a defining factor, is what is known as the fallacy (*doṣa*) of *asambhava*. Suppose someone says, "I broke a hare's horns." A hare having no horn being a well-known fact, this statement is wrong because of the *asambhava doṣa* (contradiction) it involves.

What is the one primeval causal Reality in essence? That it is Consciousness (*cit*) in essence is made clear in the next verse.

verse 7

विभज्याऽवयवं सर्वमेकैकं तत्र दृश्यते।
चिन्मात्रमखिलं नान्यदिति मायाविदूरगम् ॥७॥

vibhajyā 'vayavaṁ sarvam ekaikaṁ tatra dṛśyate ।
cinmātram akhilaṁ nānyad iti māyā vidūragam ॥7॥

When everything is divided on and on into parts, then what is perceived at the end of that is, all is but pure Consciousness (*cit*) alone, far from the delusions of *māyā*, and nothing else is seen.

It has already become evident from the discussions covered so far in this Chapter that one Ultimate Reality alone exists, and that Reality is *Brahman*. A question then arises: what that Reality or *Brahman* is in its essential content or *svarūpa*? In other words, what is Existence (*sat*) in its essence? The present verse establishes that essential substance (*svarūpa*) is pure Consciousness (*cit*) alone.

Narayana Guru lived and gave expression to his vision, in the Age of Science. He naturally imbibed the spirit of scientific thinking into his philosophical speculations. To analyse something in order to ascertain the essential content of it, is the most popular method known to modern science. The Guru was willing to adapt himself to this scientific trend. That the ancient *ṛṣis* did not resort to such a method, is not to be considered a failure on their part, for such an analytical method was not popular in those days.

The analysis summarily presented here is elaborated by the Guru himself in his *Advaita Dīpikā* (Lamp of Non-Duality) thus:

> The cloth here is thread, which is but cotton fibres, and which in turn is seen as elemental stuff, thus speculated on and on, it could be traced to pure Consciousness as its source, like water illusorily seen has desert for its source. Consciousness indeed is what exists ultimately.
>
> — Verse 3

Someone, intending to know the real content in a piece of cloth, an object that forms a part of the world, subjects it to analysis. The piece of cloth, in the first step, gets transformed into yarn, the former disappearing in the latter. Analysed further, the yarn turns out to be cotton fibres in content, again the former disappearing in the latter. Fibres are further analysed. They, according to the modern scientific view, become transformed into molecules containing atoms of elements like carbon and oxygen. These atoms, analysed further, are found to be different energy particles in essence, all of them being various forms in which one energy-reality appears.

What is the nature of that energy-reality? No one knows. It simply is. Its existence is undeniable because we know that it exists. That means, what is undeniably real is knowledge or consciousness alone. It is consciousness, in its functional states, that assumes the forms of energy, atoms, molecules, fibre, yarn, cloth and even the visible world of which the cloth is a part, all disappearing in the reality of Consciousness. This Consciousness is what is termed as *cit* in the present verse.

According to the traditional Indian perspective, the cotton fibres, when analysed, get disintegrated into five basic elements called *pañca-bhūta*s, namely, earth (*pṛthivī*), water (*ap*), fire (*agni*), air (*vāyu*), and space (*ākāśa*). These elements in their pure state do not exist anywhere. They are simply principles or "things in themselves" (*tanmātra*s). All the visible elements like the physical earth and water are combinations of all the five, one predominating in each. That means, the elements as such exist only in knowledge or consciousness. Something that exists in consciousness alone naturally is consciousness in essence. It is this Consciousness-Substance, called *cit* here, that appears as *tanmātra*s, the five visible elements, cotton fibres, yarn, cloth and even the world.

How is it that this invisible consciousness appears as everything visible? The Vedāntin's answer to the question is: it is because of *māyā*. What then is *māyā*? A clear definition of it and its detailed examination are reserved for Chapter 4. Let us, for the present, understand this much about *māyā*. The one all-underlying *cit* is, in the normal course, not perceived by us, the countless forms assumed by it are perceived, and are counted as forming the world which we presume to exist. Some mysterious factor that causes this phenomenon is there in the *cit*, and that unknowable potential is called *māyā*.

Let us put the same in a different way in terms of the law of causality. We do not directly perceive the cause; effects alone are seen and are thought of as really existing. The absolute Reality must be having within it some mysterious power that emanates both cause and effect from within Itself. This power is called *māyā*.

Our life is subject to this *māyā*, yet we remain completely ignorant of its being so. Freedom from this *māyā*'s grip is possible only in case by chance a yearning to know Reality arises within you, and you, again by chance become fortunate enough to meet with a proper *guru* to guide you towards your goal. The confluence of these two chance elements is to take place by the Grace of God. Only if favoured thus, you realize the causal Reality in yourself as *cit*, that you are *cit* alone.

Cit was thus ascertained as the all underlying *sat*. The next verse states that this *cit* itself is what manifests phenomenally as everything, and that it does not remain without manifesting thus.

Verse 8

चिदेव नान्यदाभाति चितः परमतो न हि ।
यच्च नाभाति तदसद्यदसत्तन्न भाति च ॥८॥

cid eva nānyad ābhāti citaḥ param ato na hi ।
yacca nābhāti tad asad yad asat tan na bhāti ca ॥8॥

> *Cit* alone and nothing else manifests as the world; nothing is there higher than *cit* existing. That which does not manifest as the world is unreal (*asat*); that which is unreal cannot manifest as the world either.

All Vedāntins admit that the ultimate Reality is *sat-cit-ānanda* in essence as does Narayana Guru also. These three words put together become the well-known compound word *saccidānanda* that defines *Brahman*. *Sat* (Existence) is experienced by each person as his or her own existence called *asti*; likewise, *cit* (Consciousness) is experienced as the bright functional facets of one's own mind called *bhāti*; and *ānanda* (value sense) becomes actual in life as one's own likes and dislikes (*priya*). *Saccidānanda*, as actual personal experience, thus becomes *asti-bhāti-priya*.

Cit sometimes is called *caitanya* in Vedāntic textbooks; then, the one unconditioned *caitanya*, when manifesting as specific knowledges, experiences or moods, is called *ābhāsa-caitanya* or *cid-ābhāsa*, literally "semblance of consciousness." It could well be stated in more technical terms that *cit* when subjected to *māyā* becomes *ābhāsa-caitanaya* or *cid-ābhāsa*. One *cit* manifesting as many *bhāti*s or subjective experiences could be compared to one formless clay assuming the various forms of pots, plates and so on.

Cit does not manifest itself merely in the form of mental states and experiences. Being the essential content *sat* (Existence), it alone is the substance that appears as everything. When manifesting as concrete or gross forms, it assumes the forms of physical entities; and when manifesting with subtle forms it appears as mental states or as the world of ideas. All these are to be dealt with in detail later in Chapter 5 *Bhāna Darśanam*. What is underscored here is the basic truth that it is one *cit* alone that manifests as everything both physical and mental, gross and subtle, external and internal, as both cause and effect. This manifest form of *cit* is termed *bhāti* as we have already noted. In other words, when the Reality is considered as *sat*, its manifest form is called *asti* in the personal sense, and the same in impersonal context is called *bhāva*. When considered as *cit* its conditioned form is *bhāti* or *bhāna*.

It may look easy to think of such dualities as the unmanifest and the manifest, the unconditioned and the conditioned, the one and the many, *sat* and *bhāva*, *cit* and *bhāti* or *bhāna*; but how are the limbs of these pairs related to each other? The Guru clarifies this point thus:

That which does not appear in manifest forms has necessarily to be unreal (*asat*); and that which is unreal never manifests. Something existing alone can become manifest. How can something non-existent find expression in some apparent form? What really exists (*sat*) never remains without manifesting either. Put otherwise, without *sat* there is no *bhāva*, and without *bhāva* there is no *sat* either. It is equivalent to say, without *cit* there is no *bhāna* or *bhāti*, and without *bhāna*, *cit* never exists either. Non-existent gold never appears as ornament-forms, and gold never remains without having some transient form either. Likewise, *Brahman*, *sat* and *cit* at the same time, never exists without appearing as the world, and the world never exists without having *Brahman* for its essential substance. The separateness of *Brahman* and the world, of gold and ornament-form, is merely an idea we have created in our mind. Actually the two always remain non-dual, inseparably one. This is the real non-duality (*advaita*) that gets revealed to a real seeker's yogic eye, though never to a logical mind. A subtle secret that only gets revealed to a genuine visionary of ultimate Reality (*tattvadarśin*) hides in this highly delicate situation, as is clearly forewarned in the *Bhagavad-Gītā* thus:

nāsato vidyate bhāvo nābhāvo vidyate sataḥ ।
ubhayor api dṛṣṭvo 'ntastv anayos tattvadarśibhiḥ ॥

— II.16

The unreal cannot manifest, the real never remains with no manifestations. The inherent truth of these two has thus been perceived by the seers of Ultimate Reality.

It is *cit*, the essential content of *sat*, that was earlier called cause (*kāraṇa*). Then the word *ābhāti* (manifests here as the world) stands for effects (*kārya*). The secret of non-duality or *advaita* hides in the inseparable oneness of cause and effect, of *Brahman* and the apparent world.

Having seen that *sat* is *cit* in essence, now we go to the next step of perceiving this Reality as *ānanda* (value-experience) in essence.

Verse 9

आनन्द एवास्ति भाति नान्यः कश्चिदतोऽखिलम् ।
आनन्दघनमन्यन्न विनाऽनन्देन विद्यते ॥९॥

ānanda evāsti bhāti nānyaḥ kaśid ato 'khilam ।
ānanda-ghanam anyan na vinā 'nandena vidyate ॥9॥

Ānanda alone exists and *ānanda* alone manifests, nothing else is there existing at all. The entire world, therefore, is purely *ānanda* in essence. Nothing other than *ānanda* has real existence.

First it was asserted that one Reality alone has existence, and it is called *sat*. It is this *sat* that manifests as the existence of everything phenomenal. This *sat*, in essence, is none other than *cit*, as was given emphasis to thereafter. Effulgence in essence, this *cit* (Consciousness) is always luminous in the form of everything apparent. This self-manifestation of *cit* is called *bhāti*.

We have experiences when consciousness becomes luminous in ever-changing forms, and each such experience is about something. The existence of that something could either be physical or mental. In either case, it is a *bhāna* (specific manifestation of consciousness). Along with knowing something there occurs an evaluation of that which is known. This is undertaken by relating it to our likes and dislikes. This normally takes place unconsciously, especially in the case of knowing insignificant things. Usually we remain oblivious of this evaluation taking place.

Suppose, for example, we come across a pebble lying in our study. Immediately we feel its irrelevance there, so we pick it up and throw it away. This is done only after the unconscious evaluation that the stone is of no value there and that its place is not in the neatly-kept study. This evaluation takes place right along with recognizing it as a pebble. Suppose, as we are about to throw away, we recognize it as a gemstone. Then instead of throwing away, we keep it in a secure place. This also follows an act of evaluation. Along with knowing anything, thus, takes place an act of evaluation. This particular aspect of the function of consciousness is called "affection" in Western Psychology.

Every evaluation ascertains whether the object known arouses favourable feelings (*iṣṭa*), unfavourable feelings (*aniṣṭa*) or indifference (*udāsīna*) in us. This evaluation requires a standard of measurement that helps us decide which is liked, which is disliked and which arouses indifference in us. This standard is nothing other than *cit* or consciousness, and when so functioning the same *cit* is called *ānanda*. Put otherwise, what we experience as pleasure and pain are nothing but this neutral *ānanda* manifesting positively or negatively, the same way as *cit* manifests as both knowledge and ignorance. Such being *cit* and *ānanda*, the two cannot be separated from each other.

Why is it so? *Cit* is *ānanda* also in essence. *Ānanda* understood here is not simply pleasure understood in the worldly sense. It, on the other hand, is the value-sense that renders one experience pleasurable and another painful, and therefore is neutral between pain and pleasure, and is what underlies both pain and pleasure. It is because of this *ānanda* content of *ātman* that pleasure is experienced as pleasure and pain as pain. Nothing that cannot be evaluated as pleasurable, painful or indifferent, occurs anywhere, hence the assertion in the verse, "Nothing other than *ānanda* has real existence" (*anyat na vinānandena vidyate*).

It is in the form of our experience that the world exists as far as each of us is concerned. We are not sure whether the form of the world each of us perceives is exactly the same. A world not at all experiencable, either physically or in imagination, cannot be thought of as existing either. We have an idea of the world, and we think it exists externally exactly in the form we perceive it. But we do not have any means to check the correctness of this notion. Therefore we simply assume that the world exists outside in the form we perceive. That means, the external existence of the world is as a form of *cit*. It was earlier seen that this *cit* is the essential content of *sat*. The knowledge of the world, as we have seen, is not simply an event of knowing it. It arouses value-sense also in us; so it is *ānanda* also in essence. It could therefore well be said that the being of *sat* means the being of *cit*; the being of *cit* means the being of *ānanda*. The self-manifestation of *sat* is the self-manifestation of *cit*, and so is of *ānanda*. Other than as the manifestation of *sat* and *cit*, the world has no being. *Sat* and *cit* being *ānanda* also in essence, the being of the entire world could then be seen as of *ānanda* in essence. It is stated therefore here, "The entire world therefore is purely *ānanda* in essence" (*ataḥ akhilam ānanda-ghanam*).

First everything was seen as *sat* in essence, then as *cit* in essence, and finally as *ānanda* in essence. The next verse discloses that everything ultimately is nothing but *saccidānanda*, and the Chapter concludes by revealing what would be the peril of those who do not see themselves and the world thus.

Verse 10

सर्वं हि सच्चिदानन्दं नेह नानाऽस्ति किञ्चन।
यः पश्यतीह नानेव मृत्योर्मृत्युं स गच्छति ॥१०॥

sarvaṁ hi saccidānandaṁ neha nānāsti kiñcana ।
yaḥ paśyatīha nāneva mṛtyor mṛtyum sa gacchati ॥10॥

Everything is *saccidānanda* alone; the many here have no being at all. He who perceives what exists as many proceeds from death to death.

This is the concluding verse of the chapter *Apavāda Darśanam* (Vision by Negation). It was the world constituted of gross and subtle entities seen in the first verse that was negated later. The same world, thereafter, was seen as the effect of a cause. On negating the effect, what was seen as undeniably existing was the one causal Reality or *sat*. *Sat* was then seen as *cit* as well as *ānanda* in essence. This finding leads us to the conclusion, "Everything indeed is *saccidānanda* alone." "Everything" (*sarvam*) here stands for the world seen as an effect and is then negated. What is asserted is not the unreality of the world, but that *Brahman* alone ultimately exists, of which the world merely is a manifest form. This manifesting of *Brahman* as the world is caused by *māyā*.

The speculation that began with negating the world, thus ended up in perceiving *Brahman* alone, *saccidānanda* in essence, as existing. Negating the world in this context is simply of methodological significance. That the effect is unreal and cause alone is real is not the final doctrine of Vedānta, it is merely the method that directs us to the realization of the non-duality of cause and effect, of *Brahman* and the world, the final goal of Vedāntic speculation.

One Reality alone exists; it is *saccidānanda*. Multiplicity is seen simply in the world, the transient and apparent manifest forms of that Reality. This world of multiplicity has no existence apart from the one *saccidānanda*, even as ornament-forms have no being apart from gold.

Saccidānanda, the one Reality always existing, is birthless and deathless, birth and death being phenomena seen only in the realm of multiplicity. The phenomenon of one form emerging, existing for a while and disappearing in the total Being, is natural with the apparent world. This process of self-manifestation of what really exists goes on beginninglessly and endlessly. The seeker who realizes that *saccidānanda* alone appears as all these interlinked phenomenal entities, awakens to the fact that he or she, one among such interlinked phenomenal forms, is simply that one Reality in essence. One's self-identity with this birthless and deathless substance, in effect, is one realizing one's own birthlessness and deathlessness, one's own immortality.

Yet we are used to looking at these interlinked apparent forms as existing separately. This is the perception of those who are ignorant of what ultimately exists, and in their view birth is real, and death is real. They anxiously think, "What will happen to me after death?" They believe, as taught by unenlightened religious teachers, that they would have to be reborn in order to eat the fruits of their meritorious or sinful actions (*karma*s) of this life. Furthermore, they believe this process continues endlessly. All such beliefs are covered and cautioned against in the Guru's words here, "He proceeds from death to death." (*mṛtyor mṛtyum sa gacchati*).

All sufferings in life, the most fearful of them being death, are basically caused by perceiving reality as many. All sufferings, including that of death, simply vanish on realizing that one *saccidānanda* alone assumes the emerging and merging forms of multiple worldly entities, including we human beings.

3

Asatya Darśanam
(Vision by Non-Existence)

TREATING the apparent world as effect and searching for its cause by negating the effect, was the method resorted to in the *Apavāda Darśanam*. The final conclusion then arrived at was that what appears as both cause and effect was nothing but *Brahman*, in essence *saccidānanda*. In the vision that *saccidānanda* alone exists, there is no room for discriminating cause from effect.

Who perceives this non-existent differentiation as existing? It is the mind (*manas*). The present chapter, *Asatya Darśanam* (Vision by Non-Existence) centres around the imaginative power of this mind. The mind not only conceives the unreal world as real through its power to fancy, but also enjoys the very world it imagines to be. These two potentials of mind put together are called *māyā*.

The picture of this *māyā* becomes complete only when we understand that the mind also has no existence of its own. The non-existent mind thus fancies and enjoys a non-existent world. All this takes place in the ever-existing *saccidānanda*, while itself remaining unaffected even as all such things happen in itself. It is comparable to a piece of stone remaining stone even when sculpted into a *śivaliṅga* or any other idol. That the appearance of the illusory world is seen in the really existing *Brahman* is the vision that fills the whole of this chapter.

Verse 1

मनोमयमिदं सर्वं न मनः क्वापि विद्यते।
अतो व्योम्नीव नीलादि दृश्यते जगदात्मनि॥१॥

manomayam idaṁ sarvaṁ na manaḥ kvāpi vidyate |
ato vyomnīva nīlādi dṛśyate jagad ātmani ||1 ||

> Everything indeed is imaginative mind in essence, and that mind in its turn has no being of its own anywhere. Therefore, like the blueness and other colours of the sky, is seen the world in the being of the Self.

We live in this world, and we encounter it always. It is formed of countless entities, living and not living, each having its own specific characteristics. As we encounter each object, there gets formulated in our mind an idea about that object. We simply assume that the object seen has the same form we formulate in our mind as an idea. Is it really so?

It is with the aid of our five sense organs that we perceive the world. The nature of this world could well be thought of as analysable as five sense objects. The sense organs, by nature, are such that, when one of these fully concentrates on its object, the others fade out functionally. When enjoying the visual beauty of an artwork, for example, our ability to hear, touch, taste and smell remain dormant for the moment. In short, our perceptual capability provided by our sense organs and mind together is such that one of them alone functions fully at a particular moment.

But, is it possible to perceive the world fully at any moment in its real form with one sense organ alone functioning at that moment? Is it not that all the senses have to be fully open at the same time to perceive the world in its wholeness? We are also not sure whether the world will be perceived wholly in its real form even when the five senses function all at once. We are compelled, therefore, to presume that the form of the world we constantly perceive is not the real one.

Then of what sort is the world we do see? It is the world our mind gives form to with the help of the limited capabilities of our senses. We never see the real world. We experience an imagined world, a subjective world, as if really existing objectively. In other words, *manas* (mind), in essence, is the entire world we perceive (*manomayam idam sarvam*).

The same problem could be viewed from yet another point. Suppose a red hibiscus flower is placed before a group of people. Everyone of the group is fully convinced that it is red in colour. But as they are of different age groups, the perceptive capability of their sensory system has necessarily to be different. Some might even be colour-blind, and that too of varying degrees. All these factors decide the nature of the stimulus the red rays arouse in the retina of the eye of each. The nature of the electrical impulses conveyed to the brain depends also on the capacity of the nerves connecting the retina with the brain. The chemical changes taking place in the brain, in turn, depend on its own functional nature. All these and many other factors together decide the nature of the colour-experience each has. Naturally this will be different for each person. The only common factor is that the name "red" is given to the colour by each. When you and I agree on the redness of the flower, there exists no means to check whether both of us had the same kind of colour experience inwardly.

It is, in fact, inevitable that the subjective experiences of the two will be different. This is true not only with the flower, but with the entire world, of which the flower is a minute part. What I call "the world" is not what you call "the world." The experience I have is called by me "the world"; and the experience you have is called by you "the world." The two experiences have necessarily to be different. What then, is the real form of the world, irrespective of your or my experience? No one knows! Vedānta says, as we have already seen, it is nothing but *saccidānanda.* In this sense also we could say, the world I see is a creation of my mind, and the world you see is a creation of your mind. To be so, at least the mind should exist.

What is mind? Is there such a thing existing? Modern science asserts that mind has no real existence. The Guru also categorically denies the existence of mind. What exists is *saccidānanda* alone. Its existence is multifacetedly creative in its different capacities as *sat*, *cit* and *ānanda*. As *cit* it appears as innumerable functional states of consciousness. One such functional aspect is willing and imagining (*saṁkalpa*). *Cit*, when having *saṁkalpa* for its function is called *manas* (mind). That means, *manas* on its own has no existence; its being is simply as a functional facet of *cit*. The world, according to this view, gets formulated in the willing and imagining function (*saṁkalpa*) of the non-existing mind. Therefore it is but natural that such a world has no existence of its own. The world, thuswise, is unreal; the *manas* that imagined its existence is also unreal. Then what is real? *Ātmā* alone, *saccidānanda* alone, is real.

Though actually we perceive blue colour in the sky, we are well aware that such a canopy does not exist there. In the sky of *Ātmā* also we see the appearance of the mind and the world willed by it, though both are ultimately unreal. The fact that the mind is flickery by nature is well known. Thus the world willed/imagined by it also has to be so. This is the reason for calling the world *jagat* in Sanskrit, meaning "that which is always changeful."

Ascertaining the unreality of the mind and the world willed by it does not negate the existence of *Ātmā*, the substratum underlying such illusions. On the contrary, the very unreality of the mind and the world confirms the existence of consciousness or *cit* that is aware of their non-existence.

Even the unreality of all these would remain unknown unless *cit* exists functionally. The *cit* that is aware of all this is the *Ātmā* or Self.

Verse 2

मनसोऽनन्यया सर्वं कल्प्यतेऽविद्यया जगत्।
विद्ययाऽसौ लयं याति तदालेख्यमिवाऽखिलम् ॥२॥

manaso 'nanyayā sarvaṁ kalpyate 'vidyayā jagat ।
vidyayā 'sau layaṁ yāti tadālekhyam ivā 'khilam ॥2॥

All the worlds are imagined to be existing by nescience (*avidyā*) that has no being besides the imaginative mind. This nescience in its turn just vanishes upon attaining proper knowledge (*vidyā*). The entire world, thus, has being only like that of a drawn picture.

A gold bangle is before us. It, in the normal course, is treated as an ornament to be worn on the wrist to add to a lady's beauty. What we perceive in this case is the external form and its utility value. We, for the time being, forget that what is real in the bangle is gold, and that the bangle is simply an evanescent form assumed by it. A sort of darkness here veils our mind, rendering it incapable of seeing what is real. This veil is called *avidyā* (ignorance or nescience). This *avidyā* is always there in the mind even when it wills and imagines. *Avidyā* thus is inseparable from the mind.

When afflicted with a disease we trace its cause and then treat it. We'll naturally be anxious until the illness is completely cured. No such anxiety affects us if we realize that this physical body is part of physical nature, that nature (*prakṛti*) is nothing but what appears as the ever-existing Reality creatively finding self-expression, that such a nature is always changeful, that the present disease is nothing but part of the changefulness of nature, and that the chance for every such change is there in nature. We'll then be able to face the disease boldly and to treat it with a calm mind. Treating a disease means correcting an unfavourable modification of nature with another induced one. Becoming anxiously concerned with a disease and thus frightened happens because of our lack of knowledge about ourselves, because of the shrinking of Self-knowledge (*ātmavidyā saṁkoca*), in other words; because of *avidyā*. This *avidyā* will be defined in the next chapter as that which causes one not to see the real as real and to see the unreal as real, or not to see the Self as real and to see the non-Self as real.

The idea that the external objects are real on their own, implies the corresponding idea that I am the observer of those objects. I, at that moment, remain oblivious of the fact that I am also part of the external visible world. This misconception causes the impression that the knowing subject and the known object exist separately. And the rest of the search takes place based on this initial misconception. This is the nature of the search for reality as undertaken by modern science. No one cares to ask or to answer the question, "Is it right or wrong to think that subject and object are separately existing realities?" It is as if a veil overcovers our understanding resulting in this forgetfulness. This veil is called *avidyā*.

Even in the case of the gold and ornament analogy, the gold-reality and the ornament-form do not ever exist separate. Yet the ideas we conceive in our mind of the gold and the ornament are separate. Moreover, the gold-substance is eternal and the ornament-form is transient. The eternal and the transient remaining non-dual is not acceptable to any logic, but the fact is that the two do exist as inseparably one. A logical untenability or mystery thus hides in the being of the gold ornament, but no logic is required for the inseparable oneness of gold and ornament-form; the two always remain one. It was our reasoning mind that separated the two out as eternal and transient, and this separating created the problem. The imaginative power of our mind, in short, divided into two a reality that has never existed as dual. This duality thus exists only in our imagination, never actually, and hence is unreal. The real is one and non-dual alone. Not seeing that one reality as real and seeing the unreal duality as real is what we call *avidyā*. Just as we imagine the gold-substance and ornament-form as two, we see the *Ātman*-reality and the world- appearance also as two. This mistaken perception is because of *avidyā*. The Guru therefore says, "All the worlds are imagined to be existing by nescience (*avidyā*) (*sarvam jagat avidyayā kalpitam*).

This *avidyā* vanishes when *vidyā* or knowledge shines, just as darkness vanishes when light comes. Then it becomes evident that the world, thought to have its own existence, also has no being. *Vidyā* is that function of consciousness by which it becomes clear that *Ātmā* alone is real and that *anātmā* or whatever is other than *Ātmā*, has no existence. To go back to our analogy, the function of consciousness by which one realizes that gold alone is real and ornament-forms have no reality of their own, is *vidyā*. The ornament-forms are simply superimposed on the gold-substance. Likewise, the world-form also is projected on *Brahman* or *Ātman*, which remains changeless while the apparent forms constantly appear and disappear.

He who is immersed in *avidyā*, taking the apparent world to be real, does not realize that he is in such a state. He remains happy with the worldly joys. Only by chance it strikes his mind, on his own or by the proper guidance of an enlightened *guru*, that the visible aspect of the world is ever-changing, and that there should he existing a changeless substance that gives room for all these forms to appear and disappear. At that moment alone he realizes, he was remaining in darkness till then. At that very moment the darkness of *avidyā* disappears as well. *Avidyā*'s disappearance is nowhere else than into the *cit* or consciousness that caused its emergence. The disappearance of its effects, i.e. the realness of the world, that happens along with it, would be into the *sat* aspect of Reality or *Brahman*. In the ultimate sense, *sat* and *cit* are not different. This realization results in the contentment of having known what was being searched for. This feeling of contentment (*ānanda*) also added, the Reality realized would be *saccidānanda*. The status of the apparent world would then be seen like that of an art work painted on and rubbed off the canvas of *saccidānanda*.

An art work is the materialization of the creative imagination of an artist. Likewise, the world is the materialization of the creative imagination (*saṁkalpa*) of *saccidānanda*. Treating such a world as real on its own and looking at life in the light of that perception renders life miserable and fearful. How does this happen, and how the seers of Reality become saved from it, are made clear in the next verse.

Verses 3

विजृम्भते यत्तमसो भीरोरिह पिशाचवत्।
तदिदं जाग्रति स्वप्नलोकवद् दृश्यते बुधैः ॥३॥

vijṛṁbhate yat tamaso bhīror iha piśācavat I
tad idaṁ jāgrati svapnalokavad dṛśyate budhaiḥ II3 II

Mere darkness in the work-a-day realm may loom like a frightening ghost to the vision of a coward. Likewise is this world considered by the wise, as a dream seen in the waking state.

Buddhism builds up its philosophy on the firm ground of the notion that life is steeped in sufferings. Vedāntin's goal also is crossing the ocean of sufferings of worldly life, called *saṁsāra-sāgara*, and wisdom is counted as the means. Wisdom implies realizing the one Reality that underlies the apparent being of everything in all the worlds, as the substance that assumes the form of the seeker's own being. The substance that underlies thus in the cosmic system as well as in the individuated system, is not an inert entity. It is a creative one. It creatively finds self-expression as everything. Forming part of this creative self-unfoldment of Reality is the emerging of new apparent forms and the disappearing of the older ones. What we feel as suffering then is nothing more than momentary sparks arising out of this creative process. Nothing to be frightened or complained about is there in such happenings. If the Reality is thought of as a boundless ocean, then our sufferings are simply momentary bubbles that appear as a result of the rolling on of the waves. This realization results in the vanishing of all sufferings. Then we directly perceive that our personal existence is simply as a transitory wave arising in the ocean of *saccidānanda* and that that existence is blissful.

It will then become evident that the reason for seeing life as full of sufferings is our own ignorance about the Reality of life. Why didn't we know this Reality earlier? The darkness of *avidyā* (ignorance) was veiling the clarity of our vision. In the presence of darkness we see many non-existing entities, like ghosts, as if existing. The ghost seen in darkness just disappears when a lamp is brought near. The ghost-form was simply something seen imagined by a fearful mind in darkness. The existence of the world, along with all its sufferings, likewise, is imagined by our minds steeped in the darkness of *avidyā*, and in that darkness we perceive it as frightening and full of miseries which really are nothing more than momentary sparkings of the one *saccidānanda*. This Truth becomes revealed only when the lamp of wisdom is brought closeby, and life examined in its light. This point is clarified by the Guru himself in his *Advaita Dīpikā*, thus:

> Closely examined, this world is found non-existent; it being mere *avidyā*. To those who are ignorant of Being as such, It simply looms as world because of delusion. When a lamp is lit nearby no devil appears to be, but for those who are afraid of darkness, the very same darkness looms as devil.
>
> — Verse 5

How does one perceive what was earlier seen as frightening and full of sufferings, when this awakening of Reality happens? The Guru clarifies this with the help of yet another analogy. While asleep one sees some dreams. Many terrible scenes appear and one becomes frightened, and as a result begins to shiver. In the shivering feeling one wakes up, and then becomes fully convinced that what one was till that moment seeing were all dreams. Likewise, the enlightened one sees the notion that life is full of sufferings, as only a past dream.

Verse 4

सङ्कल्पकल्पितं दृश्यं सङ्कल्पो यत्र विद्यते।
दृश्यं तत्र च नान्यत्र कुत्रचिद्रज्जुसर्पवत् ॥४॥

saṁkalpa-kalpitaṁ dṛśyaṁ saṁkalpo yatra vidyate ।
dṛśyaṁ tatra ca nānyatra kutracid rajju-sarpavat ॥4॥

> A willful imagination indeed is this visible world. Wherever there is willful imagination, and nowhere else, does the visible world seem to exist, as when a piece of rope appears to be a snake.

A piece of rope seen lying in twilight is easily mistaken for a snake. No snake really exists there. It is the idea of the snake already in the mind and the common fear of snakes together that make it appear so. This analogy suggests that the nature of what is perceived depends upon the perceiver's state of mind and understanding, a fact true in the case of perceiving the world also. What really exists is *saccidānanda* alone. We, with a deluded state of mind, perceive it as the world, treating life in it as full of miseries. The cause of this delusion and confusion is our own willful imagination. How this willful imagination and the world seemingly existing objectively are related to each other, is the point pondered on in this verse.

How do we logically arrive at the conclusion that this visible world is merely a willful imagination of the mind? By two means: one, only where there is imagination or ideation the world also appears, and two, where there is no mental conception the visible world also has no meaningful existence. The former position alone does not make sure that in the absence of imagination the world does not exist. Therefore, in order to establish that the visible world is merely a phenomenal appearance, it is to be negatively asserted that the world has no being, or rather the existence of the world is of no relevance, where there is no willful imagination or ideation.

This double method of asserting a logical truth is known as the method of agreement and difference. The two, in Indian logic, are known as *anvaya* and *vyatireka*. Something can be inferred to be certain only when these two contrary positions agree. Both the methods together are applied by the Guru here in order to logically establish that the world's being is merely as a willful imagination of mind.

The word *saṁkalpa*, rendered here as "willful imagination" denotes a vast range of mental faculties like meditation, firm decision, determination, presumption, willing, cogitation, purposefulness, imagination and so on, and none of these is to be excluded from what the word signifies here.

The first verse asserted, "Everything here indeed is imaginative mind (*manas*) in essence," and *saṁkalpa* is the function of *manas*. The point clarified in the present verse is that unless this *saṁkalpa*-function happens, no world would appear to exist. The search for Reality is only one among the many functions of mind. We do actually see a world existing around us, and a yearning to know what is real in it also arises in us. Suppose no mind is there to think, "This is the world," then the existence as well as non-existence of the world becomes of no relevance. Then there would be no search for Reality either. Our mind, when in deep sleep, remains functionless. At such time no world-experience is there. As the mind becomes functionally awake, the existence of the world is also experienced. In short, the existence of the world is meaningful only when the mind functions, and when the mind is not functional there is no world-experience either. The logical method of agreement and difference (*anvaya* and *vyatireka*) is thus made use of by the *Guru* once again, to assert the dependence of the world-experience on the *saṁkalpa* or function of mind.

The role played by mind's power to will, imagine and ideate is crucial in the nature of happiness and sufferings we experience in life. The mind not only formulates and perceives the world as existing, but also each entity thus perceived is assumed to have a value in relation to our likes and dislikes. Moreover a castle in the air is built on that foundation. Such world of hopes imagined by each would naturally be different. These hopes need not necessarily go in line with the actualities of life, and when this variance is felt, one starts to think of life as valueless and full of miseries. Then begins the search for the device to avoid these sufferings, completely oblivious of the truth that all the problems are the creation of the *saṁkalpa* of one's own mind. All search for their solution is like searching for a stick to kill the snake seen in a piece of rope. The unreality of the snake becomes evident only when looked at it in the light of a lamp. Likewise, it is the lamp of a Guru's proper guidance that makes it clear to us that the problems are our own mind's making and therefore unreal.

There is also an opposite side to this perception. Human life is impossible with no *saṁkalpa* guiding it. Then the question is, how to transform our *saṁkalpa*s in such a way that they do not become the cause of sufferings. This requires an overall awareness as to in which *saṁkalpa* or in whose *saṁkalpa*, all the worlds, all the beings in them, our minds, and the *saṁkalpa*s arising in them, have their origin and being. That *saṁkalpa* is of *Brahman*. The world exists only as *Brahman* wills so. *Brahman*, we have already seen, is *cit* or *sat-cit-ānanda* in essence. How the *saṁkalpa* of *Brahman*, of the Supreme God, materializes as the world was explicated under Verse 1 of this chapter.

Verse 5

सङ्कल्पमनसोः कश्चिन्नहि भेदोऽस्ति यन्मनः ।
तदविद्यातमः प्रख्यमिन्द्रजालमिवाद्भुतम् ॥५॥

saṁkalpa-manasoḥ kaścin nahi bhedo 'sti yan manaḥ ı
tad avidyā tamaḥ prakhyam indrajālam ivādbhutam ॥5 ॥

Between willful imagination and the imagining mind, there exists no separateness at all. That which forms the imagining mind, known also as nescience and darkness, is a marvel indeed, like a grand magic show.

It was established in the last verse that the existence of the visible world is simply an effect of the *saṁkalpa* of mind. That between *saṁkalpa* (willful imagination) and mind there exists no difference is the idea pinpointed in the present verse. The truth that mind has no being of its own was seen as early as the first verse of this chapter. There should be no need then to say that what is imagined by that mind also has no reality. One Reality, *saccidānanda,* alone exists.

Manas and *saṁkalpa* are not different. The willing and imagining (*saṁkalpa*) function of consciousness is what in the Indian context is called *manas* or mind. One and the same phenomenon, existentially is called *manas*, and functionally *saṁkalpa*. The word *saṁkalpa* used here is to be understood as inclusive of *vikalpa,* its opposite, also.

The famous Sanskrit lexicon *Vācaspatyam* defines *saṁkalpa* as *karma-sādhanāya abhitapa-vākye* (signifies a statement uttered encouraging certain action to take place). Yet another definition given is *āśāsya ca śubham kāryam uddiśya ca manogatam* (an idea formulated aimed at something desirable and propitious). *Saṁkalpa* could be of two kinds: *bhāva* and *abhāva* (positive and negative). The *saṁkalpa* of the nature "This is to be done or achieved" is *bhāva-saṁkalpa,* and of the nature, "This is not to be done or achieved" is *abhāva-saṁkalpa.*

Vikalpa denotes many mental functions such as variant imagination (*vibhinna-kalpanā*), various imaginations (*vividha-*

kalpanā), attributing proximity (*saṁsargāropaḥ*), arriving at a conclusion taking into account only one side of the context (*pakṣataḥ prāptiḥ*). This *vikalpa* could be of two kinds: *vyavasthitam* (that occurs unwillingly) and *aicchikam* (that happens as opted by oneself or someone else). Eight different possibilities of this *vikalpa* misleading us are enumerated. This is the reason why wise ones always forewarn us that *vikalpa* causes sufferings.

The word *saṁkalpa* as used by the Guru here in a general sense does not exclude *vikalpa* from its denotation. As was seen earlier, behind the emergence and existence of the world there is a cosmic will and imagination. Also called God, this cosmic *saṁkalpa* always remains unperceived, while its materialization — the apparent world — is taken to be real. The veil that overcovers Reality causing this delusion is here called *tamas* (darkness). An individuated human being, being nothing more than a minute part of the materialization of the cosmic will, his or her understanding also is subject to the same veil of darkness, and this darkness in the individuated being is called *avidyā* (ignorance or nescience). The veil thus could be called *tamas* as well as *avidyā*.

How does *saṁkalpa* take place in consciousness? How does this non-existent *saṁkalpa* materialize and appear as this world? How do both *saṁkalpa* and *vikalpa* and many such functional aspects, most of them having an opposite side, emerge in consciousness? How does this function so happen that the phenomenal world appears to really exist? Many such questions are possible. One overall answer to all these is this: all this is a great mystery comparable to a grand magic show.

Is it to conclude that all this is a magic-like mystery, that we undertake all the scientific and logical enquiries about the world? Any scientific thinking, as we understand it, should prove something based on unquestionable demonstration of facts and logical thinking. Yet something different is the notion of certainty the *ṛṣis* of ancient India had. They prove that all scientific and logical enquiry leads us to the final conclusion that the Reality is a great mystery, invisible and unthinkable. All the schools of Indian thought originated from the vision of these *ṛṣis*, for this reason, admit the mysteriousness of Reality in one way or another. We are tempted to be unwilling to admit it to be so only because our minds are already coloured and conditioned by the Western concept of scientific thinking. A close study of the most modern studies in the West clearly reveals the fact that a definite notion of what is ultimately real cannot be arrived at unless the seeker's mind has its legitimate place in it. Put otherwise, the nature of reality a scientist arrives at, according to the most modern scientific findings, depends on the preferences of the scientist's mind. Scientists therefore now stand in awe, asking themselves, "What next?" At least some of them, who do not care to be fully orthodox, have begun to think that no definite conclusion about reality can be arrived at without acknowledging the intuitive visions of the seers of the East. Scientists also, though through a circuitous route, thus come to where the *ṛṣis* of India had already reached.

The proof of the existence of an all underlying Reality is nothing other than the unreality of the apparent world and of the mind that imagines it. The phenomenon of the mind, of its imaginations and of the world it imagines — all these are appearances. Then there should be a Reality that makes these appearances possible. That Reality is nothing other than *ātmā* or *Brahman*.

Verse 6

मरीचिकावत्प्राज्ञस्य जगदात्मनि भासते।
बालस्य सत्यमिति च प्रतिबिंबमिव भ्रमात् ॥६॥

marīcikāvat prājñasya jagad ātmani bhāsate ।
bālasya satyam iti ca pratibiṁbam iva bhramāt ॥6॥

In the perception of the enlightened, the changeful world simply manifests in the Self, like a mirage. A reflected image might well be thought of as a real entity by an indiscriminate child owing to mistaken identity.

The attempt made in this chapter called *Asatya Darśanam* (Vision by Non-existence) is to ascertain what really exists if all that appears to be is unreal. It has already been shown that the world's existence is imagined by the mind and that the *saṁkalpa* (willful imagination) and *manas* (mind) are no two. This mind, in its turn, has no existence either. The world thus is a willful imagination of a non-existent mind, caused by *avidyā* (nescience). The world, in short, is unreal; the mind that imagines it also is equally unreal.

Does all this mean that nothing has existence? No, at least the idea or feeling of the existent world is there. Where does this idea or feeling get formulated? The search for this substratum of appearance takes us to the Reality which is none other than *Ātman* or *Brahman*. The first five verses of this chapter concentrated on how the apparent world and the mind that imagines it are all unreal; the next five verses show how the phenomenal appearance of all these take place in the one Reality.

A child, looking at a mirror, sees its own image in it and thinks of it as yet another child wanting to play with him or her. The child then is completely ignorant of the existence of the mirror and of the fact that what he/she sees is simply his/her own image.

What is called the Self (*Ātman*) here is oneself in its purest sense. The substance that pervades (*ātatam*) the being of oneself, that assumes the form of oneself as well as of everything, is called *Ātman*. One who realizes oneself to be *Ātman* in essence, just like a pot realizing itself to be formed of clay, is called *prājña* here, meaning "the enlightened." One who knows what oneself really is in essence, perceives the same substance as forming the essential content in everything and thus sees oneself in everything. Then alone one becomes awakened to the reality that what one was perceiving till that moment as the world is simply one's own mirror reflection, it having no being separate from oneself.

What then is the mirror in which *Ātman* becomes reflected as the world? It is the mirror of *māyā*, as will be stated later in Verse 8. The child's delusion was due to its ignorance of itself and of the existence of the mirror. Similar is the ignorance each one of us has about what is real in our own being, and of the mysterious power of *māyā* inherent in that Reality. We too are child-like in that ignorant state, which is the reason for calling an ignorant person *bāla* (child) in Sanskrit.

How does the enlightened one (*prājña*) treat the self-reflection-like apparent existence of the world? He or she considers it comparable to a mirage. The water seen in mirage will be found to be simply an illusory appearance as we go nearer to it. Likewise, the apparent existence of the world also will be realized to be unreal when we closely examine it. What exists and appears as the world is *Ātmā* alone, oneself alone.

Ātmā is the reality nearest to everyone, as is gold to an ornament. Our personal existence is as part of the world, and we should search for the substance in our being by going nearest to it. Then alone we realize that what appears as the world, including ourselves, is nothing other than an illusory reflection of that one substance or *Ātmā*. What is causal to the illusory appearance of water is space alone. There is a space, likewise, causal to the phenomenal appearance of the world; it is the Self or *Ātmā*. The appearance of water makes no intrinsic change in space; so too is the changelessness of *Ātmā*. It undergoes no substantial change even when it appears as the world, even as gold remains gold while appearing as ornaments. This point is made clearer in the next verse.

Verse 7

आत्मा न क्षीरवद्याति रूपान्तरमतोऽखिलम् ।
विवर्त्तमिन्द्रजालेन विद्यते निर्मितं यथा ॥७॥

ātmā na kṣīravad yāti rūpāntaram ato 'khilam ।
vivartamindrajālena vidyate nirmitaṁ yathā ॥7॥

Ātmā, as with milk curdling, does not undergo transformation substance-wise. Everything therefore seems to exist because of illusory projection alone, as though created by a grand magic performance.

The conclusion we have come to from the speculations done so far in this chapter is this much: everything apparent is a willful imagination (*saṁkalpa*) of mind (*manas*). The mind that so wills has no existence of its own. Therefore, everything perceived as forming the world is simply unreal (*asatya*). Still the feeling we have of the existing world does not just vanish with this intellectual conviction. Something that exists in our feeling or imagination only is called a *pratibhāsa* in Vedānta, the word meaning "illusory appearance," like water seen in a mirage. This illusory appearance of the world has *Ātmā* for its substratum. How does this illusory appearance emerge in the *Ātmā*-Substratum? This is the point meditated on in the present verse.

How does the appearance of individual entities that are many arise in the one reality? This has been a question that has tormented the minds of thinking men ever since they discriminated appearance from reality. Each school of thought has tried to answer the question in its own way, adhering fully to their respective ontological concepts, methodology and axiology. The answer of Indian thinkers could be classified into two: the theory of evolution (*pariṇāma-vāda*) and the theory of illusory appearance (*vivarta-vāda*).

The process in which the causal substance undergoes irreversible intrinsic change to assume the form of an effect, is known as *pariṇāma* (evolution). Milk curdling, for example, is a *pariṇāma*. The content of milk undergoes total change to become curd, and curd can never be brought back to the milk-form. Similarly, when *Ātmā*, the causal substance is thought of as undergoing basic change to appear as the world, the theory is known as *pariṇāma-vāda* (the theory of evolution). Certain Upaniṣadic texts, for instance, depict pictures interpretable as *pariṇāma*, as when these say, from *Ātmā* emerged space (*ākāśa*), from space air (*vāyu*), from air fire (*agni*), from fire water (*ap*), from water earth (*pr̥thivī*), from earth vegetation (*oṣadhayaḥ*), from vegetation food (*annam*), and from food living beings. Though some Vedāntins treat this creation picture as involving evolution, strict non-dualists (*advaitins*) treat this as a portrayal of a hierarchy of apparent forms ranging from the most subtle to the most gross. It indirectly admits also that cause is always subtler and effect grosser.

An evolution-like picture of creation depicted in the *Bhagavad-Gītā* is as follows:

> From food emerge all beings, from rain emerges food, from *yajña* (fire-sacrifice) arises rain, from actions (*karma*) arises *yajña*, from Brahmā (the Creator) arise actions, and from the imperishable arises Brahmā.
>
> — III.14, 16

Taken separately, these lines might sound like supporting the theory of evolution, but seen as forming part of a whole section, it will become evident that these words show only how something becomes the cause of something else as part of the overall rolling on of the wheel of Nature (*prakṛti*). On the other hand, Kṛṣṇa, while describing how Reality and the world are related to each other, clearly says, "The entire world is pervaded by me the indistinct Reality." (*mayā tatam idam jagad avyakta-mūrtinā* — IX.4).

Sāṁkhya is the one school of Indian Philosophy that bases itself on the evolution theory. The reality, according to this school, is twofold: *puruṣa* and *prakṛti* or Person and Nature. The former is unchanging pure consciousness, but the latter always evolves into twenty-four *tattva*s (basic categories) and is changeful. This evolution results in the ever-changing appearance and disappearance of everything in nature. The Sāṁkhya school being very systematic and rationalistic, many of its basic tenets have been adopted to Vedānta. For example, all the twenty-four *tattva*s became acceptable to Vedānta though in a slightly revised sense. Vedānta does not treat *prakṛti* as an inert reality existing on its own, and the twenty-four *tattva*s as its evolutes. On the contrary, *Brahman* or *Ātman* alone is counted as real, and all the twenty four *tattva*s, constituting the illusory appearance, gradable from the most subtle to the most gross, are superimposed on *Brahman* owing to Its own *māyā*-power. This argument of Vedāntins is known as *vivarta-vāda* (the theory of superimposed illusory appearances). According to this argument, the causal substance, while itself undergoing no intrinsic change, appears as all the effects, i.e. as the apparent world. This argument is clarified with the help of an example. A piece of rope seen at twilight may appear to be a snake, making you frightened. Not seeing the real rope and seeing the unreal snake as real do not make any intrinsic change in what really exists there, it always remains a piece of rope. It is in the wrong perception of the observer that the rope appeared as a snake. The unreal snake-appearance is thought of as *vivarta* on the real rope. Similar is the perceiving of the apparent world in the really existing *Brahman* or *Ātman*, effected by *māyā*. Narayana Guru also following the line of thought of Śaṅkara, the propounder of the Advaita school of Vedānta, admits this *vivarta-vāda* and rejects the theory of evolution, as is evident from many references to it in his philosophical works.

How do the illusory appearances emerge in the one Absolute Reality or *Ātman*? The answer is, it is like a grand magic show. A magician makes his spectators see certain non-existent phenomena. Similar is the way the Self makes itself appear as the unreal world.

Is this a sufficient explanation? Of course, this is not a logical explanation. Yet the analogy of magic makes it clear how an element of mystery inheres in what we are trying to understand. Our minds, in a way, are so conditioned that only logical explanations based on analysis satisfy us when trying to understand something. In philosophy too we attempt our best to represent reality in a logical way. Most of the philosophers of the West think with a mind conditioned by the preconceived notion that philosophical thinking means logical reasoning about what is ultimately real.

Such a prejudice has never corrupted the Indian thinkers. They do not hesitate to declare openly that the Reality as a whole is a Great Mystery. Their goal has never been arriving at a "reasonable" conclusion about what is real, but to directly and intuitively perceive their own inseparable oneness with what they are searching for, and to make life meaningful by realizing their identity with the meaningfulness of the Total Existence. Such is the ultimate goal of Indian thinkers, particularly of Vedāntins. They therefore have no reluctance to declare as part of their scientific thinking, "All this is a magic-like mystery!", "How could any recognized valid means of knowledge help us know this!", "Ineffable and unthinkable indeed is this!" and so on.

The scientific term Vedānta prefers to give to this seemingly unscientific aspect is "*māyā*." Therefore the next verse is centred round the concept of *māyā*.

Verse 8

मायैव जगतामादिकारणं निर्मितं तया ।
सर्वं हि मायिनो नान्यदसत्यं सिद्धिजालवत् ॥८ ॥

māyaiva jagatām ādikāraṇam nirmitaṁ tayā ।
sarvaṁ hi māyino nānyad asatyaṁ siddhijālavat ॥8 ॥

Māyā indeed is the primordial cause of the appearance of the world. Fashioned by it, everything here has no being apart from the *māyā*-making substance, and is as unreal as the effects of psychic powers.

The apparent world has no existence of its own, and to that extent it is unreal. What really exists is *Ātmā* alone. It is *Ātmā* on which the appearance of the world is projected.

How does this projecting of the unreal world-appearance on *Ātmā* occur? An indefinability, a mystery, is inherent in it, and this indefinability is called *māyā*. A detailed study of *māyā* being reserved for the next chapter, we do not have to enter into its intricacies here.

How does it so happen that we do not see the real and see the unreal as the real? This question has always been a perplexing one. Each of the schools of thought of India has tried to answer this question in its own way, and their arguments put together are known as *khyāti-vāda*s. Vedāntins' stand in this respect is known as *anirvacanīya-khyāti-vāda*, meaning, the argument that there is an indefinability in it.

A touch of this argument can be sensed in the second half of the present chapter of *Darśanamālā*. The argument could be summarized thus: The world-appearance seems to be there in *Ātmā* because of *māyā*. We do experience this world, and it arouses in us the feelings of pleasure and pain. To say that such a world is totally non-existent is meaningless. Ontologically, the world has no existence of its own. The world thus is existent in one sense and non-existent in another sense, and to this extent it is indefinable.

Where does this indefinability abide? In the Self, or *Ātmā*. If this idefinability could be called *māyā*, then *Ātmā* is the *māyin* or the wielder of *māyā*. No *māyā* exists apart from *Ātmā*; *Ātmā* alone is what really exists. The next chapter therefore begins with the definition, "That which does not exist is called *māyā*." There would be no world appearance unless this mysterious *māyā*-power abides in *Ātmā*, and in this particular sense it could be said, "*Māyā* indeed is the primeval cause of the world."

It was made explicit in the last chapter that *Brahman*, in essence *saccidānanda*, is the original cause of the world. Here it is claimed, *māyā* is the primeval cause. How are these two stands to be reconciled? The search made in the last chapter was for the ontological cause, for the one all-underlying substance, for the material cause. That *Brahman* or *Ātman* is that causal substance was the finding. The enquiry in the present chapter, on the other hand, is on how the unreal world appears to be in the real *Ātmā* the material cause. In other words, the question answered here is, "How does it so happen to us that we do not see *Ātmā* as real and see the unreal world-appearance as if it is real?" This problem, concerned as it is with how our knowledge in this case goes wrong, is rather of epistemological ordero.

The knowing function takes place in consciousness, as a functional aspect of *cit*; sometimes it goes wrong and sometimes it takes a right direction. How does it take to the wrong way of knowing instead of remaining right in respect of knowing reality? This is the problem before us now. The answer is this: it is the mysterious *māyā* abiding in *Ātmā* the material cause, that misleads us. The cause of the appearance of the world in this epistemological context is *māyā*, and this *māyā* has no being apart from *Ātmā* or *Brahman* or *saccidānanda*.

Magicians are capable of showing their spectators something quite unreal as real. *Ātmā* too is a sort of magician.

What is illusory seen because of *māyā*, and what is the reality that wields this *māyā*? These two have to be discriminated properly. This discrimination lacking, we unwittingly fall into the delusion caused by *māyā*, treating life, *Ātmā*'s magic show, as full of miseries. This point is made clearer in the next verse.

Verse 9

विभाति विश्वं वृद्धस्य वियद्घनमिवात्मनि।
असत्यं पुत्रिकारूपं बालस्येव विपर्ययम् ॥९॥

vibhāti viśvaṁ vṛddhasya viyadvanamivātmani ।
asatyaṁ putrikārūpaṁ bālasyeva viparyayam ॥9 ॥

In the perception of the one of well matured minds, the world is what looms in *Ātmā*, like forests appearing in the sky. Even a lifeless puppet might be seen by a child as a living entity.

The world is a willful imagination of mind. It is the *tamas* (darkness) of *avidyā* (nescience) that assumes the form of mind and imagines the existence of the world. This appearance, like a grand magic show, is a great mystery — all these ideas were covered in the first half of this chapter. What exists really is *Ātmā* alone. It is in this *Ātmā* that the existence of the world is illusorily imagined by mind. This mistaken perception of the world in *Ātmā* is caused by *māyā* inherent in the very same *Ātmā* — these points have just been clarified in the second half. Discriminating what is really real and what is really unreal, and realizing the real to be one alone, becoming awakened to the reality that it is this one reality alone, because of its own *māyā*, that appears as the world, as our life, as all the problems we face in life, makes one enlightened, and this awakening is what is known as attaining wisdom (*jñāna*). Those who are awakened thuswise are to be called *jñānin*s, and those of fully matured wisdom are often figuratively qualified as "the elders" (*vṛddha*s) as against treating the ignorant as children (*bālāḥ*).

You can easily imagine a forest existing in the sky and you can even describe how beautiful it is. This does not mean such a forest exists. Likewise, we can assume the existence of the world in *Ātmā* and make a detailed study of it, ascertaining also how each entity forming part of it, is valuable in one way or another. How all the constituent parts together form a structurally coherent whole could also be studied. Many such studies are possible about the world, as we see comprising the major part of modern education. The possibility of these studies does not prove the world thus studied really exists on its own. Neither does it render the really existing *Ātmā* as non-existent. Many are the experiences we do have of the world and of our own existence. The one who perceives all such as fleeting manifestations of the one ever-existing *Ātmā*, is to be counted as fully matured in wisdom (*jñāna-vṛddha*). All others are mere children (*bālāḥ*).

A child's interest is always in playing, and being so is part of its growth. No discrimination between the real and the unreal is relevant in a child's games. A child will treat a doll as a human child, dress it up, feed it and even play with it. Only after growing up and after one's attention becoming turned from playing to thinking, does a person discriminate a doll from a human child. Such a one will no longer show any interest in dolls. Treating it as a human child or as a doll does not really affect the being of the doll; it continues to be doll. Similarly, the ignorant imagining what really exists as the world does not make any change in the being of the Reality. It continues to be *Ātmā*. Only a transformation in our understanding takes place as the darkness of ignorance vanishes in the bright light of wisdom. The overall goal of the present study also is nothing other than bringing about this transformation within ourselves.

The forest supposed to be existing in the sky is absolutely unreal. Likewise is the unreality of the world in the perception of the one of matured wisdom. What appears to be the world is *Ātmā* alone. But a child's perception of a doll is totally different. The inert doll is attributed to have qualities of a human child, and is treated like one. Similar is the case of an ignorant person. Instead of having the experience of perceiving *Ātmā*, such a one feels he or she is seeing the world by attributing the qualities of the world on *Ātmā*. How such an unreal world superimposed on *Ātmā* and the Reality *Ātmā* are inseparable is clarified in the next and concluding verse of this chapter.

Verse 10

एकं सत्यं न द्वितीयं ह्यसत्यं भाति सत्यवत्।
शिलैव शिवलिङ्गं न द्वितीयं शिल्पिना कृतम् ॥१०॥

ekaṁ satyaṁ na dvitīyaṁ hy asatyaṁ bhāti satyavat ।
śilaiva śivaliṅgaṁ na dvitīyaṁ śilpinā kṛtam ॥10॥

One alone is Real, no second reality does exist. The unreal indeed appears as though real. *Śivaliṅga* is stone alone; no second reality is created by the sculptor.

This is the concluding verse of the present chapter. The world, in the first chapter, *Adhyāropa Darśanam* (Vision by Superimposition), was taken for granted to be real. Then who created it? Why was it created? How was it created? When was it created? Such questions arising from that perception were answered then. The world's existence is merely superimposed on the one Reality. As the created world is a superimposition, so is the creator as well. What appears as the created world, the creator, the creations, their birth, life and death — all these are nothing but one Reality — *Parameśvara* — appearing variously. Such was the conclusion arrived at at the end of the first chapter.

What was seen as superimposed in the first chapter was negated in the next one, and the Reality underlying such superimpositions was perceived as *saccidānanda*. What appears as all the effects is nothing but this one causal Reality.

Going one step further into subtlety, the present chapter examined directly the unreality of the world. The entire world is mind-stuff in essence, and that mind has no being either.

What really exists is one Consciousness alone. Such is the basic idea underlying the whole of the present chapter.

Mind (*manas*) is the name given to the Consciousness-Reality when It has imagination for Its function. For this reason it was stated that mind really has no being.

The function of imagination takes place in Consciousness (*cit*), and it becomes concretized as the world. This happens because of the darkness of *avidyā* abiding in and hiding the being of the very same Consciousness-Reality. This *avidyā*, in essence darkness, existing in Consciousness that is in essence pure effulgence, is a great mystery like a grand magic show.

This very *avidyā* was then called *māyā*. The Ultimate Reality is called *Ātmā*. *Māyā*, instead of *Ātmā*, is thought of as the original cause of the world in the sense that the illusory appearance of the world in *Ātmā* happens because of *māyā*.

Mind (*manas*), willful imagination (*saṁkalpa*), nescience (*avidyā*), *māyā* — these four principles were shown in different contexts of the present chapter as causal to the illusory appearance of the world. These four really are neither four nor one, these are simply unreal; what is real is *Ātmā* alone. The world and its four causes are seen illusorily in the one *Ātmā*. In short, what the word *asatya* (the unreal, the non-existent) signifies in this chapter covers both the world and its above-mentioned causes. In other words, both cause and effect are unreal.

Where do these unreal phenomena appear to be? In the *Ātmā* that alone is Real. It is that one Reality that manifests both as cause and effect, both as *manas* and *saṁkalpa*, *avidyā* and *māyā* on the one side, and as the world on the other.

The word *bhāti* (shiningly manifests), in the Vedāntic context, denotes aspects of unconditioned Consciousness becoming conditioned as specific experiences. *Ātmā*, for example, when subjectively conditioned is called *bhoktā* (the enjoyer), and when objectively conditioned, *bhogya* (the enjoyed). As forming a group of three words, along with *bhāti* are to be seen *asti* and *priya*, the group thus being *asti-bhāti-priya*. The one all-underlying Reality, *Brahman*, in the last chapter, was defined as *sat-cit-ānanda*. The denotations of these words are of universal import, their particular counterparts being *asti-bhāti-priya*. *Asti* means existence directly experienced; the most directly experienced existence is of oneself. *Cit* (pure Consciousness), when directly experienced, becomes one's own feelings, emotions and knowledge, all together called *bhāti*. Such knowledges and emotions are always associated with one's likes and dislikes. This aspect of directly experienced value is called *priya*. *Ātmā* thus is *sat-cit-ānanda* universally, and is personally experienced as *asti-bhāti-priya*. Such *Ātmā* is what appears universally as the world and individually as oneself, both as *vivarta*, itself undergoing no intrinsic change. How the one Reality, *Ātmā*, and the many unrealities in the form of causes and effects, always remain non-dual or inseparably one is clarified by the Guru in this verse with the help of an analogy.

A *śivaliṅga* (phallus symbol) made of rock is before us. The sculptor who made it did not create something new out of the piece of rock; rock itself was made to appear as *śivaliṅga* which has no existence of its own. Seen as *śivaliṅga*, therefore, it is unreal. Seen as rock, it is real. The rock alone has real existence. The real existence of the rock is seen here as the unreal existence of the *śivaliṅga*. It could therefore easily be said, seeing the unreality of the *śivaliṅga* itself is the proof of the really existing rock.

The world is to be seen in the place of the *śivaliṅga*, and *Ātmā* in the place of stone. The appearance of the unreal world itself is the proof of the existence of the Reality of *Ātmā*. Stone and *śivaliṅga* are never separable. Similarly inseparable are the *Ātmā*-Reality and the apparent world. In other words, the unreal and the real are inseparable. This may sound like a paradoxical statement; but it would be so only from the logical point of view. This oneness of the unreal world and the real *Ātmā* constitutes the essence of non-duality (*advaita*).

What is logic? It simply is a functional facet of the unreal mind that in its turn forms part of the unreal world. Trying to make use of it as a criterion to arrive at a clear understanding of the Reality underlying the whole of the world, is senseless in itself. Then it is no wonder that our logical mind reaches a dead end at this point. Looked at totally, the relationship between the unreal and the real, and the emergence of the phenomenon of life as a result of this relationship, all have inherent in it a mystery, an undefinability. This undefinability in Vedānta is called *māyā*. The next chapter, therefore, concentrates more on evaluating the nature of *māyā* in order to realize the Reality veiled by it.

4

Māya Darśanam
(Vision by *Māyā*)

BRAHMAN is indefinable, equally indefinable is *māyā*. *Brahman* has inherent within it the mysterious and inexhaustible power to make the unreal world appear to exist and to veil from view what really exists. This mysterious power is known as *māyā*. The *māyā* concepts of various elucidators of Vedānta vary substantially. Śaṅkara, in his *Vivekacūḍāmaṇi* (Crest-jewel of Discrimination) defines it as follows:

> *Māyā* is that power of the supreme God, which is named "the indistinct" (*avyakta*), the beginningless nescience (*avidyā*) and the three nature-modalities (*guṇa*s) in essence, that which is transcendental (*parā*), the existence of which is inferred by discerning ones from its effects, and that which gives birth to all the worlds.
>
> It is neither existent nor non-existent nor is it bothwise; it is neither different from *Brahman* nor not-different from *Brahman*, nor is it bothwise;
>
> Neither has it parts nor is it partless, nor is it bothwise; it is a great mystery of indefinable nature.

The *māyā*-theory of Śaṅkara did not find favour with Rāmānuja; he found it full of inconsistencies. He could not give up the idea altogether either, for the reason that no one can deny the mystery that abides in the creation of the world. And more, a direct reference to *māyā* appears in the *Śvetāśvatara Upaniṣad*. No elucidator of Vedānta can simply ignore such direct scriptural references. The Upaniṣad says,

māyām tu prakṛtim viddhi māyinam to maheśvaram ।

Understand *māyā* as constituted of nature (*prakṛti*); then the wielder of *māyā* (*māyin*) is the Supreme God. (4.10)

Rāmānuja, therefore, admitted the *māyā*-concept into his school of Vedānta by giving it a new definition. *Brahman* in its perception is Viṣṇu in form. This Viṣṇu has in Him the mysterious power to absorb into His being, in a subtle form, all the worlds, all the living beings in them and their *karma*s together at the time of dissolution (*kalpānta*), and to make them reappear at the time of creation (*kalpādi*). This mysterious power is *māyā* in Rāmānuja's view. A detailed comparative study of the *māyā*-concepts of these two great masters has been undertaken separately by us (see Chapter 7 of *Vedānta up to Narayana Guru*).

Narayana Guru directly deals with the topic in all his philosophical works as well as in his hymns. Though he apparently sides with Śaṅkara's line of thought, the *māyā* represented by him would be found agreeable to the Rāmānuja School also.

The way of approach adopted in this work, is that of viewing the non-dual Reality from ten different angles. Of these, the viewpoint of the present chapter is that the unreal world appears to be real because of the *māyā* principle inherent in *Brahman*. The overall purpose is not to help us have a clear understanding of *māyā*, but rather to describe *māyā* in such a way that the very same *māyā* could be negated by the student in order to realize what really exists. A Vedāntin studies *māyā* simply with the intention of negating it. This chapter is no exception.

Verse 1

न विद्यते या सा माया विद्याऽविद्या पराऽपरा ।
तमः प्रधानं प्रकृतिर्बहुधा सैव भासते ॥१ ॥

na vidyate yā sā māyā vidyā 'vidyā parā 'parā ।
tamaḥ pradhānaṁ prakṛtir bahudhā saiva bhāsate ॥1 ॥

That which does not exist is *māyā*. It manifests variously as *vidyā* and *avidyā, parā* and *aparā, tamas, pradhāna* and *prakṛti.*

Māyā really is indefinable. The apparently awkward definition given here, "That which does not exist is called *māyā,*" is for the sake of formality. Closely examined, it will be found to be no real definition.

It is paradoxical to say that something non-existent becomes manifest variously. How can something that has no being manifest itself? It was clearly stated by the Guru himself, earlier in Verse II.8, "That which does not exist does not become manifest," (*yat asat tat na bhāti*). The idea conveyed in that context by the Guru was that one Reality alone, in essence consciousness (*cit*), exists. Had it been non-existent it would not have become manifest. Becoming manifest, in other words itself is the proof of the existence (*sat*) of consciousness (*cit*). The search in the present context is not for the ontological Reality (*sat*). Rather it is to examine the mysteriousness of the appearance of the unreal world in the one Reality. Even after this detailed study, *māyā* will remain a mystery, but we will be capable of overcoming it.

Māyā is not a reality. It is merely a mysterious seed-like potential that gives birth to everything and abides in what really exists, as is stated by the Guru himself in Verse 53 of his *Ātmopadeśa Śatakam* (One Hundred Verses of Self-Instruction), which reads thus:

> Latent in it is a primeval creative urge that is the original seed that gives birth to everything perceptible forming the world. The seeking mind, by immersing itself into It, should meditatively cogitate (*manana*) with a view to getting rid of the delusion caused by *māyā*.

The ocean has in it the infinite potential to give rise to waves from itself. Similar is the potential inherent in the one Reality or *cit*, that causes the emanation of all the worlds and all the beings in them. That potential has no being of its own apart from the one ever-existing Reality. This is the sense in which *māyā* is "that which does not exist." A clearer picture of the same is given in the next verse.

The *vidyā-avidyā* duality, the *parā-aparā* duality, *tamas*, *pradhānam* and *prakṛti* are the instances of the effects of *māyā* mentioned in this verse. It in no way means that these cover the entire range of such effects. The Guru himself depicts in Verse 53 of his *Ātmopadeśa Śatakam* the duality of waking and sleeping states as yet another pair becoming manifest in consciousness because of *māyā*. In yet another context (Verse 57), "many and varied bodies like water and its quality, taste, forming the various worlds," are seen as the effects of *māyā*. The subject-object duality (Verse 60), the mind-matter duality (Verse 74), the birth-death duality (Verse 78), the enjoyer-enjoyed duality (Verse 81), the appearance-Reality duality (Verse 94) are some other similar pairs. The seven aspects of the manifestation of *māyā* enumerated here, therefore, are to be treated simply as representing the vast range.

Verse 2

प्रागुत्पत्तेर्यथाऽभावो मृदेव ब्रह्मणः पृथक् ।
न विद्यते ब्रह्म हि या सा मायाऽमेयवैभवा ॥२॥

prāg utpatter yathā 'bhāvo mṛd eva brahmaṇah pṛthak ।
na vidyate brahma hi yā sā māyā 'meya vaibhavā ॥2॥

> Prior to the emerging of a pot its being is as non-existent in clay. So too, prior to the emergence of the world it has no being separate from *Brahman*, and is *Brahman* indeed. This beingness of the non-existent world in *Brahman* is what is called *māyā* of unfathomable potentials.

In view of *māyā* having already been defined as "that which does not exist," it would be inconsistent even to say that something called *māyā* exists. Yet no Vedāntic speculation can do away with the *māyā* concept either. Śaṅkara was the propounder of the *māyā* theory. Though both Rāmānuja and Madhva questioned Śaṅkara's non-dualism and the *māyā* theory, they could not do away with the concept altogether. Instead they too admitted the concept in redefined senses. And above all, there is direct reference to *māyā* in the *Śvetāśvatara Upaniṣad*. Such being the *māyā* concept, Narayana Guru thought it appropriate to define it logically. Nyāya, the Indian school of logic, admits *abhāva* (non-existence) as one of the basic philosophic categories. This made it easier for him to define *māyā* logically.

Abhāva simply means, "non-existence." It may sound odd to say that "non-existence" is of different types. Yet as related to what really exists, its nature could vary, and based on it *abhāva* is thought of as of four kinds in Indian Logic. These are *prāg-abhāva* (anterior non-existence), *pradhvaṁśa-abhāva* (posterior non-existence), *anyonya-abhāva* (mutual non-existence) and *atyanta-abhāva* (absolute non-existence).

Pots are made of clay. Before appearing as pots, they were simply existing as clay, with the potential to assume the form of pots already hidden. Such potential existence of an effect in its cause is called *prāg-abhāva* (anterior-non-existence), *prāk* meaning "anterior" or "previous." The non-existence just opposite to this is called *pradhvaṁśa-abhāva, pradhvamsa* meaning "destruction." When destroyed, the pot continues to exist in the form of shreds. Then the shreds are thought of as having in them the *pradhvaṁśa-abhāva* of pots, meaning the pots' non-existence is there in the existence of shreds.

There will be no darkness where there is light, and vice versa; one's existence means the non-existence of the other. Such mutual non-existence is known as *anyonya-abhāva.*

That which does not and cannot exist anywhere is called *atyanta-abhāva.* The child of a barren woman, a flower growing in the sky, the horns of a horse, are all examples of *atyanta-abhāva.*

The Guru shows here how the otherwise indefinable *māyā* could easily be logically defined with the help of the *prāg-abhāva* concept of Nyāya. As the anterior non-existence of the pot was already there in clay, so is the anterior non-existence of the world already existing in *Brahman.* This anterior non-existence of the world in *Brahman* could be considered the best available logical definition of *māyā.* The anterior non-existence of pot and the existence of clay are identical; so is the oneness of *māyā* and *Brahman.*

Though definable thus logically, *māyā* remains a mystery. The way in which it finds expression is also mysterious. Totally inconceivable is how the indomitable potential of *māyā,* hidden in *Brahman,* becomes actualized as the apparent worlds and the events in them. It is infinite, unthinkable and unpredictable, as is denoted by the word *ameya-vaibhavā.* The rest of the chapter shows some instances of the ways in which this inconceivable *māyā* finds expression conceivably. This well-defined listing of *māyā*'s manifestations provides us with an occasion to see intuitively the nature of *māyā*, and also to negate it and realize the one *Brahman* from which it is inseparable.

Verse 3

अनात्मा न सदात्मा सदिति विद्योतते यया।
सा विद्येयं यथा रज्जुसर्पतत्त्वावधारणम् ॥३॥

anātmā na sad ātmā sad iti vidyotate yayā ।
sā vidyeyaṁ yathā rajjusarpatattvāvadhāraṇam ॥3 ॥

That because of which the non-self (*anātmā*) is understood as unreal and the Self (*Ātmā*) as real, is what this *vidyā* is, as in the case of ascertaining that the snake is unreal and the rope alone is real.

The first verse of this chapter made it clear that the possibility of *māyā* manifesting variously is endless. Of these possibilities, how it manifests as *vidyā* (knowledge) is discussed in this verse. How the same *māyā* manifests as *avidyā* (ignorance or nescience), the opposite of *vidyā*, will be stated in the next verse. What the word *vidyā* signifies is not the clear understanding we gain that *Ātmā* (the Self) alone is real and *anātmā* (the non-self) is unreal. The ultimate Reality, as was seen earlier in Verse 2.7, is *cit* or pure Consciousness in essence. Consciousness never remains functionless, and as a result everything that appears as the endless world emerges from Itself.

The nature of the variety of this self-unfoldment of consciousness decides what our world-experience is. The function of consciousness in the form of knowing the Reality in the right way and in the wrong way, both happen in the same *cit*. *Vidyā* is defined here as that particular function of consciousness because of which we come to the correct understanding that *Ātmā* alone is what exists, and that all that appears to be existing, called here *anātmā* (the non-self), is unreal. This *vidyā* is one of the endless specific manifestations of *māyā*. In short, *vidyā*, as understood here, does not mean the correct knowledge of Reality; on the other hand, it denotes the specific function of consciousness by which we gain a correct understanding of Reality. The correct knowledge of Reality is called *jñāna*, and *vidyā* is the mental function that leads us to *jñāna*.

A piece of rope seen at twilight sometimes appears to be a snake. Such a misperception is caused by a deluding mental function. It is yet another mental function that enables one to realize that it really is a piece of rope and that the snake-appearance was merely an illusion. It is a mental function similar to this second-mentioned disillusion that makes you realize what really exists is *Ātmā* alone, and that the apparent world is a snake-like illusion.

According to Śaṅkara, the propounder of the *māyā* theory, *avidyā* is a synonym for *māyā*. He thinks of *māyā* as the illusion universally prevailing, and *avidyā* as the same illusion affecting each individual's perception of reality. In other words, *māyā* exists in each of us in the form of *avidyā*, and this *avidyā* could be destroyed only with *vidyā*, the enlightenment of the real. Slightly variant is the *māyā* concept of Narayana Guru. He treats both *vidyā* and *avidyā* as two apparent opposite facets of the function of consciousness, and this multi-faceted functional manifestation of consciousness is caused by *māyā*. This variance of the line of thought of the Guru from Śaṅkara's cannot simply be treated as incidental. *Darśanamālā* was written by the Guru towards the end of his life. He, in his prime of life, had presented his philosophy in his own original way in his *Ātmopadeśa Śatakam*. In that work also the Guru underscores the point that it is because of *māyā* that the one consciousness manifests functionally both as *vidyā* and *avidyā* (see verse 72).

Ātmā is pure Consciousness in essence, and this Consciousness is creative in itself, and as a result various functions find expression in it. These functional modes appear as infinite manifest forms ranging from the most subtle mind, to the most gross matter. This phenomenon results also in our treating these manifest forms, called *anātmā* (the non-self) by the Guru in the present verse, as real, completely oblivious of the Consciousness-Reality underlying all these. Making this possible there is a mysterious *māyā*-power in the very same Consciousness, and it is called *avidyā* in Vedānta.

Each "I" thus is subject to this *avidyā*, and is in need of release from its grip. The only way to accomplish this goal is realizing that each "I" is really one of the apparent forms of pure Consciousness (*cit*), the underlying Substance, just as a pot realizing itself to be clay in essence. By chance there emerge a few who, with such an end in view, turn their search towards what is real in themselves. Such search for Reality is also a functional mode of the very same Consciousness, a manifestation of Consciousness. And that manifest form of Consciousness is called *vidyā* here. Consciousness could thus function in two extremely opposite ways, and this is caused by *māyā*. But a transcendental state of enlightenment that goes beyond this duality is also there, and it is called *turīya* by the Guru in Verse 72 of the *Ātmopadeśa Śatakam*.

Consciousness (*cit*) is what ultimately exists, and what exists always manifests itself as well. The manifest form of *cit* is called *bhāna*, and that of *sat* is *bhāva*. Without *cit* there is no *bhāna*; and wihtout *bhāna* no *cit* exists either. Likewise, without *sat* there is no *bhāva*, and without *bhāva* no *sat* can exist. This is just like saying, no ornament-form can exist without gold, and no gold can exist without assuming some form. Though logically conceivable as two, ornament-form and gold, *sat* and *bhāva*, *cit* and *bhāna*, none has ever existed separately, and will never exist so either. Likewise is the oneness of Consciousness and its functional modes. The non-duality of the two is not to be logically conceived, but is to be directly experienced as constituting one's own being, the seeker becoming lost in it!

Verse 4

आत्मा न सदनात्मा सदिति विद्योतते यया ।
सैवाऽविद्या यथा रज्जुसर्पयोरयथार्थदृक् ॥४॥

ātmā na sad anātmā sad iti vidyotate yayā ।
saivā 'vidyā yathā rajjusarpayor ayathārthadr̥k ॥4॥

That because of which *Ātmā* (the Self) is understood as unreal and *anātmā* (the non-self) as real, is what this *avidyā* is, as in the case of wrongly seeing the rope as unreal and a snake as real.

Avidyā is defined here as the opposite of *vidyā*: the function of consciousness that makes one wrongly think of the Self as unreal (*asat*) and the non-self (*anātmā*) as real (*sat*) is called *avidyā*.

Those who are under the spell of *avidyā* or nescience usually do not discriminate between the Self and the non-self, the real and the unreal. Treating the Self as unreal and the non-self as real after having known the Self, is not what they do. Those who discriminate between the two never become subject to *avidyā*. *Avidyā* causes one to simply see whatever is presented to the sense organs as real as such. That mysterious function of mind or consciousness which, unable to discriminate the real from the unreal, treats whatever is experienced through the senses as real, thinking of nothing beyond it, is the *avidyā* form of *māyā*. The traditional example of mistaking a piece of rope for a snake is also cited to make the point clear.

The definitions of *vidyā* and *avidyā* in Verses 3 and 4 include indirectly the definitions of *Ātmā* (the self) and *anātmā* (the non-self) also. What is *sat*, that means, what ultimately exists underlying the appearance of everything, is *Ātmā*; and what is *asat*, that means, what appears to exist but has no real being of its own, is *anātmā*. The word *asat*, though literally meaning that which is unreal, in Vedāntic parlance means, that which appears to exist but really does not.

To make the point clear, let us take the case of a gold ornament. What is *sat* in it is the gold-substance. It could therefore be said, gold is the *ātmā* and the ornament-form is its body. Everyone of us is in the place of an ornament. The ornament-form could be altered, but never the gold-substance; it never ceases to exist either. Likewise, what is real in us is immutable, is unceasingly existent, whereas our external form, the body, always changes; it appears and disappears as well. *Ātmavidyā* (self-knowledge) in essence means realizing, "I am not the changeful form, but am the changeless Reality or *Ātmā*," just like a gold ornament realizing "I am really gold, not the ornament-form." It is when this real substance in us remains unknown, that each of us is tempted to think of ourselves as constituted of the visible form called *śarīra*, meaning, that which perishes.

We, in the usual course, think of *śarīra* or body as consisting of the physical or gross aspect of our being. But wider is the sense in which the word *śarīra* is used in Vedānta. For instance, the *Bhagavad-Gītā*, after equating *śarīra* (body) with *kṣetra* (the field), defines it as constituted of everything that is perceivable and conceivable in a human individual. To quote the *Gītā* verses:

महाभूतान्यहङ्कारो बुद्धिरव्यक्तमेव च।
इन्द्रियाणि दशैकं च पञ्च चेन्द्रियगोचराः ॥१३.५॥

इच्छा द्वेषः सुखं दुःखं सङ्घातश्चेतना धृतिः।
एतत्क्षेत्रं समासेन सविकारमुदाहृतम् ॥१३.६॥

mahābhūtāny ahaṁkāro buddhir avyaktam eva ca ।
indriyāṇi daśaikaṁ ca pañca cendriya gocarāḥ ॥13.5॥

icchā dveṣaḥ sukhaṁ duḥkhaṁ saṁghātaś cetanā dhṛtiḥ ।
etat kṣetraṁ samāsena savikāram udāhṛtam ॥13.6॥

The great physical elements, I-sense, reason, and also the unmanifest, the ten senses and the one (mind), and the five sense-experiences; wish, dislike, pleasure, pain, the organic aggregation, conscious vitality (*cetanā*), firmness of mind — these in brief constitute the changeful field. — XIII.5-6

Every aspect that forms an individual being, from the grossest physical elements to the subtlest conscious vitality (*cetanā*), which latter is equivalent to the soul principle in theology, forms part of what is thought of as *śarīra* or *kṣetra* in the *Gītā*. All these, including the *cetanā*, are changeful. The one Substance that assumes the form of all these apparent aspects together, is what is called *Ātmā* in Vedānta. In short, what those who are under the spell of *avidyā* see as forming their own essential content is the body aspect or the apparent aspect of their being, whereas, those who discriminate between *Ātmā* and *ānātmā*, and are fully aware that *Ātmā* alone is *sat*, perceive the one *Ātmā* alone as Real, as really constituting their own being. They remain firm in this enlightened awareness, no matter the happenings of the changeful world.

Avidyā, in short, is not the state of complete ignorance, it too is a state of knowledge — the mistaken knowledge of thinking of the unreal as the real. To be more precise, *avidyā* is that mysterious function inherent in *cit*, that makes this kind of misconception possible.

Verse 5

इन्द्रियाणि मनोबुद्धी पञ्चप्राणादयो यया ।
विसृज्यन्ते सैव परा सूक्ष्माङ्गानि चिदात्मनः ॥५॥

indriyāṇi mano buddhī pañca-prāṇādayo yayā ।
visṛjyante saiva parā sūkṣmāṅgāni cidātmanaḥ ॥5॥

That, because of which the subtle aspects such as sense organs, mind and intellect, the five vital flows of energy and the like emanate from *Ātmā*, that is *cit* in essence, is indeed the *parā*.

The *parā-aparā* (transcendental-immanent) duality is an important topic that comes up for discussion at various stages in the context of Vedānta. The *Muṇḍaka Upaniṣad*, at its very beginning, differentiates *parā-vidyā* (transcendental wisdom) and *aparā-vidyā* (worldly knowledge). All the sciences, including scriptures like the Vedas and the Upaniṣads, are learnt by people with varying interests — all these form part of *aparā-vidyā* only. Yet there is another science, a Science of sciences. All the sciences and discipline are various ways in which the mind or consciousness functions and finds expression through branching out multifariously. There is a science that deals with this homogeneous Consciousness-Substance, and that science, in effect, is the Science of sciences.

This Consciousness-Reality is felt by each individual as one's own self-being, and thus this Science of sciences, in essence, is *Ātma-vidyā* (Self-knowledge). This Science is called *parā-vidyā* or transcendental wisdom. In this wisdom, the subject itself is the object studied. The subject merging in the object marks the finality of this wisdom, whereas the subject and object always remain separate in *aparā-vidyā*.

Such is the duality of *parā-vidyā* and *aparā-vidyā* described in the *Muṇḍaka Upaniṣad*. Apparently such is not the *parā-aparā* discrimination made by the Guru here in the *Darśanamālā*.

Para-Brahman and *apara-Brahman* are yet another pair of concepts that came into vogue in Vedānta after the time of Śaṅkara. He called the eternal, all-underlying, inconceivable and immortal Reality or *Brahman* in its unconditioned state, *para-Brahman* (higher *Brahman*). It is this causal Reality that appears as the world, as its conditioned manifestation, and in that state it is called *apara-Brahman* (lower *Brahman*). The names *kāraṇa-Brahman* and *kārya-Brahman* (the causal Absolute and the Absolute appearing as effects) are also sometimes given to these two. Another pair of words signifying the same differentiation is *nirguṇa-Brahman* and *saguṇa-Brahman* (unqualified *Brahman* and qualified *Brahman*). The pair of *parā* and *aparā* pertaining to *māyā* introduced by Narayana Guru here in the *Darśanamālā* is apparently different from Śaṅkara's *parā-aparā* concepts as well.

The basic deviation noticeable here is that the *parā-aparā* differentiation, as conceived by the Guru, pertains not to *Brahman*, but to *māyā*, and this *māyā* on its part is non-existent, and undifferentiable from *Brahman*. *Māyā*, as we know, is the mysterious power inherent in *Brahman* that makes possible the emerging of the world appearance from Itself. *Brahman* alone is the reality that exists. Our not seeing this one Reality and seeing many apparent forms as real, is caused by *māyā*. It thus becomes clear that it is because of *māyā* that the non-dual *Brahman* is conceived as having *parā* and *aparā* aspects, the non-dual Consciousness (*cit*) as having *parā-vidyā* and *aparā-vidyā* facets, the non-dual Reality as *kāraṇa-Brahman* and *kārya-Brahman*. What the chapter *Māyā Darśanam* thus shows as *vidyā-avidyā*, *parā-aparā* and so on are all various contexts in which the non-dual Reality appears as many because of *māyā*.

That *Ātmā* alone, or *Brahman* alone, is the one existing Reality is the basic stand of Vedānta. This *Ātmā*, in essence, is pure and unconditioned Consciousness (*cit*), and therefore it at times is called *cidātmā* by the Guru, meaning *ātmā* that is *cit* in essence. The present verse is one such instance. It is this one *cidātmā* that appears as everything, ranging from the most subtle mind aspect to the most gross physical bodies, all because of *māyā*. Of this, that aspect of *māyā* which gives rise to the subtlest aspects of our being, like mind, intellect and vital forces, is called *parā* by the Guru. These factors form part of our being. We can also think of a universal mind, intellect and vital forces that control the cosmic system.

The power of *māyā* that makes the very same *cit* appear as gross objects will be defined as *aparā* later.

The subtle aspects like mind, intellect and the five *prāṇa*s may at first sight look like pertaining to individual beings, and the gross objects to the cosmic being; but it is not so. Similar to these subtle factors are imaginable the same subtle factors of a cosmic dimension. The Upaniṣads prefer to refer to that which is related to individuated beings as *adhyātma*, and that which is of universal dimension as *ādhidaivata*. It is the five *prāṇa*s functioning that maintains an individual being as a coherent whole. Likewise, cosmic *prāṇa*s that uphold the cosmos as a coherent whole are also conceived by the Upaniṣads. And, on the other hand, gross aspects are seen as pertaining to individual beings also, as the well-known concepts of *sthūla śarīra* (gross body) and *annamaya-kośa* (sheath made of food) of Vedānta denote. All this considered together, it is difficult to say whether the subtle and gross aspects mentioned here belong strictly to individual existence or universal existence. Rather, the two belong to both at the same time.

The next verse shows how this *parā-māyā* inherent in *cidātmā* (the Self that in essence is pure Consciousness) causes delusion to the very same *cidātmā*.

Verse 6

अङ्गान्येतान्यवष्टभ्य सुखी दुःखीव मुह्यति ।
चिदात्मा मायया स्वस्य तत्त्वतोऽस्ति न किञ्चन ॥६॥

aṅgāny etāny avaṣṭabhya sukhī duḥkhīva muhyati ।
cidātmā māyayā svasya tattvato 'sti na kiñcana ॥6॥

By appropriating such subtle factors, the *Ātmā* that is *cit* in essence, deludedly thinks of itself as happy or unhappy because of its own *māyā*. Basically nothing of it is real at all.

Those who are familiar at least with a little bit of Vedāntic thinking would have the general notion that the ever-fluctuating appearance and disappearance of pleasures and pains in life are merely an effect of *māyā*, though they need not necessarily have a clear understanding of what this means. The Guru, in the present verse, gives a clear elucidation of this picture.

The one absolute Reality, called *Brahman* or *Ātman*, as we have already seen clearly, is pure and unconditioned Consciousness (*cit*) in essence. Being the all-pervading (*ātata*) substance, this *cit* is called *cidātmā*, here meaning, *Ātmā* that is *cit* in essence. It is the *cidātmā* that manifests itself as all the apparent worlds, owing to its own *māyā*. This apparent world, in its turn, includes in it everything from the subtlest mind-phenomenon to the grossest matter-phenomenon of worldly existence. That the subtle phenomena emerging from *cidātmā* cause a delusion to itself is the point underscored in the present verse.

It is with conceiving our own existence, the existence of "I" as the centre that we perceive our life and the world as well. What is this "I"? The direct experience we have of "I" is that it is a consciousness of existence. This existence is attributed to have an individuatedness whenever we refer to "I" in the ordinary sense. This individuated "I," which could be many, really is something superimposed on *cidātmā* which always is one alone.

Space is all-filling and in that sense it is called *mahākāśa*, the great space. A fragment of the same space is sometimes referred to as *ghaṭākāśa* (pot-space), taking into account its filling the inside of a pot. Similarly, *cidātmā,* because of its own *māyā*, delimits its own being and thinks of it as "I," the individual being. Those who become cognizant of this shortcoming in themselves, make it a point that they perceive life and the world with *cidātmā* for its centre, letting the "I" vanish from its centre. *Cidātmā* in its turn being the all-pervading Substance, is no centre of anything at all. When perceiving life with such a *cidātmā* for its centre, all the pains and pleasures that were seemingly relevant when seeing life with "I" for its centre, simply vanish.

Cidātmā is one alone, but the "I" senses that get formulated in it are many. How does this happen? It is comparable to treating the all-filling space as many pot-spaces. Pots here serve as the factors that condition space to make it appear as many. Similarly, there are certain conditioning factors in the *cidātmā* that make it appear as many "I"-s, and these conditioning factors emerge in *cidātmā* because of its own *māyā*. These conditioning factors were what were referred to as *sūkṣmāṅga*s (subtle factors), like sense organs, mind, intellect, the five *prāṇa*s and so on, in the last verse.

The indistinct gold-substance, by becoming conditioned by an ornament-form and becoming identified with that conditioning factor acquires the status of a distinct ornament, so too, the *cidātmā*, becoming conditioned by and identified with the above-mentioned subtle factors, appears as many "I"-s.

Each of the sense organs gets into contact with its respective object. What are these objects really? They are also nothing but the same *cidātmā*, that assumed the subtle form of senses, become differently manifest by assuming gross forms, as will be stated in the next verse. Contact with these objects results in perceptions causing pleasures and pains. Instead of treating such feelings as yet another way of the *ānanda* content of *Ātmā* becoming manifest, they are mistaken for happiness or suffering happening to the individual "I."

Ātmā, the one all-underlying Substance, as we know, is *cit* in essence. *Cit* never remains inactive either. It is spontaneous for *cidātmā* to unfold the infinite potentials hidden in itself for the sheer joy of actualizing its own *ānanda* content. As a result of this self-creativity, various ideas, imaginations and wills get formulated in it. When functioning like this the *cidātmā* is termed *manas* (mind). In short, all of us emerged from the one *cidātmā* as an effect of its creative willing. We are thus tiny fragments of *cidātmā*, and in that capacity we have abiding in us fragments of its willing power as well. The *cidātmā* enjoys itself by emanating the entire world from itself. Ignorant of this mysteriousness of *cidātmā* and our being part of it, we think we derive pleasures from sense objects and engage our mind in search of enjoyable objects. Even such sense objects, it is to be remembered, are the very same *cidātmā* appearing differently, but we remain oblivious to this fact. The tragedy that befalls us as a result of the mind's wandering after pleasurable objects is well portrayed, in the *Bhagavad-Gītā* thus:

ध्यायतो विषयान्पुंसः सङ्गस्तेषूपजायते।
सङ्गात्सञ्जायते कामः कामात्क्रोधोऽभिजायते॥२.६२॥

क्रोधाद्भवति सम्मोहः सम्मोहात्स्मृतिविभ्रमः।
स्मृतिभ्रंशाद्बुद्धिनाशो बुद्धिनाशात्प्रणश्यति॥२.६३॥

dhyāyato viṣayān puṁsaḥ saṅgas teṣūpajāyate ।
saṅgāt sañjāyate kāmaḥ kāmāt krodho 'bhijāyate ॥2.62॥

krodhād bhavati sammohaḥ sammohāt smṛti-vibhramaḥ ।
smṛti-bhraṁśād buddhi-nāśo buddhi-nāśāt praṇaśyati ॥2.63॥

Meditating on objects of sense-interest there is born in man an attachment for them; from attachment rises passion, in the face of passion (frustrated) arises rage.

From rage is produced distortion of values, and from distortion of values memory-lapse, and from memory-lapse comes loss of reason, and from loss of reason he perishes.
— II.62, 63

It is this mental factor that makes us feel like canoes lost in the winds, that is referred to in the present verse as the delusion caused by the *māyā* of *cidātmā*. Instead of letting it lead our life, the very same mind could well be made use of for attaining the ultimate goal of life.

Intellect (*buddhi*) too sometimes deludes us the same way. Relating every effect with its cause, and then thinking in terms of causality is what our reasoning faculty is familiar with. Trying to regulate the course of events in life with causality as the one guiding principle and even trying to perceive the total world likewise, is what our reasoning mind does. We then stand aghast when face to face with the fact that things do not happen strictly according to the law of causality. We do not even hesitate to evaluate the events that do not comply with the law of causality simply as impossible. A human mind simply evaluating an event as logically impossible does not actually stop the event taking place. The reasoning mind merely becomes confused as it comes across things in life and events in the world that do not take place fully in accordance with its reasoning. There is only one way out of this riddle: the reasoning mind realizing that it is one of the countless functional manifestations of the one *cidātmā*. Apart from that *cidātmā* no mind has existence, no reasoning has existence, no sense organs and their perceptions have existence, no sense-object has existence, no sense-experience has existence. All these appear to be there in the one *cidātmā* because of its own *māyā*, none of these having real existence of their own.

Verse 7

इन्द्रियाणां हि विषयः प्रपञ्चोऽयं विसृज्यते।
यया सैवाऽपराऽध्यात्मस्थूलसङ्कल्पनामयी ॥७॥

indriyāṇāṁ hi viṣayaḥ prapañco 'yaṁ visṛjyate ।
yayā saivā 'para 'dhyātma-sthūla-saṁkalpanāmayī ॥7॥

That by which this world that forms the objects of the senses emanates specifically (from the *Ātmā* that is *cit* in content) is indeed the *aparā*. In essence it is nothing but the gross ideation of individuated self.

Māyā was stated earlier (3.8) as the original cause of the appearance of the world. The world-appearance being of countless facets, it is practically impossible to say exactly how extensive the effects of *māyā* are. Such effects, in general, are referred to in Vedānta as *māyā-kārya*s and what the present chapter does is simply pinpoint some such specifiable effects of *māyā*. Knowing the real as real and knowing the unreal as real, both are caused by *māyā*, and both are functions that take place in one and the same consciousness in order to quench the thirst for knowledge. As is the function of mental faculties an effect of *māyā*, so too the appearance of the external objects is an effect of *māyā*.

The objective world is inclusive of both subtle elements and gross elements as was stated earlier in Verse 2.1. The subtle elements comprise mind, intellect, the five *prāṇa*s, the sense organs and the like, and that aspect of *māyā* which makes these subtle elements emerge in *cidātmā* was called *parā*. The very same *cidātmā* has inherent in it the mysterious power to emanate the gross elements that form the external objective world, and this power of *māyā* is termed here *aparā*.

The elements that emanate because of the *aparā-māyā* serve as objects for the elements emerged because of the *parā-māyā*. One and the same *cidātmā*, in other words, gives rise to both the subjective aspect and the objective aspect of a knowledge situation. In short, both the mental and physical aspects of existence have one substance alone underlying their being, and that substance, called *cidātmā* here, is none other than *Ātmā* or *Brahman*. This peculiarity of being the homogeneous substance underlying the being of both the mental and the physical worlds makes *Brahman* the *samāna-adhikaraṇa* (the common basis) of everything.

The realms of mind and matter apparently are opposite in nature. How do these two get into contact with each other resulting in what we experience as sense-perception? This question has always been tormenting the minds of scientists and thinkers alike ever since the beginning of the history of thought. Vedānta answers it clearly: It is one *cit* or *cidātmā*, becoming conditioned because of its own *māyā*, that manifests itself both as mind and matter, both as subject and object, the one subtly and the other grossly. *Māyā* causes the superimposition of certain conditioning factors and as a result, the one Reality appears as two. These conditioning factors taken away, what remains would be the one homogeneous substance or *cidātmā* alone. An urge for realizing this oneness is there in all the conditioned appearances. A sense organ or mind getting into contact with its object simply means, each side foregoing the conditioning factors that made them appear separate, and realizing their intrinsic oneness. Oblivious of this truth, we mistake the urge as the sense organ's thirst for pleasure.

How does the *cidātmā*, in essence pure and unconditioned Consciousness, assume the form of the gross world that includes everything from mere inert objects like stone and soil to living beings? This may sound impossible. Really nothing that happens because of *māyā* is understandable to our reasoning mind, the very mind being an effect of *māyā*. How the one *māyā* functions as *vidyā*, *avidyā*, *parā*, *aparā* and many such, therefore, is not conceivable logically. The only explanation possible is that everything happens so in *Ātmā* because of its own willing or ideation.

The willing that causes the emergence of the gross world is termed here *sthūla-saṁkalpanā* (gross ideation). Where does it take place? In the one *cidātmā* or *ātmā*. In other words, the gross ideation that takes place in *ātmā* is what appears as the gross world. For this reason, this aspect of *māyā* is described by the Guru here as *adhyātma-sthūla-saṁkalpana-mayī* (in essence, nothing but gross ideation of the individuated self), and it is none other than the *aparā-māyā*.

Verse 8

शुक्तिकायां यथाऽज्ञानं रजतस्य यदात्मनि ।
कल्पितस्य निदानं तत्तम इत्यवगम्यते ॥८ ॥

śuktikāyāṁ yathā 'jñānaṁ rajatasya yadātmani ।
kalpitasya nidānaṁ tat tama ity avagamyate ॥8 ॥

> As ignorance of the mother-of-pearl is the basis of the silver-appearance, so too there is an ignorance basic for all that is seen imaginarily in *Ātmā*. That is what is known as *tamas* (darkness).

Māyā is treated as having *tamas* or darkness for its essential quality. Darkness is marked by the absence of light, and it stands here for *ajñāna* or ignorance, the absence of *jñāna* or wisdom. Knowing what really exists as it is, is known as *jñāna*. Knowing something as it is not, is called *ajñāna* or ignorance. For instance, mistaking a mother-of-pearl for silver is *ajñāna*. Even when wrongly understood what the sense organ gets into contact with is mother-of-pearl alone, not silver. The mother-of-pearl thus is seen not as a mother-of-pearl, but as something else. A sort of darkness inherent in consciousness here veils its own knowing faculty, and this darkness is called *tamas*.

In the place of the mother-of-pearl here is to be seen the all-emanating, all-underlying substance *Ātmā*. It is *Ātmā* alone that always exists, but when encountered, it is mistaken for the world's existence. Even when seeing the silver in it, the mother-of-pearl does not become anything else. So too, seeing *Ātmā* as the world does not make it anything other than *Ātmā*. While *Ātmā* alone remains really existing, its existence is mistaken for that of the world, because of a darkness inherent in the knowing consciousness, and that darkness is the *tamas* referred to here.

The *tamas* understood here, as seen by Śaṅkara, has a double function. Mistaking a mother-of-pearl for silver involves two specific misleading factors: one, something veils the being of the mother-of-pearl, and two, something other than the mother-of-pearl is projected on it, to be perceived in its stead. Śaṅkara called the former veiling power *āvaraṇa-śakti*, and the latter projecting power *vikṣepa-śakti*. Narayana Guru, on the other hand, does not treat these two powers of *māyā* as distinct anywhere in his works. The two jointly are called by him *āvaraṇa* (veil), perhaps because he sees the imaginary silver veiling the actually existing mother-of-pearl.

In the place of the mother-of-pearl in the analogy, what really exists is one *Ātmā* alone. The world-form imaginarily seen in *Ātmā* veils the very same *Ātmā* from our view. Therefore the veiling and projecting powers do not necessarily have to be treated as separate. The Guru therefore called it *āvaraṇa*, meaning to cover both what *āvaraṇa* and *vikṣepa* of Śaṅkara signify. This veiling power, which he called *āvaraṇa* elsewhere, is denoted by the word *tamas* or darkness here. It really is the darkness of *ajñāna* or ignorance.

The *ajñāna* mentioned here and the *avidyā* described earlier in Verse 4.4 have to be distinguished. When the unreal functions as a veil put on the real, knowing the real as real becomes impossible. It results in the absence of proper *jñāna*. This is called *ajñāna*. In other words, not knowing *Ātmā* as real and knowing the world-form or *anātmā* (non-self) as real is *ajñāna*. This *ajñāna* is the result of a particular kind of function of consciousness. That function of consciousness is called *avidyā*. *Avidyā*, in short, causes *ajñāna*. Both the words are usually rendered into English as "ignorance," though a more proper word for *avidyā* would be "nescience."

The next verse describes the aspect of *māyā* called *pradhāna*.

Verse 9

धीयतेऽस्मिन् प्रकर्षेण बीजे वृक्ष इवाखिलम् ।
अतः प्राधान्यतो वाऽस्य प्रधानमिति कथ्यते ॥९॥

dhīyate 'smin prakarṣeṇa bīje vṛkṣa ivākhilam ।
ataḥ prādhānyato vā 'sya pradhānam iti kathyate ॥9॥

Because the entire world is held properly in that (aspect of *māyā*), as is a tree properly contained in its seed, or because of its pre-eminence (*prādhānya*), it is called *pradhāna* (the pre-eminent).

Scientists and thinkers are ceaselessly engaged in an effort to unravel the mystery of the universe and of the phenomenon of life in it. Suppose the world and its mystery do not exist. Then the necessity of any search for reality also becomes meaningless. Let us imagine that a scientific genius arrives at a conclusive formula that reveals the secret of the world. That very moment will mark the cessation of all human enquiries about the world. And above all, the world and the life in it will become something that has no novelty, that is monotonous. Genuine scientists who are interested in the future of science therefore are compelled to think aloud, "Let us *not* find out 'the formula' that reveals the mystery of the world." Even the necessity for the existence of science would never be felt, once such a "formula" is found out, and no scientist can think of a world without science either.

That means, without the mysterious and indefinable world existing, no science would exist. Thus scientific enquiry and the experience of mystery validate each other and find a common ground in the unitive vision of the ultimate Reality.

The apparent world, though metaphysically unreal, has a place of its own in such a unitive and comprehensive vision. There can be no denial of the appearance of the world in the one ever-existing *Ātmā*. The mystery that makes this possible in *Ātmā*, is as pre-eminent (*pradhāna*) as the world-appearance itself. This mysterious factor is what is called *māyā*. This *māyā*, in this particular context, is called *pradhāna* (the pre-eminent).

Although the entire potential for the coming forth of a giant tree hides within a tiny seed, no trace of the tree is found in the seed. Similar to the relation between the seed and the tree is that between the *pradhāna* aspect of *māyā* and the world-appearance. We could, in this limited sense, say, this *pradhāna* is the cause of the origin of the world, like seed being the source of a tree.

Those who follow the Vedāntic tradition originating from the *Uttara-Mīmāṁsā-Sūtras* or *Vedānta-Sūtras* of Bādarāyaṇa, can never admit the idea that *pradhāna* is the original source of the world. The space spent by Śaṅkara in his commentary on the *Vedānta-Sūtras*, to prove that not *pradhāna* but *Brahman* is the cause of the world is very extensive.

According to the Sāṁkhya School, the ultimate realities are two: *prakṛti* (nature) and *puruṣa* (spirit). Of the two, the former is one and undergoes evolution which results in the formation of the world comprising everything physical and mental. The latter, on the other hand, is pure witnessing consciousness which undergoes no evolution and is different for every individual living entity.

Advaitins (non-dualists) can never tolerate the idea that two realities exist. For this reason, the main opponents attacked by Bādarāyaṇa in his *Sūtra*s and by Śaṅkara in his comments, are the Sāṁkhyans for whom *pradhāna* is merely a synonym for *prakṛti*. Bādarāyaṇa and Śaṅkara alike base themselves on scriptural evidence (*śruti*), logical reason (*yukti*) and direct perceptual experience (*anubhava*) and try their best to substantiate that *Brahman* alone and not *pradhāna*, is the original source of the world.

Attacking opponents and then arguing for one's own stand, the method adopted by both Bādarāyaṇa and Śaṅkara, did not find favour with Narayana Guru. His method has always been that of presenting his own vision in a direct and succinct way with no reference to any opponent or supporter. Therefore, instead of denouncing the *pradhāna* concept of the Sāṁkhyans, what the Guru did was admit it as a particular aspect of *māyā*. Anything other than *Brahman* conceived as existing, according to *advaitins*, has to be an effect of *māyā*. With the Sāṁkhyans, *prakṛti* and *pradhāna* are simply synonyms, but with the Guru the two are different aspects of *māyā*'s effect. What he means by *prakṛti* is stated in the next verse.

Verse 10

करोतीति प्रकर्षेण प्रकृत्यैव गुणान् पृथक् ।
निगद्यतेऽसौ प्रकृतिरिति ह त्रिगुणात्मिका ॥१० ॥

karotīti prakarṣeṇa prakṛtyaiva guṇān pṛthak ।
nigadyate 'sau prakṛtir iti ha triguṇātmikā ॥10 ॥

In the sense that it, by its very nature, separates out the *guṇas* in its own proper way, it is well known as *prakṛti* (nature), the three *guṇas* in essential content.

Prakṛti is a term that has acquired a noticeable place in India's philosophical thought. It is the Sāṁkhya system that considers *prakṛti* as one of the two ultimate realities, the other being *puruṣa*. A term as old as the Vedic tradition, it has found place in almost all the philosophical schools, with variance in what it denotes in each school. Śiva and Śakti are two concepts basic to the Śaiva and Śākta cults, where *śakti* becomes synonymous with *prakṛti*. In the Vedānta of Śaṅkara, *prakṛti* is yet another word for *māyā*.

Prakṛti, according to the Sāṁkhya concept, is one in number and comprises the three *guṇas* or nature-modalities, namely, *sattva* (the pure and clear), *rajas* (the active), and *tamas* (the dark and inert). These *guṇas*, undergoing constant permutations and combinations, result in the evolution of the twenty-four first principles or *tattva*s, and consequently in the emergence of the world.

The twenty-four *tattva*s (first principles) are: *prakṛti* (nature), *mahat* (the great), *ahaṁkāra* (I-sense), *manas* (mind), the five sense organs [*śrotra*, the sense organ that hears; *tvak*, the sense organ that feels; *cakṣus*, the sense organ that sees; *rasanā*, the sense organ that tastes; and *ghrāṇa*, the sense organ that smells], the five organs of action [*vāk*, speech; *pāṇi*, hands; *pāda*, feet; *pāyu*, exeretory organs, and *upastha*, genitals], the five *tanmātra*s or subtle elements [*śabda*, sound; *sparśa*, touch; *rūpa*, form; *rasa*, taste; and *gandha*, smell], and the five gross elements [*ākāśa*, space; *vāyu*, air; *tejas*, fire; *ap*, water, and *pṛthvī*, earth]. The evolutes of *prakṛti* together are known as *vikṛti*s, meaning that which has come into being specifically. In the context of modern science, the word "nature" is translated into Indian languages as *prakṛti*.

Even though very fundamental is the word *prakṛti* to Indian philosophy, no etymological derivation of it in its philosophical sense is to be found given in any of the basic textbooks of its schools that make use of the term profusely. Narayana Guru here, as an exception, admits *prakṛti* as an aspect of *māyā* and gives a clear definition of the term beforehand. The definition in Sanskrit reads: *prakarṣeṇa guṇān pṛthak karoti iti prakṛtiḥ*, meaning, "That, by its very nature, which separates out the three *guṇa*s in its own proper way is called *prakṛti*." This Sanskrit definition could even be summarized as *prakarṣeṇa karoti iti prakṛtiḥ*. Then it would mean, "That which performs all actions in its own proper way is called *prakṛti*."

Such actions take place nowhere else than in the one imperishable (*akṣara*) Reality or *Ātmā* as made clear in the *Bhagavad-Gītā* (VIII.3), where *karma* (action) is defined as "that creative urge inherent in the imperishable Reality which gives rise to all that comes into being." Narayana Guru also takes the same stand in respect of *karma* in the *Darśanamālā*, at the beginning of its chapter *Karma Darśana*. In short, the indomitable creative urge abiding in the one *Ātmā*, when actualized, is called *prakṛti*. Put otherwise, the *Ātman*-Reality, when functional, is called *prakṛti*.

Old apparent forms disappearing and new ones emerging is but natural with the creative self-unfoldment of Reality. Which apparent form emerges and when, depend wholly on the nature of the combination of the three *guṇa*s in each context. As the human mind is one of the outcomes of the mixture of the three *guṇa*s, the nature of their mixing up and flow is ungraspable to it. The more the mind thinks about it, the more it appears to be a mystery, and that mystery is what is called here the *prakṛti* aspect of *māyā*. *Prakṛti*, for the Guru, in short, is not merely a synonym for *māyā*, it is one of the numerous facets like *vidyā*, *avidyā*, *parā*, *aparā* and so on, that *māyā* assumes.

A different picture of how the one *prakṛti*, undergoing evolution, assumes the form of both the subjective and objective worlds is portrayed by the Guru himself in his *Ātmopadeśa Śatakam* thus:

> *Prakṛti* undergoing division within itself appears on the one side as the enjoyer, and on the other as the world of enjoyables that manifests as extensively existing externally both here and hereafter, arousing this-sense.
>
> — Verse 81

Prakṛti here is seen as creatively unfolding itself as both the enjoyer (*bhoktā*) and the enjoyable worlds (*bhoktṛ-viśvam*), here as well as hereafter. Verse 75 of the same work compares the one Ultimate Reality to an ocean with numerous pearls kept underwater; then *prakṛti* is seen as forming the water content of the ocean. In short, *prakṛti* for the Guru, is a rather adaptable term.

In the concluding verse of all the other nine chapters of the *Darśanamālā*, it can be seen suggested how the non-dual Reality is to be intuitively perceived or rather attained by the seeker with the particular vision of each chapter for its backdrop. This chapter, the *Māyā Darśanam*, alone is an exception in this respect. What it accomplishes, after defining *māyā* as that which does not exist, is simply delineating certain specific effects of *māyā*, such as *vidyā, avidyā, parā, aparā*. The Guru in Verse 57 of his *Ātmopadeśa Śatakam* points out that, if the one absolute Reality could be compared to a waveless ocean, then *māyā* will be the mysterious power in the ocean that gives rise to waves, their water content, the taste-quality of water and all such specific manifestations. The waveless ocean, being merely conceptual, remains always imperceptible. It can only be conceived as the reality underlying the specific manifest forms such as water, the column of waves emerging in it, the taste-quality of water and the like. Likewise, the non-dual Reality or *Ātmā* is to be meditatively perceived by the keen student as the Consciousness-Substance that underlies the apparent forms such as *vidyā, avidyā, parā, aparā* — all effected by *māyā*. The Reality searched for is that which is intuitively perceived when all these appearances are realized to be unreal and therefore negated.

5

Bhāna Darśanam
(Vision by Manifest Forms of Consciousness)

This chapter is named *Bhāna Darśanam*. *Bhāna* means "to shine perceptibly." That one *cit* alone has real existence has already been made amply evident. This *cit*-Reality, on its own, is unmanifest. Though having no apparent form, it manifests as everything that forms the world. The one formless *cit* or Consciousness shining by assuming some specific manifest form is what the word *bhāna* signifies here. The overall intention of the present chapter therefore is enabling the seeker to realize that the world appearance is merely an incessant manifestation of the one *cit* or Consciousness that alone is *sat*, and thus to help him realize his identity with the *cit* that manifests so.

What a real philosopher does is correlating three undeniable basic factors or facets of reality in a systematic way. These three factors are, "I" the observer, the observed world and the one all-underlying unknown Reality. Seen thus, the *Darśanamālā* could be found adopting a clearly defined method of approach. The first half shows how inseparably related are the causal unknowable Reality and the world-appearance. The second half shows how the individual "I" and the same underlying Reality are related. Each half shows different levels of such a perception. How the world originated from the Causal Reality is made clear all through the first five chapters, each chapter taking a different vantage point. The idea that God created everything from Himself is introduced in the first chapter. The speculation then proceeds to end with the present chapter where the world is seen as constantly changing conditioned manifestations of the one all-abiding *sat* that is *cit* in essence. First, all such manifest forms are categorized, giving full honour to the structural coherence of the world. Then all such manifestations are treated as conditionings superimposed on what really exists, the *sat*. The chapter ends by stating categorically that the unconditioned alone is what ultimately exists.

Verse 1

अन्तर्बहिर्वदासीनं सदा भ्रमरचञ्चलम् ।
भानं द्विधैव सामान्यं विशेष इति भिद्यते ॥१॥

antar bahirvad āsīnaṁ sadā bhramara-cañcalam ।
bhānaṁ dvidhaiva sāmānyaṁ viśeṣa iti bhidyate ॥1॥

Presenting itself as existing both inside as subject and outside as object, and also fluttering constantly like a bee, manifestation of Consciousness is divisible into two kinds: generic and specific.

The world we are familiar with, first of all, is seen as having two aspects: the subjective and the objective. Of the two, the external visible aspect alone is taken into account by modern physical sciences. As every specific external aspect is perceived, a corresponding form, called idea, of the object or of the world, gets formulated in the subjective mind. In fact, everyone's experience of the world is in the form of that idea or mental image. No means is available to check whether such images correspond exactly to the external objects of which they are supposed to be reflections.

Which of the two — the external object or the internal image — is real? Those who insist that what is external is the real are called materialists, and those who hold that what is real is the mental image are known as idealists. The Guru here underscores that what appears externally as the object and internally as the mental image are merely two different modes in which the one non-dual Reality — *Ātmā* or Consciousness — functionally finds expression, as its own simultaneous manifestations or *bhāna*s. What the Vedāntins call "the world" (*prapañca*) thus comprises both the subjective and the objective modes of expression of Reality. The absolute Reality, in other words, is neither external nor internal, but it is the one *cit* that finds expression as both. It is neither material nor mental; it is non-dual. All this is suggested in the words, *antar bahirvad āsīnam* (presenting itself as existing both inside as subject and outside as object) of the verse.

In what manner does the non-dual *cit* manifest itself? It is comparable, the Guru says, to a bee fluttering its wings. The movement of the wing from one side to the other is so fast that it remains invisible. Likewise, *cit* too moves from its external manifest form to the internal and the other way round so fast and constantly that no one is able to say at which point of time it is externally manifesting, and at which point internally. Consciousness takes no time to shift its attention from an external object to what happens within; so too the other way. For the reason that this imperceptible motion takes place all the time, even its taking place is not noticed in the usual course. Instead, we feel, two parallel worlds, one objective and the other subjective, exist simultaneously and continuously. The perpetual flow of events in each of these two worlds is often compared by thinkers to the continuity of cinematographic pictures. It is when numerous pictures flow through the projector constantly that their manyness goes behind the scene and the oneness of the flow of events comes to the fore, creating the phenomenon of a motion picture. Likewise, the flow of recurring interior pictures that appear because of the fluttering-like function of *cit*, creates the impression of the existence of a world of mental images, and of it having an unbrokenness. So is the case with the impression of the existence of the external objective world as well.

Every experience, either subjective or objective, when analysed, will be found as having two opposite factors cohering in it: the one, universal (*sāmānya*) and the other particular (*viśeṣa*). A forest, seen together, is generic or universal, whereas each tree in it, seen separately, is specific or particular. The one remains unperceived when the other is seen. Both the universal forest and the particular tree pertain to the realm of external visibles. The totality of such visibles is what we call the physical world, each individual entity then forming the particular.

Hearing the word "human," referring to no individual entity arouses within us a general idea of a kind of living being. But the word "Mahatma Gandhi" is not so, it reminds us of a particular human being. "Human" here is universal (*sāmānya*) and "Mahatma Gandhi" particular (*viśeṣa*). It could well be said that the universal quality "humanness" is there in all particular humans.

As experiences, the subjective is distinct from the objective; so are the universal (*sāmānya*) and particular (*viśeṣa*) distinct. Where do all such well-defined experiences take place? In the one *cit* alone. That *cit* is neither subjective nor objective, neither *sāmānya* nor *viśeṣa*. It, on the other hand, has the potential in it to give expression to many such duals. Put otherwise, what we call the subjective and the objective, universal and particular, are all different ever-fluttering *bhāna*s of the one *cit*. We will see more details of this in the verses to follow.

Verse 2

स्थूलं सूक्ष्मं कारणं च तुर्यं चेति चतुर्विधम् ।
भानाश्रयं हि तन्नाम भानस्याप्युपचर्यते ॥२॥

sthūlaṁ sūkṣmaṁ kāraṇaṁ ca turyaṁ ceti caturvidham ।
bhānāśrayaṁ hi tan nāma bhānasyāpy upacaryate ॥2॥

That on which the manifestation of Consciousness depends, is of four kinds — gross, subtle, causal, *turīya* (the fourth). The very same division is applicable to the manifestation of Consciousness as well.

This verse makes it clear that what we experience as the world is comprised of four types of *bhāna*s (manifestations) of *cit*, each having in it the universal-particular subdivision. The "world" referred to here includes the knower's mind also. There are four conditioning factors that make the one *cit* manifest as these four *bhāna*s. Termed *bhānāśraya*s (that one which *bhāna* depends) in general, the four are named *sthūla* (the gross), *sūkṣma* (the subtle), *kāraṇa* (the causal) and *turīya* (the fourth). What the word *bhānāśraya* signifies here is denoted by the term *upādhi* (conditioning factor) in the Śaṅkara School of Vedānta. When conditioned by the *sthūla-śarīra* (gross body), *sūkṣma-śarīra* (subtle body) and *kāraṇa-śarīra* (causal body), according to Śaṅkara, the one non-dual Reality appears as the gross or material world, the subtle world or the world of vitality and the causal world. These are respectively experienced by each of us as the waking state (*jāgṛta avasthā*), dreaming state (*svapna-avasthā*) and deep sleep state (*suṣupti-avasthā*). *Turīya* (the fourth), in this context, is the fourth state that transcends all the other three and is in essence a purely mystical non-dual experience.

Differentiating the above-said three bodies forms part of the primary lessons for a student of the Śaṅkara School of Vedānta. But in his non-dual vision, Narayana Guru gives no room for such body concepts. In this regard his philosophy stands apart from Śaṅkara's. In the Guru's vision presented here, the gross, subtle, causal and *turīya* are the factors on which different *bhāna*s of the one *cit* depend, resulting in the world-appearance. The world, according to Śaṅkara, appears to be as one Reality become conditioned by the above-said three bodies. He compares it to the phenomenon of one and the same water assuming various forms as it is poured into different cups or vessels.

The *sthūla, sūkṣma* and *kāraṇa* (gross, subtle and causal) aspects, in the vision of the Guru, thus are not *śarīra*s or bodies, but are *bhānāśraya*s (factors on which the manifesting of *cit* depends). This vision or concept of the Guru is more in line with the perception that the ultimate Reality is in essence pure, unconditioned Consciousness. For instance, what is more substantial is not that the gross world exists, but is that *cit* has a gross experience in the form of the material world, or that *cit* manifests as the gross world experience.

Bhāna thus means, *cit* or pure Consciousness becoming manifest dependent on some conditioning factor called *bhānāśraya*. In accordance with the nature of these conditioning factors *bhāna* also becomes various in kind. As are the *bhānāśraya*s of four kinds, so the *bhāna*s also naturally are of four types: *sthūla-bhāna, sūkṣma-bhāna, kāraṇa-bhāna* and *turīya-bhāna*. Every such *bhāna*, as was stated earlier, has a universal or generic facet and a particular or specific facet. The *bhānāśraya*s (the factor on which the manifestation of *cit* depends) thus are eightfold as follows:

1. *sāmānya-sthūla-bhānāśraya* (the gross one that is universal in nature),
2. *viśeṣa-sthūla-bhānāśraya* (the gross one that is particular in nature),
3. *sāmānya-sūkṣma-bhānāśraya* (the subtle one that is universal in nature),
4. *viśeṣa-sūkṣma-bhānāśraya* (the sublte one that is particular in nature),
5. *sāmānya-kāraṇa-bhānāśraya* (the causal one that is universal in nature),
6. *viśeṣa-kāraṇa-bhānāśraya* (the causal one that is particular in nature),
7. *sāmānya-turīya-bhānāśraya* (the fourth one that is universal in nature),
8. *viśeṣa-turīya-bhānāśraya* (the fourth one that is particular in nature).

Likewise, *bhāna*s are also of eight kinds:

1. *sāmānya-sthūla-bhāna* (the *bhāna* that is gross and generic),
2. *viśeṣa-sthūla-bhāna* (the *bhāna* that is gross and specific),
3. *sāmānya-sūkṣma-bhāna* (the *bhāna* that is subtle and generic),
4. *viśeṣa-sūkṣma-bhāna* (the *bhāna* that is subtle and specific),
5. *sāmānya-kāraṇa-bhāna* (the *bhāna* that is causal and generic),
6. *viśeṣa-kāraṇa-bhāna* (the *bhāna* that is causal and specific),
7. *sāmānya-turīya-bhāna* (the *bhāna* that is *turīya* and generic),
8. *viśeṣa-turīya-bhāna* (the *bhāna* that is *turīya* and specific).

Each of these noticeable *bhāna*s is to be seen as having a subjective side and an objective side. Such *bhāna*s are defined in the verses to follow.

The clear picture that emerges here is of how the one Reality or Consciousness manifestingly shines as all the worlds, subjective as well as objective.

Verse 3

दृश्यतामिह कायोऽहं घटोऽयमिति दृश्यते ।
स्थूलमाश्रित्य यद्भानं स्थूलं तदिति मन्यते ॥३॥

dṛśyatām iha kāyo 'haṁ ghaṭo 'yam iti dṛśyate ।
sthūlam āśritya yad bhānaṁ sthūlaṁ tad iti manyate ॥3॥

That manifestation of Consciousness that depends on gross aspects, and finds expression as perceptual experiences, is considered gross; for example, "I am the body," "This is a pot."

Verse 4

अत्र कायो घट इति भानं यत्तद्विशिष्यते ।
तथाऽहमयमिति यत् सामान्यमिति च स्मृतम् ॥४॥

atra kāyo ghaṭa iti bhānaṁ yat tad viśiṣyate ।
tathā 'ham ayam iti yat sāmānyam iti ca smṛtam ॥4॥

Of such instances, the manifestation of Consciousness that assumes the forms such as "I" and "this" is to be known as the generic gross manifestation, and similarly, that which assumes the forms such as "body" and "pot," is specific gross manifestation.

What *sthūla-bhāna* (gross manifest form of Consciousness) means is clarified in Verse 3 with the help of two examples, and how the generic and specific aspects in those two instances are to be differentiated, is shown in Verse 4.

The word "world" in modern physical sciences signifies the physical one perceptible to the sense organs. Vedānta, on the other hand does not exclude the perceiving mind and the subjective world of ideas and mental images from what the word *prapañca* (world) means.

The perceiving experience of the perceiver is an internal subjective phenomenon, whereas the externally perceived world is an objective phenomenon. World-experience, then, for a Vedāntin, means, the inseparableness of the subjective and objective experiences. It would then be equally correct to say that what is objective gets transformed into a subjective experience, or that what is subjective is projected externally and then perceived as the physical world.

The world, objectively seen, is an aggregate of numerous individually existing entities, organic as well as inorganic. One such entity, a pot, is taken here as an example. On seeing it we say, "This is a pot." Pot is an externally existing gross object. When the mind functions and becomes transformed as an idea of that pot, it becomes the objective (*bahiḥ*) aspect of the *sthūla-bhāna*. It is not the object (here the pot) existing externally itself that is what *sthūla-bhāna* signifies, but it is the experience we have of it, like, "This is a pot." The actual pot existing externally on which this *sthūla-bhāna* depends is the *sthūla-bhānāśraya*.

Both *bhāna* and *bhānāśraya*, in the experience, "This is a pot," has each in it a generic side and a specific side. The generic-specific duality or the universal-particular duality, as understood here, pertains rather to the realm of formulation of ideas as the mind functions, than as it is understood in the material level. If "tree" in the material level is generic, then "mango-tree" is specific. Likewise, the quality of being pot, potness, is there in all the pots. Potness is then generic and each pot specific. The generic and specific sides, as understood by the Guru here pertain to the context of discriminating a particular entity as such and such. "This is such and such" is the natural way we understand things. For example, an object is identified as "This is a pot." Suppose the one who identifies the object says only "This." The listener then gets no specific idea other than that something is going to be said about something. "This" is a common pronoun usable in relation to anything. The word "This" therefore creates only a general idea of the existence of something not specific; so it is considered the generic (*sāmānya*) aspect of the particular *bhāna* "This is a pot."

Asked, "What is this 'This' and what about it?" the answer is "This is a pot." The general idea of existence created by the word "This" then gets a specificity by the added words, "is a pot." Thus in each and every context of discriminating something as "This is such and such," the *bhāna* process has implied in it a generic aspect called *sāmānya-bhāna* and a specific aspect (*viśeṣa-bhāna*). In the case of the present statement "This is a pot," pot being a gross (*sthūla*) object, "This" refers to the *sāmānya-sthūla-bhāna* and "is a pot" to the *viśeṣa-sthūla-bhāna*.

The gross world is experienced by each individual, by each "I." Being part of the gross world, this "I" also, we presume, has to be a gross entity; so each of us thinks, "I am this body," for the gross aspect of "I" is this body.

One identifying oneself with the body, in Vedānta, is known as *deho 'ham buddhi* (the idea that the body constitutes one's being). The "I" then is first identified with the gross aspect of self-existence, and thereafter one conceives the idea

"I am this body." The function of consciousness that causes this sort of self-identity is referred to initially in Verse 3. In the statement "I am this body" also we can differentiate a generic aspect and a specific aspect. Uttering the word "I" alone makes no sense other than a general idea that something is going to be stated about oneself. This vague and general idea attains distinctness as the words "am this body" are added. As the generic sense created by "I" is given specificity by "am this body," we could very well say, in the context of the gross concept of oneself "I am this body," the "I" is *sāmānya-sthūla-bhāna*, and "am this body" is *viśeṣa-sthūla-bhāna*.

This generic-specific differentiation could be noticed in concepts that are otherwise related to realities purely generic in nature as well. For example, as we have already seen, "forest" is generic and "tree" is specific. But in the idea "This is a forest," the "This" is generic and "is a forest" specific. We should therefore avoid mixing up wrongly the existential *sāmānya-viśeṣa* concepts relevant in the Nyāya system and the epistemological *sāmānya-viśeṣa* discrimination pertaining to the context of the knowing function of consciousness as understood in Vedānta here.

Verse 5

इन्द्रियाणि मनोबुद्धिविषयाः पञ्चवायवः ।
भास्यन्ते येन तत्सूक्ष्मं अस्य सूक्ष्माश्रयत्वतः ॥५॥

indriyāṇi manobuddhi viṣayāḥ pañca-vāyavaḥ ।
bhāsyante yena tat sūkṣmaṁ asya sūkṣmāśrayatvataḥ ॥5॥

That owing to which the senses, mind and intellect and their corresponding objects as well as the five vital airs, appear manifestly, is known as the subtle manifestation of Consciousness for the reason of its dependence on subtle factors.

The total world is seen in the *Bhāna Darśana* as one Consciousness or *cit* manifesting in accordance with various conditioning factors. What the gross world is comprised of was examined in Verses 3 and 4. The world, as seen by Vedāntins, is not merely an aggregate of perceptible physical entities. An idea concerning everything thus perceived also gets formulated in the mind, and it is in the form of this mental image that the external world is experienced. Whether this mental image and the world actually existing externally correspond exactly to each other is a matter no one can decide. Still it is undeniable that the subjective experiential side can never be kept aside from the context of perceiving the physical world. It is also not sure whether the subjective experience I have of the world is exactly the same as the one you have.

This experiential side is given shape by the unified activity of our senses, their objects, the *antaḥkaraṇa*s (mental faculties) and the five vital airs — *pañca-prāṇa*s that according to Indian psychologists activate all these. Ears (*śrotra*), skin (*tvak*), eyes (*cakṣus*), tongue (*rasanā*) and nose (*ghrāṇa*) are the five sense organs, and their corresponding objects (*viṣaya*s) are sound (*śabda*), touch (*sparśa*), form (*rūpa*), taste (*rasa*) and smell (*gandha*). The contact between the senses and their respective objects is controlled and transformed into world-experience by the mental faculties known as *antaḥkaraṇa*s, comprised of *manas* (mind), *buddhi* (intellect), *citta* (the faculty that stores up memories and recalls them), and *ahaṁkāra* (ego).

Probing into everything, asking the question "What is this?" is the job of *manas* or mind. *Buddhi* (intellect) answers this question. Finding out an answer mostly requires the help of previous experiences already stored up as our memories. Putting the ideas and images in storage in our memory is done by *citta*, itself recalling them as and when needed to help *buddhi*.

What is thus ascertained is then evaluated, relating it with one's own value notions or likes and dislikes in life. This is done by *ahaṁkāra* (ego). The four together — reduced here to the two *manas* and *buddhi* — is what is known as the *antaḥkaraṇa*s (inner faculties).

Prāṇa, apāna, vyāna, udāna and *samāna* are the five vital airs, called *pañca-prāṇa*s. The function of each is seen by the Upaniṣadic *ṛṣi*s and Śaṅkara, with slight variations among them. These, in short, constitute the vital functions that sustain an organic being. All the above-mentioned factors together constitute the subtle elements in the existence of individual beings, forming what is known as *sūkṣma-śarīra* or *liṅga-śarīra* in the Vedānta of Śaṅkara. As the one Consciousness functionally manifesting, assuming the form of the above-mentioned subtle factors, it is called *sūkṣma-bhāna* by Narayana Guru.

The first five chapters of the *Darśanamālā* show from five various perspectives, how the world is related to the one absolute Reality. That Reality being pure Consciousness (*cit*) in essence, what appears as the world is the functional modes (*bhāna*) of that one *cit*. Such is the overall point of view adopted in the *Bhāna Darśana*. The *bhāna* understood here is to be seen, not merely as something that happens within individual minds alone, but as having a universal dimension also. It is for this reason that the Upaniṣads often think of a *samaṣṭi puruṣa* (universal person), sometimes also called *virāṭ puruṣa*. The word *virāṭ* simply means "that which finds expression assuming all specific forms." A universal counterpart of what takes place within an individual mind could well be imagined as what takes place in a cosmic mind or the mind of God, as was pointed out as early as in Chapter 1. It was stated then that the world was imaginarily created by God as if in a dream. The idea that the world is a prolonged dream seen by God or the universal mind is repeated by the Guru himself in many of his other works also. It is where God dreaming the world and individuals dreaming the world find oneness that the real non-dual nature of the *sūkṣma-bhāna* is to be intuitively perceived by the seeker. The Guru in his concise work in the Malayalam language, called *Aṛivu* (Consciousness Examined), says:

> All the dreams that well up within one consciousness have being only as (functional modes of) the very same consciousness. So is the case with everything. — Verse 3

To elucidate: A dream experience happens within an individual's mind. What is substantial in such dreamsights is merely the mind or consciousness of the dreamer. Let us see God's mind in the place of an individual dreaming mind. Then the dream seen by God's mind becomes the world, and the essential content in it is nothing other than Gods' mind.

The *sūkṣma-bhāna* also has to have its generic and specific sides. All the experiences we have are the outcome of a creative fusion of the functional states of our sense organs, their objects, mental faculties or *antaḥkaraṇa*s and the vital forces or *prāṇa*s. Every such experience could well be treated as a specific form of knowledge or mental image. In either case, it is a functional mode of consciousness having become specifically manifest, and concerning each such experience we could say, "This is knowledge," "This is yet another knowledge." Such process of knowledge knowing itself, in psychology, is known as apperception. Its Sanskrit equivalent is *pratyavasāya*.

In the statement "This is knowledge" also, the "This" stands for its generic side, because uttering that word alone creates only the general impression that something is going to be said about something, and because the word "This" could be used referring to anything. This generic "This" gains a specificity as the words "is knowledge" are added, and therefore, "is knowledge" is here the specific or *viśeṣa* side of the statement "This is knowledge." "This is knowledge" again is a general statement that could be made concerning any knowledge. The word "This," here therefore, represents the generic aspect of all such knowledges generally; in other words, it is the genus of all genera. This peculiarity of "This" in "This is knowledge" provides us with a clue to meditate on the nature and content of pure Consciousness, the essential content of the Self or *Ātmā*. Every knowledge we gain is referable as "This is knowledge" and has in it a generic "This." This "This," thus representing the generic-most aspect of knowledge, could be meditated upon to realize the nature and content of the Self. Narayana Guru himself gives direction to do this in Verse 42 of his *Ātmopadeśa Śatakam* (One Hundred Verses of Self-Instruction). This meditation reveals that "This" in "This is knowledge," referring as it is to the generic content in all knowledges, denotes the ineffable content of Consciousness, thinkable neither as that of an individual person nor of a cosmic Person. This meditation leads us to the realization of the ultimate Reality or *sat* as the Self (*Ātmā*).

Verse 6

अज्ञोऽहमिति यद्भानं तत्कारणमुदाहृतम् ।
अत्राऽहमिति सामान्यं विशेषोऽज्ञ इति स्फुरत् ॥६ ॥

ajño 'ham iti yad bhānaṁ tat kāraṇam udāhṛtam ।
atrā 'ham iti sāmānyaṁ viśeṣo 'jña iti sphurat ॥6 ॥

The manifestation of Consciousness in the form "I am ignorant" is said to be causal; of it the "I"-part is generic and the "am ignorant"-part specific.

When asked "Do you know this?" one may answer, "No." The one who says so could be considered ignorant (*ajña*) about that particular matter. The "ignorance" understood here is not of that sort. Those who are not enlightened, in Vedānta, are often referred to as *ajña*s or *ajñānin*s, both meaning "the ignorant." Therefore, those who are interested in Vedānta, but are not enlightened, prefer to call themselves *ajñānin*s. Such an ignorance also is not what is intended in the statement *ajño 'ham* (I am ignorant) of this verse. The knowledge "I am ignorant" as understood here has the status of being *kāraṇa-bhāna* (causal manifestation of Consciousness). Causal to what? Causal to both the *sthūla-bhāna* and the *sūkṣma-bhāna* (gross manifestations and subtle manifestations of Consciousness). It points to the one causal Consciousness that unfolds itself both as *sthūla-bhāna* and *sūkṣma-bhāna*.

Though we are sure that such a Consciousness has to exist and does exist, no one knows what it is like, for the reason that it has no manifest form. In other words, both the *sthūla-bhāna* and *sūkṣma-bhāna* are the *kārya*s (effects) of this one *kāraṇa* (cause). This causal Consciousness is directly experienced by each of us in our deep sleep alone, where we are conscious of nothing. On getting up from a deep sleep, one feels "I had a sound sleep." While actually sleeping soundly one remains completely unaware of sleeping soundly, and even of being ignorant. The knowledge "I am ignorant" therefore arises, not when one is really ignorant, but when one wakes up and becomes conscious of the world. It is out of that unconscious Consciousness-content that all the specific knowledges about everything emerge on waking up. For this reason it is called *kāraṇa-bhāna* (causal manifestation of Consciousness). It could be compared to the phenomenon of the one causal substance H_2O appearing variously as vapour, steam, snow, ice, water and the like.

It cannot be said that no experience at all is there in the *kāraṇa-bhāna*. We say about it, "I had a sound sleep." That means a happiness was being experienced while sleeping — the happiness of being aware of nothing at all, a happiness experienced unaware of doing so. The knowing faculty in that state remains non-functional and dormant, like a tree does in its seed. Śaṅkara thinks of it as the state in which the darkness of *avidyā* (ignorance) veiled the Consciousness. Removing this veil reveals the pure effulgence-content of Consciousness, and the knower's being becoming merged in that effulgence is known as *turīya*, the fourth state, according to Śaṅkara. This final state is also one in which nothing is specifically known; it is rather the state in which everything specific becomes merged in the One — the One that is not in essence darkness but is pure effulgence in which the Self is experienced without conditions, where the Self remains pure and simple.

The *kāraṇa-bhāna* "I am ignorant" (*ajño 'ham*) also has in it the generic and specific aspects. When one says "I," nothing specific is communicated other than the vague idea that something is going to be stated about oneself, and for this reason the "I" in the sentence "I am ignorant" is *sāmānya* (the generic aspect). Adding the words "am ignorant" (*ajñaḥ*) gives specificity to the intention. Therefore *ajñaḥ* is its *viśeṣa* or specific aspect. *Kāraṇa-bhāna* also thus has its *sāmānya-kāraṇa-bhāna* and *viśeṣa-kāraṇa-bhāna* sides. What the two depend on forms the *bhānāśraya* (that on which a *bhāna* depends), though that factor in the present case is not clearly discernible. What we can say about what the *kāraṇa-bhāna* depends on, would be that it is simply the darkness of ignorance.

Verse 7

अहं ब्रह्मेति यद्भानं तत्तुर्यमिति शंस्यते।
सामान्यमहमित्यंशो ब्रह्मेत्यत्र विशिष्यते ॥७॥

aham̐ brahmeti yad bhānam̐ tat turyam iti śam̐syate ।
sāmānyam aham ity am̐śo brahmety atra viśiṣyate ॥7॥

The manifestation of Consciousness owing to which one experiences "I am *Brahman*," is glorified as *turīya* (the fourth). Of it, the "I"-part is generic and the "am *Brahman*"-part is specific.

Turīya also, like *sthūla*, *sūkṣma* and *kāraṇa*, is treated here by the Guru as a *bhāna* (a manifest form of Consciousness) unlike in the traditional textbooks of Advaita Vedānta, where *turīya* is always treated as the experience of the non-dual oneness of the unmanifest Consciousness.

What is *turīya*? Literally it means only "the fourth." In the context of *avasthā*s (states of consciousness), it denotes the fourth state that follows *jāgṛta* (waking state), *svapna* (dreaming state) and *suṣupti* (deep sleep state). Here, in the *Bhāna Darśana*, it comes as the fourth after the *sthūla* (gross), *sūkṣma* (subtle) and *kāraṇa* (causal) manifest forms of Consciousness. *Turīya* is not definable and is unknowable. Yet claiming that such a state exists presupposes knowing something about it. An attempt has been made in the *Māṇḍūkya Upaniṣad* to define the *turīya* or the *caturtha*, also meaning "the fourth." Translated, it reads thus:

Not inwardly known,
Not outwardly known,
Not known bothwise,
Not pure knowledge concretized,
Not known, not unknown,
Invisible, indescribable, ungraspable,

Having no distinguishing marks,
Unthinkable, unnameable
The oneness-of-*Ātmā*-experienced in essence,
Wherein all the worlds merge,
Absolute Peace in essence,
Absolute Beatitude in essence,
Non-dual in essence,
Is thought of as "the fourth" —
That is the *ātmā*,
And that is what is to be known.

—Verse 7

Closely examined, this definition will be found to be mostly negative in nature; that is to say, the definition, instead of saying what *turīya* is, simply describes what it is not. The references to "the oneness-of-*Ātmā*-experienced in essence," "Absolute Peace in essence," "Absolute Beautitude in essence," and "Non-dual in essence" are the exceptions." Though the word indicates the essential content of what *yogins* experience in their non-dual state of Existence, the very same *yogins* have at times tried their best to put in words what the essential content of their experience was. One of the best examples of such attempts is found in the following words from the pen of Narayana Guru himself.

Attaining the transparent clarity of the one bottomless and topless (unconditioned Consciousness) from bottom to top, with full transparence, is understood as *turīya* consciousness. — *Ātmopadeśa Śatakam*, Verse 28

Turīya, in other words, means knowing the bottomless and topless absolute Reality, from bottom to top. This definition suggests an experiential realm where the seeker transcends all ideas of duality, a state called *dvaya-para-bhāvanā* (enlightened awakening that transcends dualities) elsewhere.

The nature of this *dvaya-para-bhāvanā* is detailed by the Guru as follows:

> Seen from one side there are various activities; they seem to be real because of nescience (*avidyā*). Seen from the other, there is perceived pure and unconditioned Consciousness alone, and this is what constitutes the realm of true knowledge (*vidyā*). It is *māyā* that makes the Real appear always thus as two-sided. The enlightened awakening that transcends this duality alone assures the *turīya* state.
>
> — *Ātmopadeśa Śatakam*, Verse 72

That such a state exists has been testified by *yogin*s who had its direct experience, who had tried to describe what they experienced. Others also say that such a state is experienced by *yogins*. Still it remains a fact that the real *turīya*-experience is beyond words.

Every attempt to define *turīya* had been the outcome of an indomitable urge from within to put in words some definite conscious experience (*bhāna-vṛtti*) the *ṛṣi*s have had. Had it been absolutely indefinable, they would not have uttered a single word about it. But that is not the case. Every *yogī* of *turīya*-experience would try in his own way to express in words the essential content of his experience. And to that extent it is to be considered a *bhāna* (manifest form of consciousness), and thus the Guru treats *turīya* also here as one of the *bhāna*s.

The conscious experience "I am *Brahman*" (*aham brahma asmi*), or one's conscious self-identity with the Absolute, is what the Guru distinguishes as *turīya-bhāna*. *Aham brahma asmi* is one of the great dicta (*mahāvākya*s) of Vedānta, made more concise here by the Guru as *aham brahma*. All *mahāvākya*s try to express this one experience using different words relevant to different contexts.

The *mahāvākyas* of Vedānta are traditionally considered as four in number: *tat tvam asi* (That thou art), *aham brahma asmi* (I am the Absolute), *ayam ātmā brahma* (This self is the Absolute), *prajñānam brahma* (Consciousness is the Absolute). All these are in the form equations; they equate the universal and particular aspects of Reality. The words *aham* (I), *tvam* (you), *ayam ātmā* (this self) and *prajñānam* (consciousness) in these denote the particular facets of Reality, and *tat* (That) and *brahman* (the Absolute) the universal. What each of these equations suggests is the experience of oneness of the essential content of Reality that becomes manifest both as the particular and the universal. Such an experience is attained by each individual, and the individual refers to himself or herself as "I." The inner certitude that the essential content in the being of "I" is none other than that in the being of all the worlds is what the *turīya-bhāna* suggests. It could be compared to a wave looking at itself and realizing itself to be water in content, and then coming to the certitude that the same water is the essential content in the being of the entire ocean. The wave thus realizes, "I am the ocean." Similar is an individual seeker's realizing "I am *Brahman*."

Another peculiarity noticeable in all these dicta — the fourth one apart — is that one limb of each equation is in the form of a pronoun. The dictum *tat tvam asi* (That thou art) is in the form of instruction given by a *guru* to his disciple. For this reason, it is known as *upadeśa-vākya* (dictum in the form of instruction). The limb that signifies the particular aspect in this equation is *tvam* (thou or you), the second person pronoun. The disciple, on hearing this word of instruction, cogitates on it meditatively and finally realizes "I am That" or "I am the Absolute" (*aham brahma asmi*). For this reason, this dictum, is known as *anubhava-vākya* (experiential dictum). The word *aham* (I) in it is the first person pronoun. The third dictum *ayam ātmā brahma* (this self is the Absolute in essence) is uttered by neither a master nor a disciple, but by a self-realized visionary intended for no one else. The limb in this sentence signifying the particular aspect of Reality is *ayam ātmā* (this self). The word *ayam* (this) is the third person pronoun. The particular aspect, in the fourth sentence is represented by *prajñānam* (consciousness) and it signifies the consciousness-content in *tvam, aham* and *ayam ātmā,* and thus transcends the realm of pronouns. These dicta altogether show thus that the Reality in what appears to be referable by all the three kinds of pronouns and even what is beyond their realm, is *Brahman* alone.

Yet another peculiarity is that these four dicta appear in four different Upaniṣads as a sort of condensed form of their teachings. *Tat tvam asi* in the *Chāndogya Upaniṣad, aham brahma asmi* in the *Bṛhadāraṇyaka Upaniṣad, ayam ātmā brahma* in the *Māṇḍūkya Upaniṣad,* and *prajñānam brahma* in the *Aitareya Upaniṣad.* These four Upaniṣads, in their turn, are appended to the four Vedas — *Chāndogya* to the *Sāmaveda, Bṛhadāraṇyaka* to the *Yajurveda, Māṇḍūkya* to the *Atharvaveda* and *Aitareya* to the *Ṛgveda.* In short, the wisdom content of the four Vedas, summarized in the four Upaniṣads, is again condensed in the form of the four dicta, each equating the individual seeker — referred to in second person, first person, third person and personlessly — with *Brahman.* Of these four, it is the experiential dictum *aham brahma asmi* that the Guru selected here as the example of *turīya-bhāna.* In fact, *aham brahma asmi* is the only example that could be cited in the case of *turīya-bhāna,* whereas the other three *bhāna*s could have many examples.

Suppose someone utters the word *aham* (I) alone. What the listener then understands would be that he is going to say something about himself. That something could be anything. So the utterence is very vague and generic in denotation. For this reason, *aham* in the sentence *aham brahma asmi* is treated as the *sāmānya-turīya-bhāna* by the Guru here. Adding the word *brahman* gives a definiteness to the statement, and thus the listener gets a specific understanding about the intention of the other person. Therefore the *brahman*-part of the sentence is considered as *viśeṣa-turīya-bhāna*.

As the connotation of the sentence *aham brahma asmi* transcends the realm of *bhāna* and attains the experience of the self having merged in the Absolute, then no more *aham* would be there, no more *Brahman* would be there. It would simply be the pure effulgence of the all-encompassing *cit*, which can never be counted as a *bhāna* or manifest form of consciousness at all.

verse 8

यत्र भानं तत्र भास्यं भानं यत्र न तत्र न।
भास्यमित्यन्वयेनाऽपि व्यतिरेकेण बोध्यते ॥८॥

yatra bhānaṁ tatra bhāsyaṁ bhānaṁ yatra na tatra na ।
bhāsyam ity anvayenā 'pi vyatirekeṇa bodhyate ॥8॥

Wherever manifestation of Consciousness takes place there appears the object made manifest as well, and wherever manifestation of Consciousness does not take place there appears no manifest object either. Certitude is attained thus by the method of agreement and that of difference as well.

The simplest meaning of *bhāna* is "to shine," "to be luminous." What we are contemplating upon in the present chapter is, how the one *sat* (*cit* in essence) specifically becomes luminous or manifest, distinguishable as gross, subtle, causal and *turīya* world-experiences. Consciousness (*cit*) becoming luminous in the form of knowing requires something to be illumined or known. That which is illumined thus by the knowing function of consciousness is called *bhāsya*. The meditation in the present verse concentrates on the one-to-one correspondence or the mutual dependence of *bhāna* and *bhāsya*.

Wherever there is *bhāna* there would be *bhāsya* also existing; where there is no *bhāna* there would be no *bhāsya* either. The co-existence of *bhāna* and *bhāsya* is thus arrived at logically with the help of the methods of agreement and difference. Positively asserting that where there is *bhāna* there would be *bhāsya* also, is called the method of agreement. In Indian logic the same is called *anvaya buddhi*. Negatively stating that where there is no *bhāna* there would be no *bhāsya*, is the method of difference, known in Indian logic as *vyatireka-buddhi*. Any assertion becomes logically sound only when these two methods agree.

On seeing smoke on a hill side, for example, we immediately conclude, there is fire on the hill. This ascertainment is made possible by the previous knowledge we had that wherever there is smoke there is fire. This way of thinking, asserting the co-existence of fire and smoke, is called *anvaya buddhi*. Its Western counterpart is the method of agreement. It is not necessary that wherever there is fire there would be smoke also, for the reason that fire sometimes flames without smoke. But we are sure that the presence of smoke would be there only where there is fire. In other words, there can be no smoke in the absence of fire. Therefore, arriving at the conclusion that there is fire on the hill, is helped also by our previous knowledge that there can be no smoke where there is no fire. This way of becoming sure of the absence of the one in the absence of the other is called *vyatireka buddhi*, called the method of difference in the Western logic. The presence of smoke here is the means or *sādhana* that leads to the conclusion or *sādhya* "there is fire on the hill." The co-existence of the two is to be ascertained by both the *anvaya* and *vyatireka buddhis* together.

Bhāna is a subjective experience, and *bhāsya* is the corresponding object existing externally. The two always emerge together wherever the one absolute Reality finds self-expression. Each one is meaningless without the other, and both together is what we call the world (*prapañca*). That the absolute Reality, pure *cit* in essence, never becomes an object of knowledge will be made clear in the next verse. In short, whenever the event of knowing occurs in consciousness, there naturally emerges — because of *māyā* — the subject-object duality, the *bhāna-bhāsya* duality. The Absolute or *Ātman* therefore is not knowable as an object. The only means available to realize *Ātman* consists of treating both the *bhāna* and *bhāsya* as two knowable manifest facets of the one *Ātmā*, as two superimposed conditionings opposite in nature. Upon knowing this we are to withdraw ourselves into the being of pure Consciousness by taking away the conditioning factors, and becoming lost in It, as a drop of water becomes lost in the ocean, as will be stated in Verse 10 of this chapter.

Verse 9

यथा दृग्दृशमात्मानं स्वयमात्मा न पश्यति ।
अतो न भास्यते ह्यात्मा यं पश्यति स भास्यते ॥९॥

yathā dṛg dṛśam ātmānaṁ svayam ātmā na paśyati ।
ato na bhāsyate hy ātmā yaṁ paśyati sa bhāsyate ॥9॥

The eye does not see itself, so too *Ātmā* does not perceive Itself; *Ātmā*, therefore, is no object of the knowing function of consciousness. Whatever *Ātmā* perceives is what becomes manifest as objects.

Already seen is the fact that wherever consciousness functions as the act of knowing (*bhāna*) there would be object of knowledge (*bhāsya*) as well, and that where the consciousness does not function there would be no object either. All experiences have their being in consciousness, as it functions and assumes some manifest form (Consciousness or *Ātmā* on its own is unmanifest). Each such experience would be about something. That something is what becomes illumined by the shining function of consciousness. When thus illumined, we call it an object of knowledge or *viṣaya*. In short, all objects of knowledge are illumined by the shining manifestation of *Ātmā* or Consciousness, and in the absence of this manifestation there would be no object or any objective world as well.

Does this *Ātmā* become illumined as an object of knowledge by its own shining manifestation? No. How this is the case is what we concentrate on in the present verse.

The eye sees everything, but it does not see itself. The eye seeing something implies the duality of the seeing eye and the object seen. Likewise, the one Consciousnes-Reality, when self-manifesting, always gives rise to the *bhāna-bhāsya* duality. That this Consciousness-Reality is the one all-underlying Substance we have seen as early as in Verse 2.7.

The ultimate goal of our search here is knowing this non-dual Reality. How are we to know this Reality that is pure Consciousness in essence? Is it an object to be known or searched for like ordinary worldly objects? In other words, does it appear as a *bhāsya*? No. Just as the eye is no object to be seen by the very same eye, this Consciousness-Reality or the Self is not an object to the very same Consciousness. *Ātmā* knowing *Ātmā* means I knowing myself. Though I am fully aware of myself, doubtlessly there are no two "I"-s there, one to function as the subject and the other as the object. Self-knowledge (*ātma-jñāna*) or I knowing myself thus means, the knowing consciousness and the known consciousness differencelessly merging in the experiential non-dual Consciousness-Effulgence. How this experience is no knowable object at all will be clarified in the next verse. What is underscored here is the fact that *Ātmā* does not become an object of knowledge. This in no way means that attaining self-knowledge (*ātma-jñāna*) is no goal at all, nor that attaining self-knowledge is impossible. Only that consciousness does not become an object of knowledge.

To think that objective knowledge alone is the only kind of knowledge possible, is a mistake. The potential hidden in consciousness to unfold itself is really infinite of such infinite possibililities, objective knowledge, i.e. subject knowing an object, is only one. Self-knowledge, on the other hand, is the experience of subject becoming the object or object becoming the subject. When known truly in this way, the differentiation between the knowing consciousness and the known consciousness disappears, and the all-filling effulgence of unitive Consciousness in which the knower and the known get lost, alone remains. This, in the ordinary sense, is not at all objective knowledge. Indicative of all this are the following words of the Guru himself in his unique composition called *Arivu* (Consciousness Examined).

> The pure Consciousness does not ever become known (as an object of knowledge); and when known, the two (subject and object) attain inseparable oneness. — Verse 5

The nature of the subjectless and objectless Self-realization is explored in the next verse.

Verse 10

यद्भास्यते तदध्यस्तं अनध्यस्तं न भास्यते।
यदध्यस्तं तदसदप्यनध्यस्तं सदेव तत् ॥१०॥

yad bhāsyate tad adhyastaṁ anadhyastaṁ na bhāsyate ।
yad adhyastaṁ tad asad apy anadhyastaṁ sad eva tat ॥10॥

> That which is made manifest by the knowing function of consciousness is superimposed. That which is not superimposed never becomes an object of the knowing function of consciousness. That which is superimposed is unreal. That which is not superimposed is the *sat* that alone is "That."

That the Ultimate Reality or *Ātmā* is pure and unconditioned Consciousness (*cit*) in essential content, we have already noticed. It, therefore, is often referred to as *cid-vastu*, *vastu* meaning "essential substance." This *cid-vastu*, as was seen at the beginning of this chapter, never remains functionless, and its functioning is comparable to the fluttering of a bee's wings. As a result of this function emerge in it all the gross, subtle, causal and *turīya* experiences, whatever is experienced in these states, and their generic and specific aspects. Finally it was seen in the last verse that *Ātmā* or *cid-vastu*, pure and simple, does not manifest as an object of knowledge, whether gross, subtle, causal or *turīya*.

Then how is this *Ātmā* to be known or realized, and as of what nature? Or is it that *Ātmā* never becomes known at all? Is there a knowledge of the Self or realization of the Self, that is totally different from knowing it as an object? This is what we meditate upon in this last verse of this chapter, which also marks the very centre of the entire work. Being the Ultimate Reality, the *cid-vastu* could as well be called *sad-vastu*, *sat* meaning "that which ultimately exists," and *vastu* "substance." Then the point we meditate on in this verse is, what that *sad-vastu* is, and how to realize it.

The Guru manages it with the help of the notion of *adhyāsa*, well known in the Śaṅkara School of Vedānta. Śaṅkara defines *adhyāsa* as *atasmin tad buddhiḥ*, meaning "the error of taking something to be something else." For example, a gold ornament is placed before us. Really it is gold in content. Nothing other than the gold-substance exists in it. The ornament-form is simply an attribute superimposed on the gold-substance for the time being. The ornament on its own has no existence at all. In that sense it is non-existent (*asat*), here meaning, that which has no real existence, but it creates the impression of existing. What exists (*sat*) here is gold alone. On seeing the gold ornament before us, used as we are to seeing appearance to be real, we treat it as an ornament. This superimposing of what does not really exist on to what really exists is called *adhyāsa* by Śaṅkara. That which is superimposed and seen as real, is called *adhyasta*, and thus the ornament-form is *adhyasta*.

Gold is the one substance that exists in all the ornaments like chains, rings, ear-rings, and bangles. Can the real gold substance be seen without having any of these assumed forms? No. When seen, it would always have some form or other, even of being dust or ore. All such apparent forms are transitory; they are all superimposed (*adhyasta*). Gold, in other words, is the invisible, eternal substance in all the visible, transitory ornament-forms. Though invisible, it can never be considered unreal (*asat*), for in its absence no ornament can be there. The invisible gold substance here therefore is *anadhyasta* (that which is not superimposed), and it fills the being of all the superimposed (*adhyasta*) ornament-forms.

The gross, subtle, causal, and *turīya-bhāna*s, their respective *bhāsya*s, their generic and specific aspects, are all meditatively to be perceived in the place of the transitory ornament-forms. Then that invisible eternal substance which fills the being of everything that pertains to the realm of *bhāna* and *bhāsya* is the Self or *Ātmā*. Nothing can be predicated of it, since all predicates are related either to *bhāna* or *bhāsya*. "That alone exists" or *sat* alone is "That" (*sad eva tat*) is all we can say about it!

Sad eva tat (*sat* alone is "That"), is a variant version of the famous dictum *oṁ tat sat* (*AUṀ*: That alone exists). The word *tat* (That) in it stands always for *Brahman*, the goal to be attained, and the Substance that underlies the being of all superimposed forms, whether gross, subtle, causal or *turīya*.

Only something that has an attribute, only a superimposed form, can become an object of knowledge or *bhāsya*. *Brahman* or *Ātman*, not being such, never becomes an object of knowledge. For an ornament, to know gold as an external object, is impossible, but to realize "I am gold" is the easiest to attain. Similarly, for each of us, being some *bhāna* or *bhāsya* form, to know *Ātmā* as on object is impossible; but to realize "I am *Brahman*" is the easiest and most direct experience with nothing coming in the middle. Just as a piece of ornament can always remain gold, each of us, every moment of our day-to-day life, can live with the awareness "I am *Brahman*." Whatever happens in life is then seen merely as part of the eternal sport of *Brahman* or *Ātman*. That means, instead of "knowing" the *anadhyasta* Reality as an object, anyone can easily "live" as the one *anadhyasta* Reality that fills the being all that is *adhyasta*, all that is apparent.

Any systematically conceived school of thought necessarily has to correlate three basic factors: "I," the world and the unknowable all-underlying Reality. Vedānta's teaching is that it is the one unknowable Reality, called *Ātmā* or *Brahman*, that manifests itself, because of its own *māyā*, both as the "I" and the world. Put otherwise, the unmanifest (*anadhyasta*) Reality becomes manifest (*adhyasta*) as both "I" and the world. The world cannot appear to be without the Reality; the Reality cannot exist without manifesting itself as the world either.

The present work, *Darśanamālā*, in its first five chapters, visualizes how the world and the Reality are related, from five different points of view. A shift in respect of what is concentrated on, from the perceptible world to the perceiving "I," after the first half of the work, is noticeable in the overall scheme of the work. The five chapters of the second half show how the "I" and the ultimate Reality are related or to be correlated, as seen from the five different perspectives of *karma* (action), *jñāna* (knowledge), *bhakti* (contemplation), *yoga* and *nirvāṇa* (final absorption).

The first half ends with the word *tat* (That), signifying the ultimate Reality, whereas the second half begins with the word *ātmā* that could also mean oneself or "I." That *tat* is what becomes manifest as "I" or *ātmā*. Thus an equation that treats *tat* and *ātmā* as its two limbs is invisibly present between the two halves of the work, which could also be treated as a hidden pendant adding beauty, value and perfection to this garland of visions. It is with such an insight that a serious seeker should wear this garland to beautify himself contemplatively.

6

Karma Darśanam
(Vision by Action)

Verse 1

आत्मैव मायया कर्म करोति बहुरूपधृक् ।
असङ्गः स्वप्रकाशोऽपि निद्रायामिव तैजसः ॥१॥

ātmaiva māyayā karma karoti bahu-rūpa-dhṛk ।
asaṅgaḥ svaprakāśo 'pi nidrāyām iva taijasaḥ ॥1॥

Ātmā alone, while being completely unattached to anything and self-luminosity in essence, performs all the *karma*s by assuming various forms by virtue of its own *māyā*.

Being active is one of the external signs of life. The peculiarity with human life is that, as part of our natural activities, we have the free will to decide what to do and what not to do. The present chapter, *Karma Darśanam*, perceives, from the point of view of actions (*karma*s), how one's own existence is inseparably one with the ultimate Reality.

Who is the doer of Karmas?

All living beings constantly remain active. But aside from humans, there is no apparent sign of living in living beings with the notion about what they do, as "This is my *karma*." Humans alone think, "This is my *karma*; its fruits are to be eaten by me." These notions respectively are known as *kartṛtva* (sense of being the doer of *karmas*) and *bhoktṛtva* (sense of being the enjoyer of the fruits of *karmas*).

Let us look at this problem more closely. Everyone of us has organs of action such as hands and feet, and each of these has its own capability to do certain works. Neither these organs nor their capabilities were created by us. No one can create these. These are simply in us as part of nature. The same is the case with the sense organs and the mental faculties.

Should we, then, take their normal functions going on, as our *karmas*, or should we consider these as nature's *karmas*? Though the latter is the proper way of understanding, the idea all of us nurture is the former. It is from this basically wrong notion that the ideas of sinful actions (*pāpa-karmas*) and meritorious actions (*puṇya-karmas*) arise. The *Bhagavad-Gītā* underscores the point that the best way one can free oneself from the sense of sin is, having the conviction "I am no doer of any *karma*." That an individual has no *karma* of his or her own is also explicitly stated in the *Gītā*. It says:

> All sorts of *karma* take place because of the *guṇas* of *prakṛti*.
> Deluded by I-sense one thinks, "I am the doer of actions."
>
> — III.27

Basically, thus, no individual has his or her own *karmas*. How can then he or she have *sañcita-karmas* (accumulated previous actions), *prārabdha-karmas* (present unfinished actions), and *āgāmi-karmas* (future actions yet to be accumulated), all subdivisions of *karma*? The Guru himself, in the concluding verse of his *Brahmavidyā Pañcakam* (The Science of the Absolute in Five Verses) says:

> How can you have *sañcita-karma*?
> How can you have *prārabdha-karma*?
> How can you have *āgāmi-karma*?
> *Karma* is itself unreal. — Verse 5

In short, it is the total nature, not any individual, that performs all *karmas*. How should then we accommodate the free will of human beings and its application in the domain of actions, into such an overall perspective? This has always been a problem that most of the thinkers on philosophy as well as religion have tried unsuccessfully to puzzle out. The problem is, how to make free will and Destiny meet each other without contradiction, in a convincing manner.

We have the capability to choose from among many alternative opportunities of action, and also to decide what to do and what not to do; and we do apply it in life. But, did we create this capability of ours? No, this too is in us as part of nature. That means, even the application of free will that we utilize in life is part of nature's *karma*, not of any particular individual. Our applying free will to interfere with the overall flow of nature, virtually means, our opposing the nature that created us endowed with the very same free will. The application of our free will, therefore, must always be in deciding freely how to live fully in line with nature's flow of events.

What is Karma?

The previous chapter ended with the note that everything superimposed is unreal, that that alone which is not superimposed and not conditioned is ultimately Real, and that this ultimate Reality never becomes an object of knowledge. That Reality or *sat* brings into being the appearance of perceptible forms emanating from Itself. Such apparent forms or *bhāvas* are not real on their own. The continuous flow of such unreal appearances is what we treat as the world. Beings emerging and merging are simply part of the flow of such appearances. This phenomenon could well be compared to waves appearing and disappearing in the ocean. Waves have no existence apart from the ocean; and in that sense they are unreal (*asat*). Yet a creative urge is there in the ocean that causes the constant emerging and merging of wave-forms. Similarly there is a creative urge in the one ultimate Reality, that is *sat* and *cit* at the same time, to emanate from Itself all the conditioned or superimposed forms from Itself, resulting in the appearance of the constantly flowing world. This creative urge becoming actualized is what we call *karma* according to the *Bhagavad-Gītā*. It defines *karma* as follows:

> *bhūta-bhāvodbhava-karo visargaḥ karma-saṁjñitaḥ* । — III.27
>
> The specific creative urge that causes the emanation of beings is to be understood by the term *karma*.

The first half of the very same verse asserts that it is in the Imperishable (*akṣara*) *Brahman* that this creative urge abides. The same Imperishable *Brahman* is the one substratum for all the superimposed *bhāvas*. Calling the Reality "the ocean of Consciousness," the Guru portrays an overall picture of life in his *Ātmopadeśa Śatakam*, thus, where the role of *karma* is also made sufficiently clear:

> Individuated forms, like waves in the ocean, emerge in sequence and so do they merge. Alas! when will this process come to an end! O! this is nothing but the *karma* of creative self-unfoldment happening within the ocean of primeval source-Consciousnes! — verse 56

What the Guru calls "the ocean of consciousness" (*saṁvit-kaḍal*) in the *Ātmopadeśa Śatakam* is nothing other than the *Ātmā* (Self) understood here in the *Karma Darśanam*. In short, it is in the one *Ātmā*-Reality that all the *karmas* (actions) have their being, and individual beings are not really the *kartās* (doers of actions). Individual entities are nothing more than wave-like appearances emerging and merging as part of the beginningless and endless flow of *karmas*. Being part of that flow, they also have necessarily to remain active, but what they do is not their *karmas*. That the individual beings have no *karma* of their own is stressed in the *Bhagavad-Gītā*:

> No doerhood of *karmas*, nor even *karmas*, are created by the Lord as pertaining to anyone in the world. Neither is created anyone's association with a particular fruit of *karma*; what works is My own self-manifestation. — V.14

In short, we think, "This is my *karma*; its fruits are also mine; I am destined to enjoy or suffer them," only because we are in a deluded state of mind.

The How of Karma

Just as the ocean has in it the innate power to make waves appear on its surface, the *Ātmā* has also inherent in it an indomitable urge to emanate beings, organic as well as inorganic, from itself. Nothing can be predicated of this power other than that it is indefinable. The *māyā* we saw in Chapter 4 is none other than this mysterious creative urge. The Guru therefore says, *ātmaiva māyayā karma karoti* (*Ātmā* alone, by virtue of its own *māyā*, performs all the *karmas*).

Whereas the ocean is one, the waves appear as many. That means, when the one unitary ocean actively finds self-expression, many waves appear. Similar is the case with the ocean of *Ātmā* or pure Consciousness (*saṁvit*). Its is an active existence, and as a result emerge the appearance of all the worldly phenomena. Just as a wave is a specific form emerging from the ocean, every being, living as well as non-living, mind as well as matter, that constitute the world, emerge as discernibly existing, from the one ocean of *Ātmā*. The Guru in this sense says, *Ātmā* performs *karma* "by assuming various forms (*bahu-rūpa-dhṛk*). Yet It does not uphold the notion, "This is my *karma*; its fruits are also mine," about the *karmas* going on in It. *Ātmā*, in this sense, remains *asaṅgaḥ* (completely unattached).

It is self-evident that *Ātmā*, being consciousness in essence, is self-effulgent (*svaprakāśaḥ*). It is the brightness of *Ātmā* that shines in the form of the existence of all the worlds. It is because of *Ātmā*'s brightness, all the luminaries shine. It therefore is often thought of as "the light even of lights" (*jyotiṣām api taj jyotiḥ*).

How do all the individuated forms and their *karmas* emerge in the one *Ātmā*? It could in one way be compared to our seeing dreams. Dream is the inexplicable phenomenon of our consciousness unconsciously creating a multi-faceted objective world from itself and enjoying or suffering the outcome of events happening in the world created thus. Vedānta textbooks call this dreaming state of consciousness *taijasa*, literally "the *ātmā* that is in a bright state." Like the phenomenon of *taijasa* creating the dream world and enjoying the events in it, is the way how the one *Ātmā* beginninglessly and endlessly creates from itself the entire world and the endless flow of *karmas*.

It was warned even at the beginning of this study that each chapter of the work is to be meditated on as representing a particular facet of the visualization of the non-dual Reality. The present chapter depicts how the flow of the eternal *karma* is seen both in the total cosmic system and in each individual being. The overall basic perception is that the eternal flow of *karmas* is a conditioning superimposed on the unconditioned Reality or *Ātmā*. The present chapter, *Karma Darśanam*, therefore, is to be contemplated upon with the ultimate intention of perceiving one *Ātmā* alone functioning in all the *karmas* that happen in one's personal life as well as in the existence of the world.

How the one *Ātmā*'s eternal flow of *karma* results in the emergence of individual beings and how they function perfectly is depicted in the next verse.

Verse 2

मन्ये वदामि गृह्णामि शृणोमीत्यादि रूपतः।
क्रियते कर्म परमात्मना चित्तेन्द्रियात्मना ॥२॥

manye vadāmi gṛhṇāmi śṛṇomītyādi rūpataḥ ।
kriyate karma paramātmanā cittendriyātmanā ॥2॥

Actions of such forms as "I think," "I speak," "I grasp," "I hear" are performed by the Supreme self, assuming the forms of mental faculties, senses and the like.

That all *karmas* take place in one *Ātmā* has by now been sufficiently made clear. Still we humans think, we are the real doers of the actions we happen to be engaged in. This misconception is the outcome of the free will we have to decide what to do, how to do, when to do, why to do, etc. Taken for granted that each of us is the doer of *karmas*, each context of performing some *karma* could then be seen as having certain constituent factors. Three such factors — *karaṇa* (instruments or organs of action), *karma* (the actual performing of actions), and *kartā* (the performer of actions) — are pointed out by the *Bhagavad-Gītā* (XVIII.18).

Each such *karma* happens as induced by certain functions of consciousness happening according to the nature of circumstances, the innate propensities, value notions of the decision-maker and many such factors. For this reason, no one can predict what kind of reaction we could expect of a person in a particular situation. Still each such decision-making content could be seen as having three unavoidable constituent factors — *jñāna* (knowledge), *jñeya* (the object known) and *parijñātā* (the knower), as pointed out in the very same verse of the *Gītā*.

What is the Reality that unfolds itself and functions as we, as our capability to perform *karmas*, as the free will that induces us to perform *karmas*, as the intelligence that takes decisions, and as the organs and instruments that enable us to carry out such decisions? One Reality alone exists, as we have already seen, to unfold as all this, and It is *Ātmā*, unconditioned Consciousness in essence. Then all the above-mentioned must be various conditioned manifestations of that one *Ātmā*. The Guru himself underscores this point in his *Ātmopadeśa Śatakam* directly as follows:

> That which is conscious of itself even when in darkness, is the *Ātmā*. It is pure, unconditioned Consciousness. And it manifests as all the names and forms, as all mental faculties and sense-organs, as all *karmas* and their doers. Lo and behold, what a Great Magic all this is! — Verse 27

The Guru, in the present verse of the *Darśanamālā*, expounds the same basic stand, but in a slightly different way. The actual performing of every *karma* needs the backing of the instruments required, of organs of action, of sense organs, and of mental faculties. All these are nothing but various manifest forms of the one *Ātmā*. It is in the one *Paramātmā* (Supreme Self) that all the *karmas*, bodily, verbal and mental, have their being. We should therefore always have the inner awareness that whatever we imagine, whatever we think, whatever we speak, whatever we do with our sense organs and organs of action, all take place in one *Ātmā* alone. It is when performed with this awareness that *karma* becomes sublimated as *karma-yoga*; that means, each *karma* we perform then becomes a particular facet of our realizing our oneness with the total Being, the *Paramātmā*.

How to prove that all the *karma*s take place in the one *Ātmā* is stated in the next verse.

verse 3

आत्मैव कर्मणः पूर्वमन्यत् किञ्चिन्न विद्यते ।
ततः स्वेनैव कर्माणि क्रियन्ते निज मायया ॥३॥

ātmaiva karmaṇaḥ pūrvam anyat kiñcin na vidyate ।
tataḥ svenaiva karmāṇi kriyante nija māyayā ॥3॥

Ātmā alone is what exists prior to the emerging of *karma*s; nothing else does exist at all. *Ātmā*, on its own, therefore is what performs all the *karma*s by virtue of Its own *māyā*.

Flow, as an event, has to take place in water or some other liquid that are not stagnant. What we see in the form of the world is also an incessant flow of events. It is as part of that flow that we too, as individuals, take free decisions and perform *karma*s as we prefer.

What is the liquid or substance that abides as the substratum of this flow of events? It was seen earlier, in Chapter 2 (Verse 10) that the causal substance is *Ātmā*, which is *sat*, *cit* and *ānanda* at the same time. *Karma*, then, is nothing other than the continuous process by which effects appear and disappear in the one causal substance. In short, *Ātmā* alone existed prior to the emergence of *karma*, and in its absence no *karma* would emerge either. *Ātmā* alone thus gives room for all the *karma*s to emerge. Understanding this much makes it clear, where all the *karma*s have their being — they happen in *Ātmā*. That is to say, if at all there is to be a doer (*kartā*) of all the *karma*s, it has to be *Ātmā*.

When in an active state with all the *karma*s, *Ātmā* is called *prakṛti*, loosely translatable as "nature." It could then be said, it is *prakṛti* that does all the *karma*s.

The same *Ātmā* emanates from itself not only the *karma*s, but also all the instruments of action, all the organs of action, and everything needed for *karma*s to take place. How does all this happen? This is not a question answerable in a logically convincing manner. The only possible answer is this: an indefinable mysterious power to accomplish it abides in *Ātmā*. It is somewhat like the power inherent in the ocean to make waves appear and disappear on its surface. This power abiding in *Ātmā* is what the word *māyā* signifies.

That this *māyā* has no existence of its own was seen in the *Māyā Darśanam* (Chapter 4, Verse 1). The appearance of all phenomena caused by this non-existent *māyā* also has to be necessarily non-existent. The conclusion we thus arrive at is that *karma*s also have no existence of their own. What exists is *Ātmā* alone. *Māyā*, thus is the mysterious power in *Ātmā*, having no existence of its own, but which makes *karma*s, and through them the world also, appear to be. The mysteriousness of this power of *māyā* is made more explicit in the next verse.

Verse 4

शक्तिरस्त्यात्मनः काचिद् दुर्घटा न पृथक् स्वतः ।
तयैवारोप्यते कर्म निखिलं निष्क्रियात्मनि ॥४ ॥

śaktir asty ātmanaḥ kācid durghaṭā na pṛthak svataḥ ।
tayaivāropyate karma nikhilaṁ niṣkriyātmani ॥4 ॥

There exists a certain vital urge in *Ātmā*, difficult to define, and not different from Itself. Because of it all the *karma*s are superimposed on the *Ātmā* which verily is actionless.

One of the peculiar characteristics of gold is that it can be shaped into any ornament. The intervention of a goldsmith who conceives the idea of the ornament-form, its utility and the know-how of making it, are unavoidable for gold to become ornaments. But no goldsmith-like agency is there for *Ātmā* to undergo the constant process of appearing as the world by undergoing constant *karma*.

Who conceives the idea of the newly emerging forms and of the world as a whole? Who thinks of their utility and workability? The power to conceive all this and of the nature of *karma* required, is there in *Ātmā* itself. Though given the name *māyā*, it really is inconceivable and indefinable. This power in *Ātmā* makes new forms emerge and old forms disappear through unending *karma*, and thus ensures the ever-present novelty of the world and of life.

Ātmā, as the causal substance, is actionless (*niṣkriyaḥ*). There is no sense of agency of actions (*kartṛtva*) nor of being the enjoyer of the fruits of actions (*bhoktṛtva*) in *Ātmā*. Similar to superimposing ornament-forms on the gold-substance, is the superimposing of *karma*s on the actionless *Ātmā* and the resultant world appearance. All this is effected by the above-mentioned power of *māyā*.

Ātmā alone is what exists; nothing else exists on its own. Thus the above-mentioned power on its own, can have no existence. That power, in this sense, is unreal (*asat*). Yet, for the reason that its effects are constantly experienced, it is not possible to dismiss it altogether as simply unreal. Being thus neither real nor unreal in logical terms, it can only be thought of as something inconceivable or indefinable, referred to by the Guru here as *durghaṭā*.

Though actionless as the abstract substance, *Ātmā* in its actual existence never remains inactive. Thus, it is difficult to say whether it has actions or it is actionless. In this sense also it is something difficult to conceive (*durghaṭā*).

Though all *karma*s take place in it, *Ātmā* has no sense, "I am doing this *karma*," "This is my *karma*," "The fruits of this *karma* would be mine" and the like. *Ātmā* thus remains unattached to *karmas*. How each of us can realize this unattached state of *Ātmā* in our own life is detailed in the next verse.

Verse 5

सर्वदासङ्ग एवात्माऽज्ञतया कर्मसङ्गिवत् ।
करोति न करोमीति न ज्ञः कर्मसु सज्जते ॥५॥

sarvadāsaṅga evātmā 'ajñatayā karma-saṅgivat I
karoti na karomīti na jñaḥ karmasu sajjate II5 II

Ātmā indeed remains always unattached to all that takes place in Itself. Only due to ignorance one performs *karmas* as if attached to them. The wise one, on the other hand, thinks "I do nothing," and does not feel himself clinging to *karmas*.

The *karma*-related enigma, crossing the bounds of religious or cultural barriers, has always puzzled the human mind. In the Western world, it arose in the form of the conflict between free will and destiny. If the happenings of life and the world are predetermined, as religions hold, by the will of God or Fate, what then is the value and role of man's freedom to think, to take decisions and to plan activities? If man's freedom to think and take decisions can control everything in life, what then is the meaning of God and His insuperable will? The predicament man faces is that the two have to be given place in life without room for conflict, but both are unwilling to come together in a reasonable manner.

Of varied significance is the notion of *karma* that has developed in the religious thought of India. The *Bhagavad-Gītā* also warns, "the way of *karma* is elusively subtle indeed" (*gahanā karmaṇo gatiḥ* — IV.17). The classification of *karma* as *nitya-karma* (daily rites), *niyata-karma* (rites invariably performed), *naimittika-karma* (occasional rites), and *kāmya-karma* (rites performed with some particular objective) pertains to the context of ritualism; whereas *sañcita-karma* (accumulated actions of the past), *prārabdha-karma* (actions already initiated) and *āgāmi-karma* (actions yet to be performed in the future), are the subdivisions meaningful in the context of actions in general performed by each individual in his/her life.

The latter division of *karma*s has for its basis the belief that the latent impressions (also referred to as *karma*s) of everything one happens to do in life cling to the soul even after death, as a deciding factor in the nature of its reincarnation. It is a common practice in India to say, when one happens to face certain peculiar circumstances, favourable or unfavourable, in life for no apparent reason, that it is the fruition of one's past *karma*s. The subdivisions of such latent impressions are what are known as *sañcita*, *prārabdha* and *āgāmi karma*s.

All the actions one had performed in all the previous incarnations, as the *karma*-theory holds, cling to a soul waiting for their fruition in one birth or another. Such *karma*s or latent impressions of actions are called *sañcita-karma*s. The same kind of impressions yet to be accumulated in the present life are called *āgāmi-karma*s. There could be certain previous *karma*s whose fruition is already initiated but not yet completed. These *karma*s are often compared to arrows already released from a bow but yet to reach their targets; an arrow already shot has necessarily to reach its destination. Likewise, the fruition of such *karma*s necessarily has to find its natural end. Even some of the enlightened sometimes have had to suffer severe bodily pains, particularly as they near the end of their life-term. Such phenomena are often explained by the unenlightened believers in the *karma*-theory, that it is because of their *prārabdha-karma*.

All these notions evidently are meaningful only when actions are thought of as performed by individuals. Who really is the performer of actions? Is it we the individuals, or is it the total nature? Our being born in this world, living here, remaining active all through life, and finally dying — all these happen as part of the overall flow of the total nature, and this flow actually is a flow of actions. Being part of this grand flow of actions, we also remain active; that is all. The overall flow of the totality is what we call *prakṛti* or nature.

The word *prakṛti* has the word *kṛti* forming part of it. *Kṛti* means "action." *Prakṛti* (nature) as a reality also has *kṛti* (action) as inseparable from it. Action or *karma* incessantly goes on in every minute element of nature. As part of nature, we too are active. All the actions (*karma*s) we happen to perform, whether physical, mental or verbal, in short, are part of the overall *karma* of nature. Of numerous mental actions, one is our willing freely. All the actions, from the most external and physical ones to the most internal and subtle free will, are simply part of *prakṛti*'s never-ending flow of actions, and not the actions of individuals. The one underlying Substance providing for this incessant flow of actions is *Ātmā*. It is with all this in mind that it was stated at the very beginning of this chapter that *Ātmā* alone performs all the *karma*s (*ātmaiva karma karoti*).

It is evident in view of this overall perception of *karma* that the *nitya-niyata-naimittika-kāmya* subdivisions, as well as the *sañcita-prārabdha-āgāmī* subdivisions, are all unreal in themselves, because *Ātmā* alone is Real. All the *karma*s then are merely superimposed on the one *Ātmā*. The *karma*s of each individual are merely each person partaking in the overall flow of the actions of nature. Nature's action and the individual's action thus become one action. One who is engaged in actions with this perception is to be called a *karma-yogin*.

My thinking "I have my own *karmas*" is naturally followed by the idea that their fruits are also mine. The idea that a certain action was done wrongly then leads to the sense of sin (*pāpa*), and the opposite idea to the sense of merit (*puṇya*). Those who are endowed with a moral sense always like to avoid doing sinful actions. Still situations arise in life, in which I, as if compelled by circumstances, helplessly commit sins. It then ends up in a state of mental conflict.

How can I free myself absolutely from sins? This problem then disturbs me. One means alone is there for attaining this freedom: realizing that all *karmas* take place in *Ātmā* alone; that, if at all there is a performer of *karmas*, it is the one *Ātmā* alone, not me the individual. *Ātmā*, having become creatively self-manifest, is what we call nature or *prakṛti*. While engaged in all natural activities, I have to realize that the *karma* I happen to perform becomes unavoidable as part of the overall flow of action of nature, and that I am not the doer of it. When a *karma* is not an individual's, it being sinful or meritorious makes no sense.

Saṅga means attachment. The idea "I am the performer of *karmas*" makes me attached to those *karmas*, and this attachment is called *karma-saṅga*. The one not attached in this way is called *asaṅga*. *Ātmā* is *asaṅga* because, though all the *karmas* constantly take place in it, it does not think, "I am the doer of these *karmas*." The individual also, when fully enlightened, finds identity with that one *Ātmā*, and thus feels unattached to all the *karmas*. He or she also thus feels what it is to be an *asaṅga*. The word *ātmā* here could be interpreted as meaning the individuated Reality or the Reality in the being of the total world, just as gold could be seen as the substance in a particular ornament, and in all the ornaments everywhere. *Ātmā*, as the total Reality, remains active without being attached to any action. But the individuated *ātmā*, oblivious of the Reality in himself or herself, mistakes the actions as his or hers, the state of being ignorant (*ajñatā*) mentioned in the verse. It is this ignorance that makes one attached to the actions one happens to perform. A *jñānin*, an enlightened one, on the other hand, even while remaining fully active, lives liberated from all such attachments.

The next verse portrays the picture of the cosmic aspect of *karma* that goes on in the one *Ātmā*.

Verse 6

ज्वलति ज्वलनो वायुर्वाति वर्षति वारिदः।
धरात्मा सन् धरति खल्वेको वहति वाहिनी ॥६॥

jvalati jvalano vāyur vāti varṣati vāridaḥ ।
dharātmā san dharati khalveko vahati vāhinī ॥6॥

One (*Ātmā*) alone is what burns assuming the form of fire, blows assuming the form of wind, showers assuming the form of rain, supports everything assuming the form of the earth, and flows in the form of rivers (universally in the world).

The world, as far as we know in detail, is not something inert. It is a living whole, and that world has in it innumerable living species. Changes always take place in it everywhere, from its subtlest mental aspect of existence, to the grossest physical aspect. All such changes imply *karma*s of one sort or another taking place. A result of such *karma*s is the disappearance of old patterns of appearance and the appearance of new ones. Unimaginably extensive is the variety and vastness of such phenomenal change and the phenomenon of life in it.

That all such changeful phenomena should be having an underlying substance is taken for granted by all thinkers, especially of the East. What is that substance? Of what nature is it? These questions are yet to be finally settled. Perhaps, settling these finally will render philosophizing or search for Reality, no longer needed, and above all it will make life monotonous for humans, for life in a fully known world will be insipid. Life continues to exist with all its novelty, new hopes and aspirations for humans, only because everything concerning it is not fully known.

The physicists' attempt is also to find out the ultimate building block of the universe; only that their search is confined to the physical reality behind the physical phenomena. Their final finding is that energy is the one all-underlying substance. But, what this energy is in its nature and content, is a question that still baffles them. Energy, according to them, is something indefinable, something mysterious, something we are uncertain about. It is this indefinable and uncertain energy that appears as everything definable and certain.

Even as all this holds true, life really is not something physical alone in nature. Without some vital principle functioning, there could be no life. This is the law that governs the organic phenomena of the world. This vital principle, called soul or spirit in religions, and mind by certain psychologists, in the perception of scientists, is no reality at all. According to them, it is simply a by-product of certain chemical actions taking place in the physical object called brain.

A man running, and a train running are both physical events in the perception of scientists. But no train will run, and no train could be made, unless some human intelligence works behind it. Which was the physical law that caused the origination of this intelligence? Which is the physical law that governs the intimacy between two lovers? What is the physical basis of the fondness a mother feels towards her child? Many such questions remain unanswered by physicists, and even biologists. They just set aside such questions, saying they do not pertain to the realm of scientific enquiry. Such unwillingness to face actualities, at least to our estimation, is also to be treated as unscientific.

Brahma-vidyā, the science of the Absolute, also known as Vedānta, on the other hand, is the comprehensive and integral science that excludes no aspect of reality from within its scope. Many phenomena discernible as material, biological, psychological and the like, are there in nature. Vedānta holds that there has to be one Reality underlying all these apparent phenomena, and that Reality is *Brahman*, realizable by every seeker as *ātman*. The ultimate reality found out by physicists, is indefinable according to scientists themselves. Somewhat similar is the case of Vedāntins who come to the final conclusion that *Brahman* or *Ātman* is the one Reality behind everything phenomenal and definable. Though not knowable as an object, this *Ātman* is realizable as what oneself really is. This doctrine of Vedānta is to be treated as scientific at least to the extent of the modern scientists' assertion that energy is the building block of the universe. Science too admits that the invisible and indefinable energy appears as everything visible and definable. Of similar nature is the doctrine of Vedānta that everything material and mental, gross and subtle, cosmological and psychological, appears to be as various manifest forms of one *Brahman* or *Ātman*.

Karma, thus, is the activity that goes on in the one *Ātmā* making it appear as all the phenomena. The Guru therefore says, the one *Ātmā*, as the result of its own *karma*, assumes the form of fire and performs the *karma* of burning; assumes the form of air and performs the *karma* of blowing; assumes the form of clouds and performs the *karma* of pouring down as rain; assumes the form of the earth and performs the *karma* of supporting everything. So are to be understood all the activities going on in nature as a whole. Despite all the *karmas* going on in it, *Ātmā* remains unattached to, and even, so to say, unmindful of, such *karmas*.

Fully enlightened on this reality concerning *karma*, one would perceive the one *Ātmā* alone actively existing not only in every apparent phenomenon of nature, but also in oneself, one being a minute element of the total nature. A picture of the *karmas* perceptible in individual beings is depicted in the next verse.

Verse 7

ऊर्ध्वं प्राणो ह्यधोऽपानः खल्वेको याति निष्क्रियः ।
नाड्यन्तराले धमति क्रन्दति स्पन्दति स्थितः ॥७॥

ūrdhvaṁ prāṇo hy adho 'pānaḥ khalveko yāti niṣkriyaḥ ।
nāḍyantarāle dhamati krandati spandati sthitaḥ ॥7॥

> The one actionless *Ātmā* alone is what moves in individuated beings upwards in the form of *prāṇa*, downwards in the form of *apāna*, pulsates within the nervous system, makes murmuring sounds within, and functions as heart-beats.

The Reality that pulsates and finds expression in the universal being is what does so in individuated beings as well. In fact, the universal-particular division with respect to *karma* as well as Reality is of no relevance. *Ātmā*, the ultimate Reality is one alone, and its *karma* is also one. It is the innumerable outcomes of this *karma* that we differentiate as universal and particular. This division exists only in our ideation. Whether something is seen as universal or particular depends upon the angle we choose to view it. Seeing an object from two angles does not make the object two, though perceived with our eyes as different. The same is true with *karma* also. The *karmas* we individuals perform also are nothing other than specific manifest forms of the one overall *karma* that goes on in *Ātmā*.

We remain unconscious of many of the activities that go on in us. Usually, particularly in the context of religion and ethics, only those actions done voluntarily and deliberately are treated as *karmas*. Breathing, the heart beating, blood circulating, food getting digested, throwing out dirt and matters not needed for the body — all these are actions going on in our system without our knowledge. None of these *karmas* happens as willed by us. The same is true with the *karmas* we do voluntarily. Our sense organs also, along with the organs of action, always remain active, as does our mind. It is mind that takes the decision as to which action to do and which not. Still the mind's capability to do so was not created by us. It is the one ultimate Reality, *Ātmā*, that decided, "Let humans be a species possessing a freely willing mind." The voluntary actions taking place in us too, therefore, in the ultimate sense, are of *Ātmā*. He who becomes fully aware of this reality with regard to *karma*, treats both his voluntary and involuntary actions, as really pertaining to *Ātmā*, and this awareness makes him unattached to, and liberated from, all *karmas*.

Verse 8

अस्तिजन्मर्द्धिपरिणत्यपक्षयविनाशनम् ।
षड्भावमिह यो याति स नान्योऽविक्रियात्मनः ॥८ ॥

asti janmarddhi pariṇaty apakṣaya vināśanam ।
ṣad bhāvam iha yo yāti sa nānyo 'vikriyātmanaḥ ॥8 ॥

That which attains the six states of, basically existing, being born, growing, evolving, deteriorating and finally becoming extinct, is not really different from the one actionless *Ātmā*.

That every action taking place universally in the cosmic system is really the *karma* of the one *Ātmā* was seen in Verse 6. In the next verse was seen that every *karma* performed by every individuated being, voluntarily and involuntarily, also is of the one *Ātmā*. The eternal flow of *karma* thus finds expression both as universal *karma*s and particular *karma*s. Thus unfolds the eternal flow of life, consisting of birth, sustenance and dissolution of beings, forming part of the cosmic phenomena.

The emergence of an individuated being, as part of the total *karma* of *Ātmā*, is what we call birth, and its disappearance, death. Both events take place in the one *Ātmā*. Birth and death are phenomena comparable to the emerging and merging of waves in the ocean. Both the birth and death of waves happen in the total being of the ocean, or in the water-content of ocean. Water remains water, and the ocean remains the ocean. While all these activities continue to take place in it, the ocean undergoes no intrinsic change. In the same way, wave-like individuated beings emerge and then merge in the water-like Consciousness-content or *Ātmā*. Throughout, *Ātmā* remains unchanged. *Ātmā* neither appears nor disappears, and in this sense it is actionless (*niṣkriyaḥ*).

The life-span is usually thought of as beginning with birth and ending with death. Looked at with a more philosophical insight, the same life could be seen as passing through many stages, of which six are particularly noticeable. They are *asti* (existence), *janma* (birth), *vṛddhi* (growth), *pariṇāma* (evolution or transformation without apparent growth), *apakṣaya* (decline) and *vināśa* (final dissolution). Something substantial has to exist before for the event of birth to take place, and it is denoted by the word *asti*. Only in an already existing substance there can emerge some new apparent form, and the emerging of the new form is called *janma*. The individual being thus born never remains changeless; it grows constantly. This process is called *vṛddhi*. This growth stops at a certain age, but transformation or evolution (*pariṇāma*) continues. This stage, in human life, is known as the middle age or the prime of life. Then the decline of the body (*apakṣaya*) begins, and finally the individual entity gets dissolved (*vināśa*) back into the total being. Destruction happens only to the apparent form. What is real in the individual being continues to exist as *asti*, as part of the total being (*asti*). These states together are known as *ṣaḍ bhāva*s (six states of apparent forms).

The underlying substance (*sat*) remains changeless, and its manifest forms (*bhāva*s) appear and disappear constantly — this is the rule that guides nature. It is like gold remaining changeless while its ornament-forms always change. It is in this changeful aspect of appearance that we discern the six different stages. They do not affect the one underlying *Ātmā*. Ornament-forms do not exist separate from gold. The ever-changing appearances also do not have being apart from the one Reality or *Ātmā*.

In short, every change, growth or decline, that happens to our bodily existence has to be treated as the varying manifest forms of the one *Ātmā*, as the *karma* in the one *Ātmā* finding expression following a system of its own.

Verse 9

स्वयं क्रियन्ते कर्माणि करणैरिन्द्रियैरपि।
अहं त्वसङ्गः कूटस्थ इति जानाति कोविदः ॥९॥

svayaṁ kriyante karmāṇi karaṇair indriyair api ।
ahaṁ tvasaṅgaḥ kūṭastha iti jānāti kovidaḥ ॥9॥

Karmas become self-accomplished with mental faculties and senses as instruments; yet I remain unattached and firm like a rock. Thus is the steadfast understanding of the enlightened one.

Each of us considers ourselves as the centre of the universe, unmindful of the fact that it has no centre at all. Moreover we imagine ourselves as the centre of all the activity in the world also. This self-centredness becomes all the more strengthened by the ability each of us has for freely taking decisions and freely engaging in activities. This self-centredness or I-sense is called *ahanta* in Vedānta. As are the decisions to perform actions ours, so are the organs of actions also ours. The factors that influence the nature of decision we take regarding each action are self-interest and one's own value notions. All these factors together create the impression in our mind, "I am the doer of this action." In Sanskrit this sense of agency of actions is called *kartṛtva.*

Mind thus becomes more and more attached to what one happens to do, and the idea, "I am bound to enjoy or suffer the results of this action" becomes more and more fixed in the mind. This sense of being the enjoyer is known as *bhoktṛtva*. This overall attachment one develops towards the actions one happens to perform and their fruits results in a mine-sense, called *mamatā* in Sanskrit. *Ahanta* (I-sense) and *mamatā* (mine-sense) together, thus bind one to the world of *karma*s. The sense of attachment that thus becomes well-rooted is called *karma-saṅga*.

As has become sufficiently clear now, all the *karma*s take place in the one all-underlying *Ātmā*. The appearance of the entire world, along with all the fleeting phenomena in it, is the end-result of this *karma*. Each of us, our ability to perform *karma*s, the capability to take free decisions, all the instruments of action — all together form a minute element of such transitory phenomena. Though unfolding itself as everything, *Ātmā* has no sense of being the doer of the *karma* of unfolding, nor the enjoyer of its fruits. What it is that happens then in *Ātmā*, is described by the *Bhagavad-Gītā* thus: *svabhāvas tu pravartate* (the Self's innate urge exerts itself) VIII.14.

All the *karmas* belong to the realm of appearances (*bhāvas*), and they do not affect the immutability of *sat*. The underlying *Ātmā*, in this context is referred to as *kūṭastha* (unmoved like a mountain peak). One, on realizing what is real in one's own being, finds one's identity with that Reality (*sat*), as opposed to what takes place apparently. The apparent aspect is always changeful, whereas the Reality is immutable. Attachment (*saṅga*) happens between two or more apparent forms, never between Reals. *Ātmā*, the Real, always remains attachmentless (*asaṅga*). One's self identity with *Ātmā* makes *Ātmā*'s attachmentlessness one's own also. One also thus finds oneself a *kūṭastha*. Such enlightened ones are referred to in this verse as *kovidaḥ* (the learned).

How would the learned perceive the nature of *karma* that happens in himself or herself? Such a one perceives that the sense organs have their own attributes and roles to play, and they function accordingly. The learned one remains a witness to all such activities, unattached to any of them. The *Bhagavad-Gītā* also puts emphasis on this attitude of the learned when it says:

> *guṇā guṇeṣu vartanta iti matvā na sajjate* । — III.28
>
> Holding the view that (subjective) modes move around the corresponding (objective) modes, he remains unaffected.

The sense organs, the organs of action and the mind becoming engaged in their normal activities result in pleasurable, painful or indifferent feelings. One usually likes pleasurable feelings and dislikes the painful ones. Whose are these likes and dislikes? Are these ours? No, they are of the senses which pertain really to the realm of appearances, not of the Reality. The same is the case with regard to the sense objects as well. The contact between the two also happens in the same realm. Attachment and aversion are felt nowhere else. None of these really affect the real being of us. The idea that these happen to our real being is our enemy. The *Gītā* warns us against the danger of our becoming subject to this wrong idea when it says:

> Attraction-repulsion abide mutually as between the senses and their objects. One should never come under their (double) sway. They indeed are one's (twin) enemies.
>
> —III.34

Verse 10

दृश्यत्वाद्भास्यमहमप्यतोऽहं शुक्तिरङ्गवत्।
अध्यस्तमेक एवाद्यश्वोऽपि सर्वोपरिस्थितः ॥१०॥

dṛśyatvād bhāsyam aham apy ato 'haṁ śuktiraṅgavat ।
adhyastam eka evādya śvo 'pi sarvoparisthitaḥ ॥10॥

> "The I" too is an object of awareness, and to that extent is a superimposition, as is the silver-glean of the mother-of-pearl. What has existence today and tomorrow above everything, is one alone.

All the *karma*s apparently take place in the visible world, as part of the changefulness of the world. That all the visible (*dṛśya*) entities are merely conditioned manifestations, that all such are superimpositions, and that the unconditioned substratum is one *Ātmā*, the *sat*, alone, was seen at the end of the last chapter. What the word *dṛśya* signifies includes all that manifests in the gross form, subtle form, causal form and *turīya* form, as was seen also in the same chapter. The ordinary physical, visible world is what we become aware of through sense perception.

This visible world undergoes constant change, and the inherent urge within, that causes this change is called *karma*. *Karma*, in this sense, forms part of the gross world of which we as the perceivers are inseparable. Still by habit, owing to our ignorance, we consider every action we happen to perform as ours. As a result what we call *kartṛtva bodha* (the sense of being the agency of actions) becomes deeply rooted. We, thus, superimpose the *karma* that really pertains to the one *Ātmā*, on ourselves as individuals.

The I-sense in each of us is also part of the visible world, only that it pertains to the realm of the subtle as opposed to the gross. To that extent it too is a *dṛśya* (visible entity). The word *dṛśya* means "object of knowledge." As the I-sense is also an object of our knowledge, it too is a *dṛśya*.

Wherever there is a perceived object, there is a perceiving subject also, and in the absence of the subject there can be no object, or rather, something will not be an object unless perceived by a subject. Subject and object, both emerge in the one *Ātmā*, and thus both are conditioned manifestations (*bhāsya*). In other words, both the subject and the object, being knowable and distinguishable as separate, form part of the *dṛśya* or perceptible aspect of existence. In that sense "I," as the doer of *karma*s, is also part of the conditioned manifestation appearing in the one *Ātmā*. To that extent "I" is a superimposition and hence unreal. The words *aham api* (even I) of the verse suggest that, not only the perceivable and enjoyable external world, but the perceiving and enjoying subject or mind also is a conditioned manifestation (*adhyasta*) and hence unreal (*asat*).

The Guru here resorts to the famous silver-and-mother-of-pearl analogy of Vedānta, in order to explicate how the non-dual perception is to be deduced from the chapter as a whole. Merely mistaking a mother-of-pearl for silver does not make it real silver. Likewise, wrongly conceiving a specific functional manifest form (*bhāna-vṛtti*) of *Ātmā* as the performer of *karma*s, does in no way make it the real performer of *karma*s.

There exists one Reality alone; It manifests itself as all the *karma*s and their doers, as all the enjoyables and their enjoyers, as all the knowables and their knowers, as all the individual entities and their *karma*s; and as the universal aspect of existence and all the universal *karma*s. That Reality is *Ātmā*, in essence pure and unconditioned Consciousness. Its manifesting as all these happens like a great magic show, as has been made clear by the Guru on various occasions in his works.

This Reality's existence, it is stated in the verse, is above everything. This does not mean that its being is spatially above all the perceptible entities. This aboveness is rather of a philosophical order, in the sense that it is far beyond our grasping power. Actually its being is as the indwelling, all-pervading, invisible and inconceivable Substance in all that is visible and conceivable. It is this imperceptible and inconceivable Reality, because of the *karma*-urge in it, that assumes the form of everything. In its absence nothing will appear to be, just as in the absence of the mother-of-pearl no silver-appearance would be seen. When, as part of the world, we remain engaged in *karma*s, we should perceive intuitively one *Ātmā* alone creatively existing in the form of the world, in the form of *karma*s, in the form of the fruits of *karma*s. This enlightened perception renders us free even when we are engaged in actions.

7

Jñāna Darśanam
(Vision by Knowledge)

THE method resorted to in the second half of the *Darśanamālā* is that of looking from five different levels at how we individual seekers are related to, or should relate ourselves with, the one absolute Reality. Of these levels the most apparent one pertaining to the grossest aspect of existence, is that of actions (*karma*s) dealt with in the last chapter. Subtler than the level of actions in the existence of individual humans is that of knowing. Though the word used in the text for "knowing" is *jñāna*, evidently it does not stand for the absolutist wisdom (*jñāna*) Vedānta aims at. The knowing function happens in us constantly, even when we remain unconscious of it. For example, it is because the knowing function works even when we are in deep sleep, that we become capable of saying after waking up, "I had a sound sleep." Though we remain fully unconscious in that state, the same unconscious aspect of our being enjoys the soundness of the deep sleep then and there. That means, the knowing function takes place constantly in us irrespective of the altering states of our consciousness, oscillating as it does between deep sleep and full wakefulness. How various are such knowing functions? How can we intuitively perceive the existence of one *Ātmā* even when the modes of knowledge vary from state to state, from object to object? It is these lines of thought through which the Guru leads us in this *Jñāna Darśanam*.

Verse 1

ज्ञानमेकं हि निरुपाधिकं सोपाधिकं च तत् ।
अहङ्कारादिहीनं यत् ज्ञानं तन्निरुपाधिकम् ॥१॥

jñānam ekaṁ hi nirupādhikaṁ sopādhikaṁ ca tat ।
ahaṁkārādihīnaṁ yat jñānaṁ tan nirupādhikam ॥1॥

Jñāna is one and unconditioned indeed, itself becoming conditioned as well. Unconditioned *jñāna* is that which is devoid of I-sense and the like.

One alone is the Reality that exists eternally. That Reality is unconditioned and unmanifest. That Reality is not an object of knowledge. Such were the assertions made as the last chapter ended.

What is that Reality in its essential content? It was stated as early as Chapter 2 (*Apavāda Darśanam*) that, in essence, it was *sat-cit-ānanda*. Of these three, the *cit* (consciousness) aspect has knowing for its main function, and it is this particular function of *cit* that is referred to as *jñāna* (knowledge) in this chapter.

The *cit* aspect of *Brahman*, also called *cid-vastu* (the thinking substance), remains always one even when finding expression as various kinds of knowledge. The variety of such functional modes of *cit* really is infinite, as the Guru himself points out in his *Ātmopadeśa Śatakam* (Verse 36). This infinite possibility of the knowing power of consciousness is classified there by the Guru into two — *sama* and *anya* ("the same" and "the other"). Almost similar is the division of knowledge made here as *sopādhika* and *nirupādhika* (the conditioned and the unconditioned).

The Guru defines the *anya* kind of knowledge as that by which things are perceived as many. The knowledge that perceives one Reality alone, in spite of the variety of appearances, is of the *sama* kind (the same). The one appears as many when conditioned by some conditioning factor, called *upādhi* in Sanskrit. That which is subjected to such conditioning factors (*upādhi*s) is called *sopādhika*.

What the word *upādhi* signifies could well be clarified with the help of an analogy. Space (*ākāśa*), having no bounds, fills everywhere. The same space, when circumlimited by the four walls and roof of a building, becomes conditioned as building-space. There could be a pot within or without the building. The same space conditioned by the walls of the pot, becomes pot-space. Neither the building-space nor the pot-space has existence apart from the one space. The building is the *upādhi* (conditioning factor) in the former case, and the pot in the latter. If these *upādhi*s are destroyed, the space confined within them merges with the one all-filling space.

The one *jñāna* becoming conditioned is similar. It could become functionally manifest both as conditioned knowledge (*sopādhika jñāna*) and unconditioned knowledge (*nirupādhika-jñāna*), of which the latter is defined in the present verse. Every situation of knowledge involves a subject, called *ahanta* and an object, called *idanta*. The word *ahanta* literally means "I-sense" and *idanta* "this-sense." That knowledge in which these two are absent is called *nirupādhika-jñāna* (the unconditioned knowledge). That means, it is the knowledge in which no object separate from the subject exists. In other words, it is the knowledge where the subject or "I" becomes the object of knowledge. Put otherwise, it is the self-awareness each of us has. Self-knowledge being the only instance of the *nirupādhika-jñāna*, it has no subdivisions.

The next verse defines *sopādhika jñāna* or conditioned knowledge.

Verse 2

अहन्तयाऽन्तर्बहिरस्ति यदेवमिदन्तया ।
भानवृत्त्याऽन्वितं यत्तु ज्ञानं सोपाधिकं मतम् ॥२॥

ahantayā 'ntar bahir asti yad evam idantayā ।
bhāna-vṛttyā 'nvitaṁ yat tu jñānaṁ sopādhikaṁ matam ॥2 ॥

That knowledge which is always accompanied internally by subjective functional modulation and externally by objective functional modulation, is known as conditioned knowledge (*sopādhika jñāna*).

Water has no form of its own. Poured into a tumbler, it assumes the form of the tumbler. Poured into a pot, it assumes the form of the pot. In a pond it exists in the pond's shape. Tumbler, pot, pond and such are conditioning factors. When conditioned by these factors, the ultimately formless water appears to have specific shapes. That means, the unconditioned water becomes Conditioned when subjected to these factors. Similar is the case of *jñāna* or consciousness also. Being pure effulgence, it has no form of its own, but it assumes the form of every object known. On seeing a chair, for example, it assumes the chair's form, and on seeing the world, it appears as having the form of the world. Countless are the forms thus assumed by the one Consciousness.

The particular form it assumes when we specifically know something is called *viṣaya* or object, and the knowledge we have about a *viṣaya* is called *viṣaya-jñāna* or objective knowledge. How did all these objects (*viṣaya*s) originate? As a result of the conditioned manifestation (*bhāna-vṛtti*) of the very same *cit*, assuming the gross (*sthūla*), subtle (*sūkṣma*), causal (*kāraṇa*) or the fourth (*turīya*) forms, as was seen in Chapter 5. All such objects together is signified by the term *idanta* or "this-sense," meaning "the objects." Objects are supposed to exist externally (*bahiḥ*). Even our mental functions and ideas, we know, could become objects of our knowledge, and thus are also to be included in what the word *bahiḥ* (externally) denotes.

Such seemingly external objects become known only when a knower or subject exists. That subject, who knows also that he knows, is called *jñātā*, meaning "the knower." This *jñātā* can never be thought of as existing externally, for it is the I-sense each knower has. In short, no knowledge occurs without this internal I-sense of the knower and the external object of knowledge. Hence these three — the knowing subject, the known object and the knowledge — together is known as *tripuṭi* in Vedānta, meaning "the three-petalled context," comparable to a flower having three petals.

Apparently an objective knowledge happens only when an internal subject gets into contact with an external object. Yet, as we have already seen, the ultimate Reality is one alone, *sat-cit-ānanda*. Then where does this subject-object duality arise from? It can only come from the one *sat-cit-ānanda*. How did the two originate from it? Being Consciousness (*cit*), it never remains devoid of *cetanā* or function, and its functioning is comparable to a bee fluttering its wings, as was seen at the beginning of Chapter 5. A bee's wings move always invisibly between two ends. So too Consciousness flutteringly moves between subjective awareness and objective awareness, creating the impression that subject and object have their own separate existences. This kind of function of *cit* was what was called *bhāna* (conditioned manifestation of Consciousness) earlier in Chapter 5. Subject (*ahanta*) and object (*idanta*) are thus merely two extreme poles between which *cit* or Consciousness flutters. Put otherwise, the one unconditioned and unmanifest *cit*, when conditioned, appears both as subject and object.

Even the external-internal differentiation is really a conditioned concept. The I-sense is within the person who knows, but he really is part of the world thought of as external or visible. Granted that the world is external, then the question arises, "External to what?" If it is external to "me," the knowing subject, then that "me" is also part of what we call external. Where then is what is to be called "the internal?" On the contrary, when the knowing subject is taken to be an internal phenomenon, then the question, "Internal to what?" arises. There is no proper answer.

In short, the world is thought of as external and the knowing subject as internal, only in a relative sense. Absolutely, nothing is external; nothing is internal.

It is in this sense that the internal-external division is thought of as *sopādhika* or conditioned. Every knowledge thought of as a knower knowing an object different from itself, thus, is a conditioned knowledge (*sopādhika-jñāna*). This event of knowing takes place in the unconditioned Consciousness or *cit* as its conditioned functional manifestation (*bhāna-vṛtti*).

The unconditioned knowledge is one alone in number, and so it is not classifiable. The conditioned knowledge varies according to the conditioning factors. Of such various conditioned knowledges, a few are touched upon in the verses that follow.

Verse 3

अनात्मनामहङ्कारादीनां येनानुभूयते ।
साक्षी तदात्मज्ञानं स्याद्येनैवामृतमश्यते ॥३॥

anātmanām ahaṁkārādīnāṁ yenānubhūyate I
sākṣī tad ātmajñānaṁ syād yenaivāmṛtam aśyate II3 II

> That knowledge by which the witnessing consciousness that is aware of the non-self factors like the I-sense, becomes known, is called self-knowledge (*ātma-jñāna*), through which one enjoys immortality.

Knowledge was first classified as the unconditioned and the conditioned. The former was then defined, followed by the definition of the latter. The former type of knowledge is unclassifiable, because there is only one knowledge of that kind. All the varieties of knowledge defined in the remaining verses are therefore to be considered as examples of the conditioned knowledge.

As we have seen, the unconditioned knowledge is the one in which there is no room for the subject-object duality, whereas the other type of knowledge is conditioned by the division of subject and object. Anything can become an object of knowledge, but the knowing subject is always *ātmā* or the self. The object then could be counted as the non-self or *anātmā*, meaning "that which is not the self." This non-self need necessarily be something external. Even one's own mental functions that one becomes conscious of, pertain to the realm of the non-self here.

It was the knowing I-consciousness that was earlier called the subject, or *ahanta* or *ahaṁkāra*. Every human being is conscious also of knowing something, or of being the knower of something. That means, the subject itself becomes an object of knowledge sometimes. The subject or *ahaṁkāra* in such contexts thus functions as the non-self or *anātmā* as well. The subject could then be treated as the subtlest of all the non-self aspects. The non-self or *anātmā*, in other words, is inclusive of everything, from the subtlest I-sense to the grossest physical world.

As the non-self ranges from the most subtle I-sense to the most gross physical world, so does the knowledge concerning the non-self as well. Its extensiveness could be thought of as extending from the fully wakeful knowledge (*jāgṛta*) to the state of deep sleep (*suṣupti*) where nothing is known. The sense, "I am the experiencer" runs through all such states, whether waking, dreaming or sleeping, and this I-sense is what the word *ahaṁkāra* signifies. This *ahaṁkāra* is consciously felt by us in both the waking and dreaming states, whereas it is felt unconsciously in the deep sleep state. Though the happiness or soundness of the sleep is experienced right when one is sleeping, one would not then be conscious of doing so. One feels to have slept soundly, only after waking up. Apparently thus, the I-sense, though unconscious, was functioning even in sound sleep.

Consciousness functions also as a witness that perceives its own altering states such as waking, sleeping and deep sleep. This witnessing function does not occur only in one particular state, but all through them, hence its name in Vedānta is *avasthā-traya-sākṣin* (the witness of the three states). This witnessing consciousness is the real *ātmā*, the real "I." It transcends the three altering states. It transcends the differentiation of the past, present and future. It transcends the bounds of the three worlds. It is beyond *tripuṭi*. Realizing one's identity with this witnessing consciousness is to be called self-knowledge or *ātma-jñāna*, and this realization transcends all the conditionings.

When we are aware of this witnessing consciousness, remaining at the back of all knowledge, it could also be thought of as something known, as an object of knowledge, as if it also pertains to the *idanta* aspect. To that extent, it is also a conditioned knowledge. What we can safely say about it is that it is the conditioned knowledge closest to, or one step below, the unconditioned and ineffable one.

Even the awareness "I am the witnessing consciousness" vanishes when self-knowledge intensifies itself to attain the status of unconditioned knowledge. The latter would simply be a blissful experience of getting lost in the primeval Greatness of the one Consciousness-Substance, as the Guru himself puts it in Verse 4 of his *Ātmopadeśa Śatakam*. The Upaniṣads prefer to compare it to the event of a drop of water falling into the ocean of pure water.

It also is the state in which one directly experiences one's own immortality. The self-knowledge (*ātma-jñāna*) described here, then, is the innermost door that opens to the *sanctum sanctorum* of immortality. Thus, it is qualified here as "through which one enjoys immortality," instead of saying "itself is the experience of immortality."

The difference among the unconditioned knowledge (*nirupādhika-jñāna*) defined in Verse 1, the self-knowledge (*ātma-jñāna*) portrayed here, and the transcendental knowledge (*para-jñāna*) to be defined later in Verse 10, really is extremely subtle. The unconditioned knowledge can be defined only negatively, i.e., as what it is not (that which is devoid of I-sense and the like), because the moment it is positively defined, it becomes conditioned (*sopādhika*). But self-knowledge and transcendental knowledge are definable positively as what these are, and to that extent they are definable, and thus conditioned.

The overall methodology resorted to in this work to reveal the secret of Vedāntic wisdom, we know, is that of portraying ten different pictures of one and the same non-dual Reality, viewing it from ten different angles. The ultimate goal of this wisdom is attaining immortality, i.e. one realizing, "I am the birthless and deathless *Ātmā*." Pots, plates, pans and such utensils are destroyable, but clay, the substance of which these are made, is indestructible; it neither has a beginning nor an end. We can safely say, a pot realizing "I am the birthless and deathless clay" is its self-realization, is its attaining immortality. Each of us is in the place of a pot. What is the clay-like substance of which we are made? That Reality is called *Ātmā* in Vedānta, translatable loosely as "the Self" in English. In the place of the pot-appearance are to be seen both the physical and mental aspects of our being.

One who realizes, "I am not an individual; I am really the one *Ātmā*," and who lives as an embodiment of this enlightenment is the one who actually experiences immortality (*amṛtatva*) while living. Such are to be called *jīvanmukta*s. Self-knowledge (*ātma-jñāna*) is the royal path that leads us to this goal. *Ātma-jñāna*, in short, means my knowing the essential content of my own being. It means, becoming aware that I am the witnessing Consciousness which remains immortal and changeless, while being fully aware of all the changes and everything changeful and their mortality.

What is to be defined in the next verse is *anātma-jñāna* (the knowledge of the non-self), the opposite of *ātma-jñāna*. *Ātma-jñāna*, in short, means, the one unconditioned consciousness becoming conditioned by assuming the form of the search for the reality in one's own being, and finally realizing, "I am the witnessing Consciousness." The same one unconditioned Consciousness, becoming conditioned in a different way, assumes the form of the knowledge concerning innumerable objects existing as if different from it. Such a conditioned knowledge is to be called *anātma-jñāna*, as the Guru defines it in the next verse.

Verse 4

अहङ्कारादि कार्यं यदनात्मकमसङ्ख्यकम् ।
येनावगम्यतेऽनात्मज्ञानं तदवधार्यते ॥४॥

ahaṁkārādi kāryaṁ yad anātmakam asaṅkhyakam I
yenāvagamyate 'nātmajñānaṁ tad avadhāryate II4 II

That knowing function of consciousness by which one becomes aware of countless non-self factors related to I-sense and similar effects, is to be understood as knowledge of the non-self (*anātma-jñāna*).

What is designated as *anātma-jñāna* (knowledge of the non-self) is the knowing function of consciousness by which the non-self aspect becomes understood. What is meant by *anātmā* or the non-self? Everything that could be considered as effects of the primeval cause could be treated as pertaining to the realm of the non-self. Everything apparent or conceivable that emerges from the one non-apparent and inconceivable causal Substance is an effect. Having examined the nature of the cause-effect relationship in Chapter 2 earlier, we know already that an effect has no existence separate from the cause.

Using the terminology of Chapter 5 (*Bhāna Darśanam*), we could safely say that whatever appears manifestly (*bhāsya*) is a non-self factor. Such manifestations of consciousness (*bhāna*) can be gross (*sthūla*), subtle (*sūkṣma*), causal (*kāraṇa*) or the fourth (*turīya*) in nature, as was seen in that chapter. Each of these specifiable functional modes of consciousness (*bhāna*) involves its own particular *bhāsya* or object aspect as well. All are superimposed (*adhyasta*) in the one non-superimposed (*anadhyasta*), unmanifest Reality or *Ātmā*. All such superimpositions are unreal on themselves and constitute the non-self or *anātmā* aspect understood here.

Śaṅkara, in his *Vivekacūḍāmaṇi* (Crest-jewel of Discrimination), makes a detailed examination of the non-self. He perceives its range as having three different bodies (*śarīra*s) — the gross body (*sthūla śarīra*), subtle body (*sūkṣma śarīra*), and causal body (*kāraṇa śarīra*). Deviating from this line of thought, the Guru here points out that the I-sense (*ahaṁkāra*) or one's feeling of being the knowing subject is the subtlest form of the non-self. Beginning with it, the range of the non-self extends to include the entire objective world.

Though it is termed *anātmā* or the non-self, a real seer does not see it as something different from the Self or *Ātmā*, but only as various manifest self-expressions of the one unmanifest *Ātmā*. That means, the one *Ātmā* manifests itself as many apparent forms, both subjective and objective, and the very same *Ātmā* becomes conscious of such forms of its own, and such a knowledge is what is meant by *anātma-jñāna*. In short, even knowing what *anātma-jñāna* is, in a way, can be a particular facet of realizing the one Reality or *Ātmā*.

Verse 5

यथावद्वस्तुविज्ञानं रज्जुतत्त्वावबोधवत् ।
यत्तद्यथार्थविज्ञानमयथार्थमतोऽन्यथा ॥५॥

yathāvad vastuvijñānaṁ rajjutattvāvabodhavat ।
yat tad yathārtha-vijñānam ayathārtham ato 'nyathā ॥5॥

That knowing function of consciousness by which things are known as they really are, as when a piece of rope is known really as rope, is known as factual knowledge (*yathārtha-jñāna*), the opposite of it is known as fictitious knoweldge (*ayathārtha-jñāna*).

Yathārtha-jñāna or factual knowledge could be defined as the knowledge of the meaning content of the object correctly as it is. Knowing an object entails formulating an image in the mind corresponding to the perceived object. Are we sure that the image thus formulated corresponds exactly to the object perceived? No. For example, when perceiving an object with our eyes the nature of the experience we have depends on many factors such as the intensity of the external light, the physical condition of our eyes, even the interest we have in the thing perceived and many such factors. A colour-blind person perceives the world in colours different from that perceived by people with normal vision.

The experience of the size of an object depends on its distance from the eyes. Something 10 centimetre in size, placed half a kilometre away, appears to be imperceptibly small. The same object, if placed close to the nose, will look too big even to see it in full. Which of such many sizes experienceable is the real size of the thing? We stand dumbfounded unable to asnwer.

Our feeling is that we are perceiving the world continuously. The actual perception of the world is the result of the functioning of our five sense organs and mind together. But, owing to some natural law, all our sense organs do not function together with equal intensity. When the mind concentrates on hearing a sound, for example, the functioning of the other four sense organs becomes dimmed, and sometimes even cut off at least for a fraction of a moment. The world in its wholeness is to be perceived with all the sense organs functioning with equal keenness, an event that never happens. Then, is the form of the world we experience, the real one? Probably not so.

What then is the real form and nature of the world? Being something not yet fully perceived with our senses, it is unthinkable and inconceivable as well. There exist, therefore, conflicting opinions about the conformity of the perceived world with the actual world. Those who opine that the actual world is different in form from the experienced one, are known as epistemological dualists. Those who think that the perceived world corresponds exactly to the world existing outside are called epistemological monists. Knowing something as it exists, is what the Guru defines here as *yathārtha-jñāna* (factual knowledge), its opposite being *ayathārtha-jñāna* (fictitious knowledge). This "something" could be a specific entity perceived with one or more of our sense organs. It could also be the one all-underlying Substance. Factual knowledge is possible concerning both.

It is possible that something is mistaken for something else, for example, a piece of rope could be taken for a snake, a mother-of-pearl could be mistaken for silver. Such examples of fictitious knowledge (*ayathārtha-jñāna*) happen in the realm of sense perception. Factual knowledge in these cases is that of seeing the piece of rope as piece of rope, and the mother-of-pearl as mother-of-pearl. The same kinds of factual knowledge and fictitious knowledge are possible concerning what ultimate exists as well. There the fictitious knowledge (*ayathārtha-jñāna*) is that of seeing the ultimate Reality as the world, and factual knowledge (*yathārtha-jñāna*), knowing the ultimate Reality as ultimate Reality, regardless of it appearing in the form of the world. This kind of factual knowledge about the ultimate Reality, in traditional Vedānta, is known as *paramārtha-jñāna* (the real knowledge of the ultimate Reality).

Gold is the reality in an ornament. But seeing the gold as gold is not common, for it becomes visible only in various ornament forms. Those forms are transitorily assumed by the indestructible gold-substance. The possibility of seeing gold, therefore, is in and through the ornament forms only. Seeing a piece of gold-ornament placed before us as gold is *yathārtha-*

jñāna, and seeing it as an ornament is *ayathārtha-jñāna*. The entire world appearance is to be seen in the place of the ornament forms. Then, knowing the gold-like Substance that the world is made of, i.e., *Ātmā*, as real is *yathārtha-jñāna*, and seeing the apparent world as such as real is *ayathārtha-jñāna*. Those of speculative insight do not perceive the world as the world, but as the invisible *Ātmā* having assumed the visible world-form.

Seeing one Reality alone existing is called *jñāna* (wisdom) in Vedānta (we have already noticed that this word in the present chapter of the *Darśanamālā* is used with a slightly variant connotation). Those of this insight perceive in each and every changeful aspect and experience of life, different transitory facets of the one *Ātmā* becoming manifest.

The *Bhagavad-Gītā* calls this aspect of wisdom *vijñāna*, and it has set apart a whole chapter (Chapter 7) to elucidate it. For example, water is a particular manifestation of the Real, and its specific quality is having taste. When sipping water and tasting it, you should see in that experience the one Reality or *Ātmā* becoming manifest in a specific way, signified by the prefix "*vi*" of the word "*vijñāna*." That kind of awareness is *vijñāna*. The original words of the verse, "*yathāvad vastu-vijñānam*" are interpretable in this way as well.

Ayathārtha-jñāna (fictitious knowledge), the opposite of *yathārtha-jñāna*, means taking what appears before us as such as real, with no search made for finding out what underlies the appearance. This is like taking a piece of rope for a snake.

The Guru, in the next three verses, defines perceptual knowledge (*pratyakṣa-jñāna*), inferential knowledge (*anumiti-jñāna*) and analogical knowledge (*upamiti-jñāna*). These are the main three of the six types of valid means of knowledge acceptable to traditional Vedānta.

Verse 6

यत्सान्निध्यादेव सर्वं भासते स्वयमेव तत्।
प्रत्यक्षज्ञानमिति चा परोक्षमिति लक्ष्यते ॥६॥

yat sānnidhyād eva sarvaṁ bhāsate svayam eva tat ।
pratyakṣa-jñānam iti cāparokṣam iti lakṣyate ॥6॥

That knowing function of consciousness because of the presence of which everything appears to exist by themselves, is knowledge by direct perception (*pratyakṣa-jñāna*). What is known as direct insight (*aparokṣa-jñāna*) also is to be understood secondarily as of the same nature.

Prati + *akṣam* is *pratyakṣam*. *Akṣam* means sense organs, and *prati*, face to face with. That which comes face to face with our sense organs could thus be termed *pratyakṣam*. What we examine here is *pratyakṣa-jñāna* or perceptual knowledge. Customarily it is defined as the knowledge we acquire when our senses come into contact with their objects. All other kinds of knowledge together are classified as *parokṣa-jñāna* or indirect knowledge. Yet another kind of knowledge that is neither direct perception nor indirect knowledge is the knowledge we each have of ourselves.

My being is not in contact with any of my sense organs. Thus my self-knowledge is not perceptual knowledge. Nor can it be said to be indirect knowledge. Vedānta invented a new name to signify it: *aparokṣa-jñāna*, meaning non-indirect knowledge. It is not a sort of knowledge in which a subject becomes aware of an object. It is simply an experience of self-beingness. In this sense, it is sometimes called *aparokṣa-anubhūti*, *anubhūti* meaning indescribable intuitive experience. Śaṅkara, with a view to expounding the indescribability of this experience, composed a Vedāntic text under the very same title.

Though differentiating direct perceptual knowledge from indirect knowledge is easily possible, doing so between direct perception (*pratyakṣa-jñāna*) and non-indirect knowledge (*aparokṣa-jñāna*) in definite terms is not an easy task. The Guru here, in his own way, treats the two as if almost synonymous. In what sense he does so, is a matter of interest to any serious student of Vedānta.

Six are the *pramāṇa*s or valid means of knowledge acceptable to Vedāntic epistemology: *pratyakṣa* (perception) *anumāna* (inference), *upamāna* (analogy), *arthāpatti* (postulation), *anupalabdhi* (impossibility) and *śabda* or *śruti* (*a priori* verbal testimony). How and in what sense these various *pramāṇa*s are acceptable to a non-dualist Vedāntin is clarified by Dharmarāja Adhvarīndra in his famous book *Vedānta Paribhāṣā* (Vedānta Expounded), one of the basic textbooks for those who learn Advaita Vedānta in the traditional manner. A separate long chapter is set apart in it for each *pramāṇa*. The word *pramāṇa* is defined by him as *pramā-karaṇam pramāṇam,* meaning, that which is instrumental to arriving at definite knowledge is *pramāṇa*.

Dharmarāja Adhvarīndra, while thinking of the perceptibility of something, differentiates object-related perceptibility (*viṣaya-gata-pratyakṣa*) from knowledge-related perceptibility. In order to contrast the two, we should first know what are the factors involved in a situation of perceptual knowledge.

A Vedāntin's basic stand, as we know, is that Reality is one alone, and it is *cit* or *caitanya* (Consciousness) in essence. This one Consciousness becomes conditioned (*upahita*) in three ways in the context of perceptual knowledge. These are *viṣaya-caitanya* (consciousness become conditioned as the object), *pramātṛ-caitanya* (consciousness become conditioned as the subject), and *pramāṇa-caitanya* (consciousness become conditioned as the means of knowledge). The one Consciousness, in its conditioned state, appearing as objects like pots and fruits with which senses have contact, is called *viṣaya-caitanya* or *viṣayopahita-caitanya*. The same Consciousness, having become conditioned, appearing as the mental faculties of the knower, is called *pramātṛ-caitanya*. These mental faculties have necessarily to function when perceiving something. The one Consciousness, in its conditioned state, appearing as these functionings of the mental faculties, is called *pramāṇa-caitanya* by Dharmarāja Adhvarīndra. Granted all these, the context of a perceptual knowledge is portrayed by him as follows:

Suppose water is stored up in a reservoir. In order to direct it to agricultural farms for irrigation purposes, first we make a hole in the wall of the reservoir. Water then flows out through the hole and enters a channel assuming its form. Finally it reaches the farm land and assumes its form. Likewise, the mental faculties (*pramātṛ-caitanya*), through the outlet of sense organs, enters the objects and assumes their form. This transformation is what is called *antaḥkaraṇa-vṛtti*s or mental functions, here termed *pramāṇa-caitanya*.

It is really one *caitanya* alone that becomes conditioned and appears both as the mental faculties (*pramātṛ-caitanya*) and their functions (*pramāṇa-caitanya*). This transformation results in consciousness becoming identified with or assuming the form of the object, which is yet another form in which the one Consciousness manifests.

What really happens in the event of perceptual knowledge taking place is this: *viṣaya-caitanya*, *pramātṛ-caitanya* and *pramāṇa-caitanya* — all give up their conditioning factors and realize their real oneness for a moment. A perceptual knowledge thus is nothing but a bit of the event of Consciousness or *Ātmā* realizing its real oneness. This, according to Dharmarāja Adhvarīndra, is the nature of object-related perceptual knowledge (*viṣaya-gata-pratyakṣa*).

Now coming to knowledge-related perceptibility (*jñāna-gata-pratyakṣatva*) such as in the case of "I know myself," "I feel happy," "I feel unhappy," what makes such knowledge different from the object-related perception (*viṣaya-gata-pratyakṣa*) is that the subjective consciousness (*pramātṛ-caitanya*) does not go out through the outlets of sense organs. In this case, the objective consciousness is where the subjective consciousness also is. Therefore, the latter going out in search of the former does not become necessary. The location of both being the same, their attaining identity, or realizing their intrinsic oneness by giving up the respective conditioning factors, also takes place at the very same spot. Though involving no sense contact, the *pramātṛ-caitanya* (subjective consciousness) and *prameya-caitanya* (objective consciousness) come together and find their identity. This sort of perceptual experience is comparable to the *mānasa-pratyakṣa* (mental perception) conceived by the Nyāya system. Involving no sense contact and being no indirect knowledge, this kind of perception could as well be termed, as is done by Narayana Guru here, *aparokṣa-jñāna* (non-indirect perception). The Guru treating both *pratyakṣa-jñāna* (perceptual knowledge) and *aparokṣa-jñāna* (non-indirect knowledge) as if synonymous, could well be pondered on in the light of the above-mentioned concept of the knowledge-related perception (*jñāna-gata-pratyakṣa*) of Dharmarāja Adhvarīndra. The Guru's definition of perceptual knowledge is thus: "That knowing function of consciousness because of the presence of which everything appears to exist by themselves" (*yat sānnidhyād eva sarvam bhāsate svayam eva tat*). A generalized definition, this could include both the perceptual knowledge and the non-indirect knowledge within its scope.

It is neither sense contact nor the functioning of the mental faculties that the Guru takes seriously here. There is within each of us a knowing faculty that enables us to discriminate every entity we come across, as "This is such and such," or "This is so and so." No knowing takes place in us in its absence, nor would the presence of the world be felt in its absence. This functioning faculty within is what the Guru designates here as *pratyakṣa-jñāna* (perceptual knowledge). It is what enables us to discriminate an object we perceive as "This is such and such an object," and the subjective experience as "This is knowledge," or "This is a subjective feeling."

Verse 7

ययाऽनुसाधकं साध्यं मीयते ज्ञानरूपया ।
वृत्त्या साऽनुमितिस्साहचर्यसंस्कारजन्यया ॥७ ॥

yayā 'nusādhakaṁ sādhyaṁ mīyate jñānarūpayā ।
vṛttyā sā 'numitiḥ sāhacaryasaṁskārajanyayā ॥7 ॥

The knowing function of consciousness that arises from the memory of some previous experience of concomittance, which helps one predicate something as something, with the help of a leading cause, is inferential knowledge (*anumiti-jñāna*).

Anumāna (inference) is the one valid means of knowledge (*pramāṇa*) acceptable to all the Indian schools of thought aside from the materialists (Cārvākas). The inferential knowledge (*anumiti-jñāna*) defined here, is the certainty we arrive at with the help of inference (*anumāna*). *Vyāpti-jñāna* or the awareness of invariable concomittance is what is instrumental in this kind of knowledge. For example, there will be fire wherever there is smoke; but it need not be true that there is smoke wherever there is fire. There can be fire burning without smoke, as in the case of gas-stoves. That means, the context of fire burning is wider in range than the contexts of fire burning without smoke. Such awareness of the comparability of the concomittance of the minor term and major term is known as *vyāpti-jñāna*.

To elucidate: seeing smoke on a hill compels us to assume the presence of burning fire there. Such kind of certainty we arrive at is called *anumiti-jñāna* or inferential knowledge. Though the fire remains unperceived, smoke is perceived directly. Seeing smoke leads us to the knowledge of the presence of fire. "There is fire there" here is *sādhya* (the major term or predicating something as something) and the presence of smoke is the middle term or *hetu* that leads to the conclusion, "There is fire there." This middle term is called here *anusādhaka* (that which helps one to predicate). All the places where we see smoke come within the range of the places having the presence of fire. Therefore, the *anusādhaka*, smoke, leads to the *sādhya*, "There is fire there." Having cognizance of this comparability of the range of the regions having smoke and that having fire, as well as the like phenomena, is known as *vyāpti-jñāna*.

How do we get at this *vyāpti-jñāna*? How do we arrive at the conclusion that fire must be there where smoke is seen? In our kitchens we have seen fire burning with smoke, and we have seen smoke only where fire burns and no where else. Such invariable co-existence of a causal phenomenon and an effect-phenomenon, is known as *sāhacarya*, literally the state of being together or moving together. In Western logic this is called "invariable concomittance." Seeing directly the co-existence of these two — fire and smoke together in our kitchen — had left in us a sort of memory or latent impression of it, called *sāhacarya-saṁskāra*. In its absence no inferential knowledge would be possible. This latent idea, *hetu* or causal sign when present (the smoke), leads us to predicate something about what we see (that there is fire in the hill). What is precisely defined as inferential knowledge (*anumiti-jñāna*) in this verse is the function of consciousness that leads us to such a conclusion or to the major premise. The traditional Nyāya system of Indian philosophy calls what is termed here as *anusādhaka* as *hetu* or *liṅga*, and the major premise *pratijñā* or *nigamana*.

In the case of inferential knowledge there also occurs the coming together of the *pramātṛ-caitanya* (subjective consciousness), the *prameya-caitanya* (objective consciousness) and the *pramāṇa-caitanya* (the function of the subjective consciousness). In this case, the objective consciousness appears as existing externally (in the hill), the knower's mind and its knowing function are within, and the knowing function happens because of the *sāhacarya-saṁskāra*. In short, in this case also, the three conditioned states of consciousness — the mind, its function and the corresponding external object — forgo their conditionings and realize their intrinsic oneness. That means, inferential knowledge, in the perception of the non-dual vision of Vedānta, is really yet another instance of realizing one's self-identity with the pure Consciousness or *Ātmā* or *caitanya*.

One of the peculiarities of inferential knowledge is that it is only possible in the case of things of which we have had previous perceptual experience. For example, unless we had seen previously the togetherness of smoke with fire, we would never be able to infer the presence of fire on seeing smoke. For this reason, any sort of guesswork or conjecturing, though valid, cannot be counted as *anumāna* or inference. Vedāntins, therefore, had to admit *upamāna* (comparison), *arthāpatti* (postulation) and *anupalabdhi* (impossibility) also as *pramāṇas* or valid means of knowledge.

Verse 8

गत्वा समीपं मेयस्य मीयते श्रुतलक्षणः ।
यया संवित्सोपमितिर्मृगोऽयमिति रूपया ॥८॥

gatvā samīpaṁ meyasya mīyate śruta-lakṣaṇaḥ ।
yayā saṁvit sopamitir mṛgo 'yam iti rūpayā ॥8॥

The function of consciousness by which an object, for example, an animal, is ascertained by going near it and discerning, "This is the animal whose characteristics were previously heard of," is knowledge by comparison (*upamiti*).

Inference, we just saw, is the kind of certainty we arrive at regarding a major premise, led by a middle term or *hetu*. This certainty becomes possible only because of our previous experience of the two existing together. The nature of *upamiti-jñāna* (knowledge by comparison or analogy) is just the opposite of inference. Suppose we have heard of something in detail, but have never seen it. Then, if after sometime, we happen to see it directly, we recognize the object to be what we have heard of. The function of consciousness that enables this kind of certainty is known as *upamiti-jñāna* (knowledge by comparison or analogy).

For example, a man hears of a wild animal known as *gavaya* which is almost like a cow. All its features are well described to him. One day he happens to go to the forest and sees an animal having all the features he had heard of. Then he decides, "This is the *gavaya* I have heard of." This is an example of *upamiti-jñāna*. Directly seeing the object about which we become certain occurs earlier in the case of inference, whereas it happens at the end in the case of comparison or analogy. In this case also the conditioned aspects of consciousness — *prameya-caitanya, pramātṛ-caitanya* and *pramāṇa-caitanya* — give up their respective conditioning factors and realize their intrinsic oneness.

Though Vedāntins traditionally admit six means of knowledge (*pratyakṣa* or perception, *anumāna* or inference, *upamāna* or comparison, *arthāpatti* or postulation, *anupalabdhi* or impossibility, and *śabda* or *śruti* or verbal testimony) as valid, only the first three are defined by the Guru here. He might have treated the fourth and fifth as coming under inference. The *para-jñāna* (transcendental knowledge) defined in Verse 10 could well be treated as marking the ultimate limit of *śabda-jñāna* or *śruti-jñāna* (knowledge by scriptural evidence).

The next verse classifies all the knowledge-experiences we have in our day-to-day life, as *jīva-jñāna* (self-related knowledge) and *indriya-jñāna* (sense-knowledge).

Verse 9

अहं ममेति ज्ञानं यदिदं तदिति यच्च तत्।
जीवज्ञानं तदपरमिन्द्रियज्ञानमिष्यते ॥९॥

aham mameti jñānaṁ yad idaṁ tad iti yacca tat ।
jīva-jñānaṁ tad aparam indriya-jñānam iṣyate ॥9॥

The knowledge by which one becomes aware of "I" and "mine" is self-related knowledge (*jīva-jñāna*). The other knowledge by which we know "this" and "that" is spoken of as sense-knowledge (*indriya-jñāna*).

Jīva-jñāna (self-related knowledge) and *indriya-jñāna* (sense-knowledge) do not find place in the classification of the conditioned knowledge (*sopādhika-jñāna*) acceptable to classical Vedānta tradition. This addition could be considered as an outcome of the influence of modernity in Vedāntic speculation.

The Guru's own *Ātmopadeśa Śatakam* (One Hundred Verses of Self-Instruction) deals with this categorization in many contexts. It is asserted at the very middle of the work that everything knowable, from the most subtle to the most gross, from the most general and abstract to the most specific and concrete, becomes sublimated as the transcendental being of the one unconditioned pure Consciousness or *arivu*.

Immediately following this assertion is the statement that the very pure unconditioned Consciousness becomes conditioned basically in two ways — as *ahanta* (subjective consciousness) and *idanta* (objective consciousness). These two conditioned aspects together, like two creepers entwining and growing over a tree with flowers and fruits, create through their intermingling, the impression of the existence of the phenomenal world (see Verses 50 and 51).

Towards the end of the same work, the Guru shows how, because of *māyā*, one *prakṛti* or nature, appears on the one side as the enjoyer and on the other as the enjoyable world (see Verse 81). Also in the very first verse of the work, the Guru underscores the reality that it is one Core-Reality (*karu*) that manifestly shines both in the form of the knower and the world known. Such a division of the internal and external worlds is all the more important in modern philosophy, science and psychology. The *jīva-jñāna* and *indriya-jñāna* defined here, referring as they are to the knowledge one has of oneself and of the objects with which one can have sense contact, correspond more or less with the above-mentioned double conditionings of consciousness.

The I-sense each of us has is what is termed *ahanta* here by the Guru. Inseparable from this I-sense are the countless mental functions and the mental images it creates. All these together could well be considered as "mine" (*mama*). The I-sense and mine-sense together constitute the interior or subjective world. This world might seem to be an extremely subtle and very tiny one, but really it is not so. Each entity existing externally has a corresponding mental image in the interior world. This latter world thus is as extensive as the former. The I-sense has also the power to imagine things and events that are quite unrelated to the external world, to create a world of its own, and in that sense we could say, the interior world is more extensive than the exterior one. Knowing the entire realm of all these mental functions together — the I-sense, its sense of being the knower, enjoyer and doer, the ideas it formulates and the imaginary world it creates, all these taken together — is termed here as *jīva-jñāna, jīva* standing for the individual living being or person, and *jñāna* for knowledge. The Guru skilfully defines the entire range of the subjective world concisely as *aham mameti jñānam,* meaning, "The knowledge of 'I' and 'mine'."

Idanta means "the state of being this or *idam*." Everything in this world is discernible as "This is such and such." All such knowledge is acquired through sense-contact. The function of consciousness by which such certainties are arrived at is defined by the Guru as *indriya-jñāna* (sense-knowledge), as if this is his observation of a prevailing popular opinion, as the words "spoken of as" (*iṣyate*) suggest.

A question now naturally arises: how to differentiate between perceptual knowledge (*pratyakṣa-jñāna*) and sense-knowledge (*indriya-jñāna*), particularly in view of the fact that the word *pratyakṣa* has in it the word *"akṣa,"* meaning sense-organs or *indriyas*. Perception, we know, is customarily defined as the knowledge we gain by means of the contact the senses have with their objects. But, as defined by the Guru in this chapter, it is much wider in scope, for it could include even what is termed as *aparokṣa-jñāna* or non-indirect knowledge (see Verse 6 above and the comment on it). We could therefore safely say that perceptual knowledge is much wider in scope than sense-knowledge. Furthermore, differentiating knowledge as perception, inference and comparison becomes relevant when our concern is for the validity of the means of knowledge (*pramāṇa*s), whereas the self-related knowledge and sense-knowledge are distinguished when we think of the interiority or exteriority of the objects known. That means, these two classifications of knowledge pertain to two different epistemological contexts, neither depending on nor affecting the credibility of the other.

Endless is the way in which the knowing function of consciousness works, and therefore classifying and defining all sorts of conditioned knowledges (*sopādhika-jñāna*) is an impossibility. Therefore, instead of going into such details endlessly, the chapter ends with the next verse defining *para-jñāna* or transcendental knowledge.

Verse 10

ॐ तत्सदिति निर्दिष्टं ब्रह्मात्मैक्यमुपागतम् ।
कल्पनादिविहीनं यत्तत्परज्ञानमीर्यते ॥१० ॥

auṁ tat sad iti nirdiṣṭaṁ brahmātmaikyam upāgatam ।
kalpanādi vihīnaṁ yat tat para-jñānam īryate ॥10 ॥

That which is signified by the words *auṁ tat sat* (*Auṁ* — That is what exists) and experientially attained as the oneness of *Brahman* and oneself, free from thoughts, imaginations and the like — that is spoken of as transcendental knowledge (*para-jñāna*).

That *jñāna* is basically one, and that the same appears both as conditioned knowledge (*sopādhika-jñāna*) and unconditioned knowledge (*nirupādhika-jñāna*) was stated in Verse 1. The transcendental knowledge (*para-jñāna*) defined here, in essence, is the state in which one finds oneself merged in the being of the one *jñāna* that appears in the above-mentioned two manifest forms. *Para-jñāna*, in other words, could be considered as the *nirupādhika-jñāna* (unconditioned knowledge) introduced in experiential terms.

Extremely subtle is the difference between the unconditioned knowledge (*nirupādhika-jñāna*) and the Transcendental knowledge (*para-jñāna*). The former was defined in Verse 1 as *ahaṁkārādi-hīnam yat jñānam* (that *jñāna* which is devoid of I-sense and the like). That means, it is the knowledge in which there is no room for the subject-object duality or the triple factors of the knower, known and knowledge. In fact, it is a sort of negative definition clarifying what it is not, or what it lacks, rather than what it really is. The Transcendental knowledge (*para-jñāna*), on the other hand, is given here a positive definition saying clearly what its essential content is — a content that is nothing other than what the great dictum *auṁ tat sat* signifies, and is experienced as *brahmātmaikya* (one's own identity with the Absolute).

The definition of *nirupādhika-jñāna* (unconditioned knowledge) given here arouses interest in clearly knowing in an academic way, what it is. But the definition of *para-jñāna* (Transcendental knowledge) is entirely of a different order. Its content, even according to this definition, is the direct experience of one's self-identity with *Brahman* or the Absolute — the ultimate goal of all Vedāntic enquiry. This definition arouses in the seeker an inner longing to attain that state of realization. The attribute *kalpanādi-vihīnam* (free from thoughts, imagination and the like), on the other hand, is almost in line with the defining factor *ahaṁkārādi hīnam* (devoid of the I-sense and the like) of the *nirupādhika-jñāna*.

Auṁ tat sat is a famous dictum as important as the four traditional *mahāvākyas* (great dicta) of Vedānta. It also is a *mantra* (sacred formula) which is sometimes made use of for meditation purposes by spiritual seekers. What it signifies is this: that Reality (*tat*) which is signified by the monosyllable *AUṀ*, is what really exists (*sat*). The significance of *AUṀ* is detailed in the *Māṇḍūkya Upaniṣad*, and what the words *tat* (that) and *sat* (existence) stand for is explicated in the *Chāndogya Upaniṣad* as it deals with the great dictum *tat tvam asi* (That thou art) in its Chapter 6. That section begins with the well known sentence *sad eva somya idam agra āsīt* (in the beginning, my dear, this world was *sat* alone). The Guru's words defining *para-jñāna* here, *"AUṀ tat sat iti nirdiṣṭam"* (that which is signified by the words *AUṀ tat sat*) are to be meditated upon with all this for its backdrop.

Brahmātmaikya (*Brahma* + *ātmā* + *aikya*), meaning "one's self-identity with *Brahman* or the Absolute," is often mixed up with the notion *jīva-brahmaikya* (the oneness of the individual soul with the cosmic soul or *Brahman*), though in a misconstrued sense of both the terms. According to that interpretation, the body aspect of our individual existence is simply ignored as unreal, considering the *jīva* or soul aspect alone as real. Similarly, the physical existence of the cosmic system is thought of as non-existent and the imaginary cosmic soul (*Brahman*) as real. Then the essential oneness of the individual soul and cosmic soul is asserted, and is treated as what non-duality (*advaita*) means. But a close familiarity with the Upaniṣads will reveal the fact that Vedānta does not treat anything as non-existent or unreal. On the other hand, it considers all the appearances as different manifest forms of the one absolute Reality (*sat*), that alone has its own existence. In other words, Vedānta holds that although apparent forms, material as well as mental, do not exist on their own, their evanescent existence derives from the eternal existence of the one *sat*, the non-dual *Brahman*. This is amply evident from the famous dictum *sarvaṁ khalvidaṁ brahma* (everything here indeed is *Brahman*), of the *Chāndogya Upaniṣad* (III.14.1). The appearances are thus not absolutely unreal. One Reality exists in all of them. One eternal *sat* manifests as all the individual evanescent entities of which "I" too is one such. "I" (*ātmā*), when striving to find out what is real in "me," realizes that that Reality is nothing but *Brahman*. Besides, the most direct way of knowing that *Brahman* is, in the form "I really am That," just as a gold-ornament realizes, "Really I am gold,"as denoted by another of the famous dicta *so 'ham* (I am That). This experience of the seeker's self-identity with what he seeks is the real significance of the compound word *brahmātmaikyam*.

The chapter began with the assertion that *jñāna* is one alone, and that it becomes manifest both as conditioned and unconditioned knowledges. We have also understood from the studies pursued so far that one primeval Substance or *sat* alone is Real and that it is pure Consciousness (*cit*) in essence.

A question then naturally arises: if one *cit* alone has existence, then where did the factors that condition it arise from? As was seen at the beginning of the *Bhāna Darśanam* (Chapter 5), the *bhāna* or functional self-expression of *cit* is like a motion fluttering in between subjectivity and objectivity, and that it results in the appearance of the gross, subtle, causal and *turīya* forms of *bhāna*, each having its own generic and specific facets. It is this *bhāna* or the restless self-expression of consciousness that becomes a sort of conditioning factor that veils the real nature of *cit* itself, resulting in knowledge of the same also becoming conditioned.

An enlightened person, even when living in this world involved in conditioned knowledges and engaged in worldly affairs, would constantly be well aware of the reality that all such are merely one *jñāna* becoming variously manifest. This awareness enables one to maintain an unceasing sense of detachment towards everything worldly and conditioned one is involved in oneself. In short, a *jñānin* or an enlightened one is not merely a person who is constantly lost in the ecstacy of the Transcendental knowledge (*para-jñāna*), but is a person who remains unattached towards one's own worldly activities, conditioned knowledges and their outcomes, with an inner transparent perception of one *jñāna* alone finding self-expression as both the conditioned and unconditioned knowledges.

8

Bhakti Darśanam
(Vision by Bhakti)

THE five chapters of the second half of the *Darśanamālā* present us with five different facets of an individual experiencing his oneness with the whole or *Brahman*. Of these facets, the most exterior one is that of actions (*karmas*). One finding one's actions as inseparably one with the flow of actions of the total nature was the topic we dealt with in Chapter 6. More interior and subtle than the field of actions is the realm of knowing (*jñāna*) we have just covered in the last chapter. Still more interiorized than knowing is the emotional coming together of the individual being with the total being — the realm of *bhakti*. Though the term is commonly translated as "devotion," it is here to be understood as having the undertones of a contemplative mood.

Bhakti is a word given varied connotations by various systems, traditions and cults. In the religious context it means a sort of emotional rapport a supplicant develops towards God or the deity he worships. One's attitude of surrendering oneself and everything to God's will, called *prapatti*, is also a form of *bhakti*. One offshoot of this form of emotional *bhakti* is the popular religious expression of singing exhilarating songs, called *bhajanas*. Temples and other places of worship developed as an extended version of this *bhakti*. Without going into the details of such varieties of *bhakti*, the Guru deals with it in the

Bhakti Darśanam, giving more weight to the philosophical insight of non-duality than to the emotional aspects. *Bhakti*, according to him, is one of the facets of experientially perceiving one's oneness with *Brahman* or the Absolute.

Bhakti is a word derived from the verb root *bhaj*, meaning, "to do service by sitting nearby" (*bhaj sevāyām*). This sitting nearby and doing service need not necessarily be a physical act. The more virtual rather than actual it is, it becomes more sublime. The root also denotes: to be seated nearby, to partake of something, to meditate, to attain, to accept, to worship, none of which needs be excluded from the sense of *bhakti* understood here.

What is it that you become emotionally attached to? You always become naturally attracted towards that which makes you happy. You will automatically like it. This is the reason why *bhakti* and love always go together. Something becomes lovable to you, not because you like that particular object, but because you love happiness or *ānanda* it gives. This *ānanda*, in its turn, really is the essential content of your own being or *Ātmā*. The object you love also is yet another form in which the same *Ātmā* becomes manifest. This is one of the secret aspects of wisdom taught by the saint Yājñavalkya to his disciple and wife Maitreyī, in the *Bṛhadāraṇyaka Upaniṣad* (IV.5.6).

> Verily, not for the sake of the husband is the husband dear, but for the sake of the self is the husband dear. Verily, not for the sake of the wife is the wife dear, but for the sake of the self is the wife dear. Verily, not for the sake of the sons are the sons dear, but for the sake of the self are the sons dear. . . . Verily, not for the sake of all is all dear but for the sake of the self is all dear. Verily, the self is to be seen, to be heard, to be reflected on, to be meditated upon; when, verily, the self is seen, heard, reflected on and known, then all this is

known.

Following along these lines, the Guru also defines *bhakti* here as "meditation upon *ānanda*."

When we like something, our feeling is that it gives us happiness. It really is not the giver of happiness, for happiness is something that wells up from within our own being. It really remains dormant in us as the essential content of our own existence. The object we like becomes only an instrument that helps arouse that latent happiness. Really, as is our being *ānanda* (happiness) in essence, so is the object we like also, but appearing in a different form. *Ānanda* (happiness) thus is the real content of the being of both the enjoyer and the enjoyed, their coming together is only helping its self-unfoldment, or actualization. The origin of happiness, thus, is nowhere else than the Self or *Ātmā*, the one ultimate Reality both in me and the object I like. Meditatively searching for this *Ātmā* (*svātma-tattvānu-sandhānam* or *svasvarūpāṇu-sandhānam*), therefore, is counted by Śaṅkara as *bhakti*. While following almost the same line of thought, the Guru here gives more philosophical perfection to the motion of *bhakti* in pursuance of *Brahmavidyā*, as will become evident as we proceed.

Verse 1

भक्तिरात्मानुसन्धानमात्माऽनन्दघनो यतः ।
आत्मानमनुसन्धत्ते सदैवात्मविदात्मना ॥१॥

bhaktir ātmānu-sandhānam ātmā 'nanda ghano yataḥ ।
ātmānam anusandhatte sadaivātmavid ātmanā ॥1॥

Bhakti is constant meditative search into oneself/*Ātman*. For the reason that oneself/*Ātman* is *ānanda* in essential content, an *Ātman*-knower always meditatively searches into oneself with oneself as means.

The Guru's overall perception of *bhakti* is based on the notion that *Ātman,* the Self or oneself, in essence is *ānanda.* It was seen as early as Chapter 2 (Verse 10) that everything in its essential content is *sat-cit-ānanda.* That means, what is real in the being of all the worlds as well as of oneself, is *sat* (Existence pure and simple), *cit* (unconditioned Consciousness) and *ānanda* (Happiness or value-sense). That everything is *ānanda* is a fact thus already admitted. The same *ānanda* is what everyone is always in search of. Oneself being *ānanda* in essence, one's search for *ānanda* has necessarily to be turned inwards, towards one's own being. Taking this stand as a firm basis in this chapter the Guru gives six definitions of *bhakti,* each complementary to the others. The first of these is *bhaktir-ātmā-anusandhānam* (*bhakti* is constant meditative search into oneself or into *Ātman*). A person in whom such a search has become fruitful, and who perceives *Ātman* alone as existing, is to be counted as a knower of the Self or *ātmavit* or *ātma-jñānin,* as is pointed out in the verse itself.

Self-knowledge, when conceptualized, could be seen as having two facets:

1. Realizing what is real is the substance in one's own being, and living as that substance; and
2. perceiving one Reality or *Ātmā* as pervading the being of everything in all the worlds, and seeing that Reality alone as functionally manifesting in and through even minute worldly phenomena.

Though conceivable as having these two facets, self-knowledge really hbas no such division. The facets imagined here are like two sides of a single coin. Reality is neither one of the two sides, but is what is in between the two. Likewise, self-knowledge is neither of the facets mentioned above, but is what is real in between the two conceivable facets. The real self-knowledge as such is simply inconceivable. One searching for one's identity with that neutral and central Reality is to be called *bhakti* according to this verse.

In the *Bhagavad-Gītā*, Chapter XII, these two facets of one's identity with *Ātmā* are depicted using a different terminology. *Ātmā*, in the *Gītā*, is conceived as *Bhagavān* or the Lord. Considering this *Bhagavān* as an abstract Reality, and one trying to attain one's identity with that Reality is one facet of *bhakti*. The other is treating the concrete universe and all the events in it as the *Bhagavān* become visibly manifest, or as the cosmic form (*viśva-rūpa*) of *Bhagavān*. Treating one's own concrete existence as inseparably one with this cosmic form, or oneself as existing as an inalienable minute element that forms part of the mysterious cosmic system, is then the essence of *bhakti*.

Being embodied beings, we individuals naturally find developing the former kind of rapport with *Bhagavān* rather difficult and inaccessible, though it is admitted as the more superior of the two. The latter being the easier way, the *Gītā* recommends it, and goes into its details. Each individual, as a living concrete entity, developing a sense of inseparable oneness with the mysterious cosmic system — represented in the *Gītā* as the cosmic form of *Bhagavān* — and incessantly experiencing this identity in one's day-to-day life, is portrayed there as the ideal *bhakti*. The *Gītā* in this sense says:

> *mayyarppita-mano-buddhir yo mad bhaktaḥ sa me priyaḥ* ।
>
> One whose mind and understanding are fully dedicated to me, is my devotee; he is dear to me.

For the reason that the *bhakti* understood here essentially consists of one's yearning to attain oneness with the absolute Reality, differentiating it from *yoga* is somewhat difficult. The *Gītā* therefore identifies real *bhakti* with *yoga*. The *Darśanamālā* also introduces *yoga* in the very next chapter where the sense of identity gains more intensity.

The ideal *bhakta* (devotee), conceived here by the Guru, is evidently none other than the one of Self-knowledge (*ātmavit*), a person who has attained his goal. But *bhakti* as popularly understood is more a means than an end, particularly according to the Bhāgavata cult which treats it as the easiest and the best means for realizing God in this Kaliyuga (the Age of Strife). Yet it is not that the Guru does not at all consider *bhakti* as a means. One who strives to attain the goal of Self-knowledge is known as *jijñāsu* (an aspirant of wisdom), and for that one, *bhakti* is a means, and that means is none other than *ātmānusandhāna* (meditative search into one's own being). This search consists of one's seeking what is real in one's own being, and finally experiencing oneness with that Reality. This constant effort is called *ātmānusandhāna*. In short, *bhakti*, with a realized person or *ātmavit*, is one's natural state of mind; and with a seeker, it is a spiritual discipline or *sādhanā* one undergoes. Both are signified by the word *ātmānusandhāna*.

Verse 2

अनुसन्धीयते ब्रह्म ब्रह्मानन्दघनं यतः ।
सदा ब्रह्मानुसन्धानं भक्तिरित्यवगम्यते ॥२॥

anusandhīyate brahma brahmānanda ghanaṁ yataḥ ।
sadā brahmānusandhānaṁ bhaktir ity avagamyate ॥2॥

Brahman is always searched for meditatively, because *Brahman* is *ānanda* in essence. Constant meditative search for *Brahman* is, therefore, known as *bhakti*.

The last chapter ended with the definition of *para-jñāna* (Transcendental knowledge) as consisting of realizing the oneness of *Brahman* and *ātman* (*brahmātmaikya*) or the oneness of the Absolute and oneself. The *Bhakti Darśanam* is visualized in this chapter with this concept of *brahmātmaikya* at its core. *Ātmānusandhāna* (meditative search for what is real in one's own being) in essence is none other than *brahmānusandhāna* (the meditative search for *Brahman* or the absolute). The absolute Reality, individuated, is understood as *ātman*, and universally as *Brahman*, both being *ānanda* in essence. Thus both *ātmānusandhāna* and *brahmānusandhāna* are *ānandā-nusandhāna* virtually and actually. *Bhakti*, defined in the last verse as *ātmānusandhāna*, therefore is redefined here as *brahmānusandhāna*. Both definitions really convey to us one inner sense only.

Verse 3

आनन्दमेव ध्यायन्ति सर्वे दुःखं न कश्चन।
यदानन्दपरं ध्यानं भक्तिरित्युपदिश्यते ॥३॥

ānandam eva dhyāyanti sarve duḥkhaṁ na kaścana ।
yad ānandaparaṁ dhyānaṁ bhaktir ity upadiśyate ॥3 ॥

Everyone meditates on *ānanda* (happiness) alone. No one meditates on sufferings. Meditation aimed at *ānanda* is taught of as *bhakti*.

Not merely humans, but all living beings as well, every moment in every way, strive to ensure happiness in life. This is a basic law that governs life. One thing that every being contemplates on always thus is the means of achieving happiness. No being desires to be unhappy. Therefore, there is no activity in life that aims at one's own suffering. This happiness or *ānanda*, the one goal of all beings, is nothing but the essential content of their own being, the essential content of *Ātmā* or *Brahman*. Therefore the *ātmānusandhāna* which is equivalent to *brahmānusandhāna*, is also *ānandaparam dhyānam* (constant meditation on happiness). *Bhakti* thus gets yet another definition, as the meditation aimed at happiness.

Suffering and happiness (*duḥkha* and *sukha*) are contrasted by the Guru here. The former is never aimed at by any, and the latter is aimed at by all. What really is happiness? Is it simply a state of the absence of sufferings? Or, is it something to be achieved positively? What is the essential content of the feeling of happiness? Almost all the thinkers of the West as well as of the East, have wrestled with these problems, but unsuccessfully. Though the Guru asserts here that no one meditates on sufferings, it is a well-known fact that Buddhism has meditation on sufferings for its firm basis, but not as something to be attained. Its search is for the means of doing away with sufferings. Buddhism accepts four noble Truths (*ārya-satyas*): that life is full of sufferings; that there is a cause for sufferings in life; that there is a means to do away with sufferings; and that following the eightfold path is the means. Though thus stemming from the actuality of sufferings in life, avoiding sufferings is Buddhism's final goal. The Guru's words here, "No one meditates on sufferings" simply mean no one aims at having suffering in life.

Realizing supreme Happiness is conceived by Rāmānuja as a two-pronged process. He compares it to a two-petalled flower. One petal is that of avoiding worldly suffering caused by ignorance (*avidyā*) and the *karmas* it produces. The other petal consists of achieving the final goal of getting the chance after death of doing eternal service to God or Viṣṇu.

Such problems concerning the nature of the experience of happiness arise when it is simply treated as a goal to be attained. Seekers, of course, treat it as an end to be reached, whereas, when, through their intense and proper spiritual discipline, they attain the goal, what they really attain is a new revelation — a revelation that really the supreme Happiness is not a goal to be reached, but is the essential content of the seeker's own being. The goal attained is not something different from one's own being. The attainment merely consists of the removal of a veil that was hiding from one the real nature — the Happiness content — of one's own existence. The revelation is directly perceiving the real *ānanda*-content of oneself. As far as a *jñānin* is concerned, *ānanda* is not a goal attained, but is what is real in oneself. Given all this, it becomes evident that all the above-mentioned unanswerable questions about *ānanda* have their origin in our ignorance of ourselves. The final solution to them, therefore, is in removing the ignorance in us. Ignorance removed, the questions also vanish; then we need no answer. As suggestive of all this are the Guru's words here, *iti upadiśyate* (is taught of as).

The first verse defined *bhakti* as *ātmānusandhānam* (meditative search into oneself), and the second one as *brahmānusandhānam* (meditative search into *Brahman*). The present verse conceived it as *ānandaparam dhyānam* (meditation aimed at *ānanda* or Happiness). *Ātmā*, *Brahman* and *ānanda* are merely three terms denoting one absolute Self or *Ātman*. Therefore, the next verse defines *bhakti* as *bhajati iti yat ātmānam* (meditative adoration of *Ātman*).

Verse 4

आत्मैव ब्रह्म भजति नान्यमात्मानमात्मवित् ।
भजतीति यदात्मानं भक्तिरित्यभिधीयते ॥४ ॥

ātmaiva brahma bhajati nānyam ātmānam ātmavit ।
bhajatīti yad ātmānaṁ bhaktir ity abhidhīyate ॥4 ॥

Ātman (oneself) is *Brahman* indeed. What an *ātman*-knower

> meditatively adores is *ātman* (oneself) alone, and nothing else. The meditative adoration of *ātman*/oneself (that is *Brahman*) is spoken of as *bhakti*.

Ātman or oneself being *Brahman* in essence, meditating on *ātman* means meditating on *Brahman*. Whether seen as *ātman* or *Brahman*, its real content is *ānanda*. The last chapter ended with giving a definition of *para-jñāna* (Transcendental knowledge), as experientially attaining the oneness of *Brahman* and *ātman*. For those who are absorbed in such an experience, meditating on *Brahman* and meditating on *ātman* mean the same. The real *bhakta* or devotee therefore is the one who meditatively adores the Self-Reality by being immersed in the experience of the oneness of *Brahman* and *ātman*. This inner feeling of self-absorption is to be counted as philosophically sound *bhakti*.

Verse 5

आनन्द आत्मा ब्रह्मेति नामैतस्यैव तन्यते ।
इति निश्चितधीर्यस्य स भक्त इति विश्रुतः ॥५॥

ānanda ātmā brahmeti nāmaitasyaiva tanyate ।
iti niścita-dhīr yasya sa bhakta iti viśrutaḥ ॥5 ॥

> *Ānanda, Ātmā, Brahman* — these three are said to be different names of this One alone. The one who is certain of this oneness is well known as a *bhakta*.

The word *"ānanda"* arouses in us the sense of an exhilarating feeling everyone longs for in life. The word *"ātmā"* makes us think of ourselves and of what is real in our being. *"Brahman,"* 1 on the other hand, is the word that makes us think of an absolute Reality that underlies the being of all that appears to be, something all seekers aspire to know. Finding the experiential oneness of these three is also implied in the philosophically sound notion of *bhakti* presented here. A real *bhakta* thus is characterized by the conviction, "I am essentially *ānanda*, and therefore I am essentially *Brahman* as well." The first line of the verse, *ānanda ātmā brahmeti,* sounds like a revisualized version of the famous Upaniṣadic great dictum *ayam ātmā brahma* (This *ātmā* is *Brahman*).

The Guru bases his examination of *bhakti* on the Vedāntic doctrine that *ātmā* essentially is *ānanda* in content, and that *ātmā* is nothing but *Brahman*. Following the same line, a real *bhakta* is defined in the next verse by introducing a revised version of yet another great dictum (*mahāvākya*) of Vedānta, namely, *aham brahma asmi* (I am really *Brahman*).

Verse 6

आनन्दोऽहमहं ब्रह्माऽत्माऽहमस्मीति रूपतः ।
भावना सततं यस्य स भक्त इति विश्रुतः ॥६॥

ānando 'ham ahaṁ brahma 'ātmā 'ham asmīti rūpataḥ ।
bhāvanā satataṁ yasya sa bhakta iti viśrutaḥ ॥6॥

I am *ānanda,* I am *Brahman,* I am *Ātman* — the one who always has this meditative insight — he is well known as a *bhakta.*

It became amply evident by the last verse that what the three words *ānanda, ātmā* and *Brahman* signify is one alone. What then is that "one?" It is referred to as *aham* here, meaning "I" in its most abstract and generalized sense. That this "I" is in essence pure, unconditioned Consciousness (*cit* or *aṛivu*) is yet another stand given emphasis by the Guru, particularly in his works *Ātmopadeśa Śatakam, Advaita Dīpikā* and *Aṛivu*. Such a meditative insight of oneness is seen here as what characterizes a genuine *bhakta,* a fully devout person. To put it more precisely: one in whom the equations *aham* = *ānanda,* *aham* = *Brahman* and *aham* = *Ātmā* become one intuitive experience is a real *bhakta*. The word *bhāvanā* in the original, rendered here as "meditative insight," really is the state in which one becomes (*bhāva*) what one meditates on. "I am *ānanda*," "I am *Brahman*," "I am *Ātmā*," are meditated on here, and the meditator becomes the "one" connoted by the three equations.

What the words *ānanda*, *Brahman* and *Ātmā* stand for was earlier (2-10) referred to as *sat-cit-ānanda*, where all the worlds together was equated to it, saying *"sarvam hi saccidānandam"* (everything indeed is *saccidānanda*). Relating to that context we could safely say concerning the present *aham* (I) that, "everything is "I" alone."

It is not merely in the spiritual pursuit that the *ānanda*-centred *bhakti* becomes meaningful. Wherever there is quest for *ānanda*, *bhakti* is also there; only that we remain oblivious of being *bhakta*s. This *bhakti* has its place even in the context of our pursuit for worldly pleasures. One of the best examples of such a *bhakti* is in the form of the conjugal relationship between husband and wife. The mutual adoration relevant in such contexts is also counted as a form of *bhakti* in the next verse.

Verse 7

भार्या भजति भर्तारं भर्त्ता भार्यां न केवलम् ।
स्वानन्दमेव भजति सर्वोऽपि विषयस्थितम् ॥७॥

bhāryā bhajati bhartāraṁ bhartā bhāryāṁ na kevalam ।
svānandam eva bhajati sarvo 'pi viṣaya-sthitam ॥8॥

What a wife lovingly meditates on is not simply her husband; what a husband lovingly meditates on is not simply his wife. It is self-happiness alone that each one meditates on, as inherent in the object concerned.

Longing for happiness is the most forceful urge that pushes life forward in the case of all living beings. But where is the abode of this happiness or *ānanda*? We have already seen that everything indeed is *sat-cit-ānanda* (*sarvam hi saccidānandam* - 2.10). Of these three aspects of the all-underlying Reality, the *ānanda* aspect is concentrated upon in the *bhakti* context. Reducing the entire scene thus to that of *ānanda*, we could as well say *"sarvam hi ānandamayam"* (everything indeed is *ānanda* in essence). That means, *ānanda* has no particular abode, but is the substance of which everything, including the *ānanda*-seeker, is made. The only problem is that the seeker remains unaware of the reality that the *ānanda* he or she seeks is the real content of his or her own being. *Ānanda* thus is not derived from any object, but the object becomes an instrument in arousing the *ānanda*-content already dormant in our being.

To like what gives happiness is but natural in life. Erotic pleasure towers over all other sense pleasures. This pleasure becomes actualized when a couple bodily unites together. It is this actualization of erotic pleasure that prompts them to love each other. Though this love, in a social sense, is considered as the husband loving the wife and vice versa, really their love is not for each other, but is for the happiness the other person causes to become actualized. The husband or wife is merely an instrument in the welling up of happiness from within themselves. That means, the wife realizes her own being *ānanda* in essence, by means of the union with the husband, and the other way round also. The mutual love they have is merely an external sign of the love each has for the happiness that already remains hidden in their own being or in the self, in other words for self-happiness.

There is a dialogue between Yājñavalkya and Maitreyī in the *Bṛhadāraṇyaka Upaniṣad* which goes into the details of this subtle aspect (Ch. II. Sec. 4 and Ch. IV. Sec. 5). Though already quoted, we repeat the relevant part of the dialogue for the sake of ready reference:

> Then, he (Yājñavalkya) said: "Verily, not for the sake of the husband is the husband dear but for the sake of the self is the husband dear. Verily, not for the sake of the wife is the wife dear but for the sake of the self is the wife dear. Verily, not for the sake of the sons are the sons dear but for the sake of the self are the sons dear. Verily, not for the sake of wealth is wealth dear but for the sake of the self is wealth dear. Verily, not for the sake of the cattle are the cattle dear but for the sake of the self are the cattle dear. . . . Verily, not for the sake of everything is everything dear but for the sake of the self is everything dear. Verily, the Self, Maitreyī, is to be seen, is to be heard, is to be reflected on, is to be meditated upon, when verily the Self is seen, heard, reflected on and known, then all this is known."

The Upaniṣad asserts that, on knowing the Self properly with seeing, hearing, reflecting and meditating as means, everything becomes transparent. Likewise, the implicit significance of the statement that adoring the Self or *ānanda* alone is involved in a husband loving his wife, and a wife loving her husband, becomes revealed only if and when we the seekers perceive its necessity, hear the secret of wisdom as taught directly by a guru, subject it to intense cogitation, and finally realize its Truth through meditation.

Only a suggestion leading the seeker to a process of undergoing the above-said reflection and meditation, is given in this verse by the Guru, in the words, *sarvo 'pi viṣayasthitam* (each one meditates on what is inherent in the object concerned).

That everything is *ānanda* in essence is now an accepted fact. Then what is it that appears as the object of enjoyment?

It is also a variant form of the one *ānanda* or *Ātmā* manifesting itself. What happens when the enjoyer gets into contact with an enjoyed object? Nothing other than realizing the *ānanda* content of oneself or of the Self, by unconsciously giving up momentarily the notion, "I am the enjoyer" and "The other is the enjoyed object." Where did the actual happiness or *ānanda* hide until it was actually experienced? Was it in the subject, or the object? In neither. It was remaining unrevealed in the one essential content of both the subject and the object, in the one *Ātmā*. Our effort to reveal to ourselves the *ānanda* content remaining in us is called *bhajanam* or meditative adoration. This *bhajanam* is what both husband and wife do when they love each other.

What happens at the union of the couple thus is both forgoing for the moment their separateness and becoming merged in the *ānanda*-content of beingness. Their mutual adoration or *bhajanam* is meaningful only because it leads them finally to experience actually their being one with *ānanda*. In short, even ordinary sense pleasures, and the love we feel towards pleasurable objects form part of this *bhajanam*.

Verse 8

एवं पश्यति कुत्रापि विद्वानात्मसुखं विना।
न किञ्चिदपरं तस्य भक्तिरेव गरीयसी ॥८॥

evaṁ paśyati kutrāpi vidvān ātma-sukhaṁ vinā ।
na kiñcid aparaṁ tasya bhaktir eva garīyasī ॥8॥

Thus a wise one perceives everywhere nothing in the least other than Self-Happiness. His *bhakti* is of the most superior order.

That everything is *saccidānanda* (*sarvam hi saccidānandam*) is now a firm spring board for us. When limiting this notion to the context of *ānanda* alone, we could very well say, *sarvam hi ānandamayam* (everything indeed is *ānanda* in essence). People still, even when they are experiencing directly the *ānanda*-content of *Ātmā*, because of their ignorance, remain completely unaware of doing so, and think of life as full of sufferings. Only one means is there to free them from their sufferings — leading them to wisdom, or removing their ignorance. Once having become enlightened, they see both in painful and pleasurable experiences, one *ānanda*-content of *Ātmā* alone as manifesting fleetingly in various ways. They would be seen engaged in worldly activities as everyone else, but in their own view, all such activities, either painful or pleasurable, are merely ever-changing new facets of directly realizing one's being *ānanda* in essence. Such a one's *bhajanam* (contemplative adoration) always will be on the one *Ātmā*. One's *bhajanam* of one's own self-content is thought of as the best form of *bhakti*.

What is the dearest for each of us? It is our own existence. This existence is nothing other than the existence of the *ānanda*-content of *Ātmā*. He who visualizes this *Ātmā* as existing not only in the form of oneself, but in the form of all the worlds also, is the real Self-knower or *ātma-jñānin*. For this reason, the love one feels for oneself gets transformed as the love for every being in all the worlds, as the love for God. Such a love, called *parama-prema* (supreme love), is considered the best mark of *bhakti* in the *Nārada-Bhakti-Sūtras*, one of the best Indian treatises on *bhakti*. This definition of *bhakti* thus becomes acceptable to Vedāntins also.

Verses 9-10

लोकस्य पितरि स्वस्य गुरौ पितरि मातरि।
सत्यस्य स्थापयितरि तत्पथेनैव यातरि॥९॥

नियन्तरि निषिद्धस्य सर्वेषां हितकर्त्तरि।
योऽनुरागो भक्तिरत्र सा परा परमात्मनि ॥१०॥

lokasya pitari svasya gurau pitari mātari ।
satyasya sthāpayitari tat pathenaiva yātari ॥9 ॥

niyantari niṣiddhasya sarveṣāṁ hitakartari ।
yo 'nurāgo bhaktir atra sā parā paramātmani ॥10 ॥

The enduring love one has for the Father of the world, for one's own *guru*, father and mother, for the one who lays the foundation of Truth, for the one who walks on the path of that Truth, for the one who puts down evils, for the one who does good to all — is all to be counted as *bhakti*. The enduring love one has for the Supreme Self, on the other hand, is to be considered *bhakti* of the highest order (*parā-bhakti*).

One thing all the religions teach is that you should love God, the creator, sustainer and destroyer of the world. This concept entails understanding that one's own life and the events in it, are not fully in one's own control, but are ultimately controlled by God. Even individuals' free decisions are subject to the control of God. Everyone's desire is as much as possible to make all events in life conducive to happiness. Fulfilling this desire requires our desires and Gods' will fall in one line, and this is what is signified by God's Grace. The fact is that even our love for God is ultimately aimed at self-happiness, though we remain unaware of it. Meditating on God and adoring God, thus means, meditating and adoring *ānanda* or happiness. The *bhajanam* (meditative adoration) of God therefore means adoring the Self that is nothing but *ānanda* in essence, which means Self-knowledge, and thus is philosophically sound *bhakti*.

Loving one's own *guru*, father and mother is a value considered lofty by all human societies, particularly in India. A *guru* is loved because he helps one make life happy by imparting wisdom. Parents are considered dear for begetting us and nurturing us with all concern for our well-being. Thus our love for *guru* and parents alike is a sort of external expression of our love for *ānanda* or love for ourselves.

Junctures in which a particular people or society in general somehow become steeped in unrighteousness, immorality, evil practices, and untruth arise sometimes in human history, for some historical reason or plain ignorance. On all such occasions, as if willed by the unknown, there emerge some persons as saviours of the society. Such are worthy of being loved by everyone. The love we feel for them also is nothing other than our innate longing to be happy in life. That means, it also is a form of adoring (*bhajanam*) *ātmā* or *ānanda*.

It is the bounden duty of rulers to protect the general public from the menace of evil-doers, and to ensure the safety of their life and properties. When performing these duties with no partisanism they are also loved by all. That love too is a sort of outgrowth of our love for ourselves, our love for *ātmā* or *ānanda*.

In short, whatever be that we love, the basic urge behind that feeling is our love for ourselves, the love for *ātmā*, a ceaseless urge in all beings. This self-love, instead of turning towards something external, could directly turn towards *Ātmā* itself, towards the most lovable content of our own being, towards *Paramātmā*, and that is considered the best kind of *bhakti* called *parā-bhakti*.

9

Yoga Darśanam
(Vision by Yoga)

WHAT we saw in the first three chapters of the second half of *Darśanamālā*, were different levels in which the seeker finds his identity with the all-underlying Reality (*Brahman* or *Ātman*). Each chapter gradually shifts its stand from grosser to subtler aspects, and from exteriority of perception to interiority of perception. We have just seen that *bhakti* is the state of meditatively adoring *Brahman* experienced as *ānanda*. Subtler and more interior than meditatively adoring the Real is finding one's unity with the Real. This latter state is what is known as *yoga*. The present chapter therefore, looks at, or rather experientially visualizes, non-duality (*advaita*) from the point of view of *yoga*, or in the perception of a *yogī*.

The biographers of the Guru, when evaluating him as a perfect *yogī*, have often made the mistake of basing themselves on the notion of *yoga* found in the *Yoga-Sūtras* of Patañjali, and other more physically biased *yoga* systems such as *Haṭha Yoga*, based on the texts like *Haṭha-Yoga-Pradīpikā* and *Gheraṇḍa Saṁhitā*. The Guru, in his early days, must have practised such *yoga*-disciplines. But the Guru has formulated his own concept of *yoga*, based on his finalized non-dualistic vision. That this stand finds expression in his *Yoga Darśanam* of *Darśanamālā* is not given proper attention by biographers. Though familiar with the body-oriented *yoga* practices, he had his own opinion about such. He once remarked, "They help easier removal of phlegm from the body." The present chapter, *Yoga Darśanam*, throws ample light on what sort of *yogī* the Guru was, as well as on how non-duality is to be perceived from a *yogī*'s point of view. In what sense the Guru is a *yogī* also is to be evaluated on the basis of his own concept of *yoga* in the *Darśanamālā*, not based on the already prevailing traditional or popular *yoga* systems or cults.

Verse 1

सततं योजयति यद्युनक्ति च चिदात्मनि।
मनो निरोधरूपोऽयं स योग इति शंसितः ॥१॥

satataṁ yojayati yad yunakti ca cidātmani ।
mano nirodha-rūpo 'yaṁ sa yoga iti śaṁsitaḥ ॥1॥

The state of mind-restraint by which one unites oneself with, and becomes united with, *Ātmā* which in essence is pure Consciousness — that is praised as *yoga*.

Derived from the verb root *yuj*, the word *yoga* means "the state of existing together (*yuja samyamane*). Literally, any situation in which two entities or factors always exist together could be considered as that of *yoga*. But in the spiritual context, it is used to denote the state of *samādhi* (*yuja samādhau*). *Samādhi* means properly (*samyak*) finding one's own proper abode (*ādhi* or *ādhānam*). *Yoga* thus means one finding out one's own real abode and remaining one with it.

What is it that makes the search for its own proper abode? Mind or *manas*. What is *manas*? A particular way in which consciousness (*cit*) functions. No one really can imagine how various are the functional aspects or modes of expression of consciousness. According to the Vedāntic stand we are already familiar with, it is one Consciousness or *cit*, having become functionally manifest, that appears as all the worlds. In Indian psychology, when this one Consciousness becomes conditioned as an individuated consciousness and functions as imagining and doubting, it is called *manas* (mind). Being thus a functional aspect of individuated consciousness, mind has its proper abode in pure Consciousness or *cit*, the source of individuated consciousness. Gold-substance, having attained a specific form, appears as an ornament such as a bangle. The proper abode of the bangle then is gold itself. The bangle finding its real abode in gold and remaining fully identified with it, is its attaining *samādhi* or *yoga*. Mind, here, is to be seen in the place of the bangle, and pure Consciousness in the place of gold. What we mean by pure Consciousness is not our consciousness *about* something; on the other hand, it is the Substance that functionally finds expression as all our items of knowledge, imagination, reasoning, feeling and all such.

This pure and unconditioned Consciousness, in Vedānta, is known as *cit*, sometimes also termed *cid-vastu*, *vastu* meaning "substance." The Guru has himself made sufficiently clear in his other major works like *Ātmopadeśa Śatakam* (One Hundred Verses of Self-Instruction), *Advaita Dīpikā* (Lamp of Non-Duality) and also in Chapter 2 of the *Darśanamālā*, that this one *cit* or *cid-vastu*, also called *arivu*, is what appears as all the worlds, owing to its own mysterious *māyā*.

This *cit* or *cid-vastu*, in the sense that it is the substance that pervades the being of everything (*ātata*), is called *Ātmā* in the Upaniṣads as also by the Guru. This pervading of *Ātmā* into the being of everything is like that of gold in the being of ornaments. This *Ātmā*, being *cit* in essence, is termed *cidātmā* here by the Guru, a term seen used only in the *Rāmapūrvatāpaṇī Upaniṣad* (6) among the ancient sciptures.

Nothing in any world, material or mental, exists other than as the manifest form of this one *cidātmā*. Each of us thus is a momentary spark of the great bonfire of *cidātmā*. Our searching mind too thus is one among such. A bangle's proper abode is the gold-substance. Its finding that abode and remaining one with gold is its state of *yoga*. Likewise, mind finding its being in *cidātmā* and remaining fully identified with it, is its *yoga* state.

A *yoga*-context naturally involves two aspects to be brought together — two separately understandable but never ultimately separable aspects, to be more precise, two counterparts. Here the counterparts are *manas* (the searching mind) and *cidātmā*. *Manas* has to look at itself and see the *cidātmā* that has assumed its own form, and realize its oneness with *cidātmā*. Unless and until this is realized, the *manas* could think of itself as having its own separate existence, its own functions, its own interests. This state of ignorance, called *ajñāna*, causes one's life to aimlessly go astray, like a canoe caught in high winds. Such a state makes life miserable, and may even lead to total annihilation. What will happen if mind is let loose like this is portrayed in the *Bhagavad-Gītā*, also a science of *yoga* (*Yoga-Śāstra*), as follows:

> Meditating on objects of sense-interest, there is born in man an attachment for them; from attachment rises passion; in the face of passion (frustrated) arises rage.
>
> From rage is produced distortion of values, and from distortion of values memory-lapse, and from memory-lapse comes loss of reason, and from loss of reason he perishes.
>
> — II.62, 63

What you should do to avoid such tragedies in life is, restrain your mind (*mano-nirodham*). It does not mean that the normal functions of mind have to be cut back. Flooding rivers are often controlled by forming embankments on both sides in the face of the possible destruction of the surrounding areas. Likewise, the free flow of mind is also to be well-guided with deliberately applied disciplines so as to make it conducive to the attainment of the ultimate goal of life. Such a discipline is what the word *manonirodham* (mind-restraint) implies.

This mind-restraint is a double-phased discipline. The first is that of withdrawing the mind from all that we are sure will lead us to unpropitiousness and disasters in life. Practising what are known as *yama* (self-control) and *niyama* (restraint) prescribed by Patañjali in his *Yoga-Sūtras*, is popularly considered the best means to actualize this withdrawal. The *Bhagavad-Gītā* reduces this elaborate practice into developing a sense of detachment (*vairāgya*) towards pleasurable objects. This phase of discipline, of course, is rather a negative one, that is to say, the withdrawal part of the discipline, as opposed to the active effort required to attain the goal. This latter positive phase of the discipline (*sādhanā*), consists of guiding the mind properly to its real goal. Mind, by nature, never remains in a state of having no interest in anything. The nature of the course of one's life is determined by that on which the mind fixes its interest. When it becomes interested in fleeting sense-pleasures, life ends up as a pleasure-seeking affair. This pleasure-seeking terminates, naturally or otherwise, at a certain stage, and then one finds that life has reached nowhere. Having lived so far without much purpose, one becomes frustrated with oneself. Treating the life's goal as realizing the ultimate Reality in oneself or as oneself, makes life as a whole, and even the momentary pleasure-seeking that forms part of it, conducive to that goal. What is that ultimate Reality to be aimed at? It is nothing other than the *cidātmā* we have just examined.

If the *manas* (mind) is fully aware that it is simply a tiny spark of the *cidātmā*, that the apparent world is the sum total of such sparks, that everything it is interested in also is nothing but other sparks of the same *cidātmā*, and that even the happiness it derives from such objects is nothing other than the momentary spurting of the *ānanda*-content of *cidātmā*, then whether it is engaged in worldly affairs or absorbed in meditation, the *manas* is in its constant state of *samādhi* or *yoga*. This inner perception and discipline together that enables the mind to see its own functional existence in *cidātmā*, whatever be the changeful states it goes through, is what the word in this verse *yojayati* (one unites oneself with) suggests. This discipline is suggested in the *Bhagavad-Gītā* by the word *matparaḥ* (having Me alone for goal) and *tatparaḥ* (having That alone for goal). The same is enjoined by the Guru in his *Ātmopadeśa Śatakam* thus:

> The searching mind, by immersing itself into It, should meditatively cogitate with a view to getting rid of the delusion caused by *māyā*. — Verse 53

The discipline of *yoga* (*yoga-sādhanā*), in short, has two facets: that of disentangling your mind from situations of temptation that render life aimless like a canoe lost in high winds; and that of uniting your mind with what is of ultimate value in life. Together these two sides of *yoga*-practice are signified in the *Gītā* by the compound word *tatparaḥ-samyatendriyaḥ* (being intent on "That" and having the senses subjugated). On becoming interested in what is of the highest value in life, the mind's longing for things of lesser values becomes subdued, whereas the deliberate withdrawal of the mind from momentary interests of pleasure-seeking makes it more and more capable of attuning itself with the ultimate goal. *Yoga*-discipline thus finds its finality when the disentangling process on the one side, and the uniting process on the other, meet at a neutral ground in the seeker, as mutually compensatory.

The process of the mind finding its real abode in *cidātmā* also is seen here by the Guru as having two sides. The mind deliberately uniting itself with *cidātmā* is the one side of it. This is signified by the word *"yojayati."* As a result of this effort, the mind finds its natural union with *cidātmā* spontaneously, denoted by the word *"yunakti"* (becomes united with). This latter is the experiential side of the mind merging in the being of *cidātmā*. In the traditional *yoga* system, this state is known as *amanībhāva* (the state in which mind becomes a non-entity).

After outlining the nature of *yoga* in a general way in the first verse, the verses to follow go into more details of the *yoga*-principle as applicable here.

Verse 2

न द्रष्टा दर्शनं दृश्यं विद्यते यत्र तत्र हृत्।
योजयेद्वासना यावद्योगोऽयमिति योगवित्॥२॥

na draṣṭā darśanaṁ dṛśyaṁ vidyate yatra tatra hṛt ।
yojayed vāsanā yāvad yogo 'yam iti yogavit ॥2॥

As long as incipient memory factors are present in oneself, the heart should be united to That wherein is present no distinction of perceiver, perceived and perception. This is considered as *yoga* by *yoga*-knowers.

Every moment of our wakeful life we continue to acquire knowledge about something or other. A constant flow of such experiences comprises life for us human beings. Each such experience necessarily involves three factors: *dṛk* (the perceiver), *dṛśya* (the perceived) and *darśana* (perception); or simply, the knower, the known and knowledge. These factors together in Vedānta are known as *tripuṭi*, literally a three-petalled entity.

All that appears as the knower, the known and knowledge, according to the basic teaching of Vedānta, is none other than the one Reality (*Ātmā* or *Brahman*), *sat*, *cit* and *ānanda* at the same time, manifesting Itself variously. This one Reality is neither an object perceived, nor a perceiving subject, nor even the event of perceiving. This one Reality alone existing, there is no "other" to be known or perceived. It is, therefore, neither a subject nor an object; and in the absence of these two no event of knowing is relevant either. One's identity with that Reality is simply an experience of oneself becoming lost in the pure effulgence of Beingness, the final state that marks the final attainment of a *yogī*.

Philosophically understanding the nature of this state of attainment does not make one a *yogī*. Such a one is the knower of the basic Truth; the Truth is the object known; and the act of knowing the Truth takes place within oneself. A sort of veil, so to say, obstructs transforming one's *understanding* of the Truth to *experiencing* the Truth and *becoming* the Truth. This obstruction is called *vāsanā* here, rendered as "incipient memory factors."

Modern genetics reveals that all the experiences we acquire in life are encoded in our genes and are carried to our next generation. The same natural phenomenon was conceived by the ancient *ṛṣi*s of India as the notion that the incipient memories of the actions we perform in the present life are carried into future births. Such inborn traits are called *vāsanā*s, and sometimes *karma-vāsanā*s. Each person, in addition to having such inborn traits, acquires also new experiences in the present life, which also leave their impressions in the genes or in the subtle body; such impressions are known as *saṁskāras*. *Vāsanās* and *saṁskāra*s together give shape to the personality of the individual. The influence of these factors is always there in the way a person understands and appreciates things and life-situations, and in the way he or she reacts mentally as well as physically. Countless are such *vāsanās* and *saṁskāras* underlying the being of each individual. One such is the tendency to see the perceiver or oneself, the perceived object and the act of perceiving as separate. As long as this tendency prevails, transcending these threefold factors (*tripuṭi*) and attaining unity with the absolute Reality remains only as a concept. Thus, it never becomes the realization of oneself becoming lost in the Reality. A genuine seeker, therefore, having not realized the experiential oneness, should remind oneself that one's own *vāsanās* are there as hindrance. One means alone is there to overcome this — subjecting oneself to the insistent practice (*sādhanā*) of uplifting oneself from the tribasic prejudices (*tripuṭi*) and of uniting oneself with the unconditioned realm of Reality. Incessant practice of this discipline weakens the unhealthy tendency to remain subject to *tripuṭi*, and also strengthens the healthy trend to become attuned to the one Effulgence. Those who know the secret of *yoga*, consider this aspect of discipline as constituting the essence of *yoga*. Giving predominance to the knowledge-aspect or the epistemological aspect, this concept of *yoga* does not exclude other facets of *yoga*-discipline.

It is the seeker's own heart (*hṛt*) that is to be attuned to the Reality that transcends the bounds of *tripuṭi*. *Hṛt* (heart) is a word having different connotations according to the context. With biologists, it is the bodily organ that pumps blood all through the body. In the perception of a poet, it is the epicentre of all feelings and emotions; and philosophically it could be understood as the imaginary central point of one's own personal being. Our personal existence is a part of the total existence that is not conditioned by *tripuṭi*. We do not feel the relevance of *tripuṭi* in the context of experiencing our own existence either. Our feeling ourselves merged in that experience is the essence of *yoga* as understood here.

Verse 3

नामरूपमिदं सर्वं ब्रह्मैवेति विलीयते ।
यद्ब्रह्मणि मनो नित्यं स योग इति निश्चितः ॥३॥

nāma-rūpam idaṁ sarvaṁ brahmaiveti vilīyate ।
yad brahmaṇi mano nityaṁ sa yoga iti niścitaḥ ॥3॥

That which is comprised of mind remaining constantly merged in *Brahman* by the realization that all this (world) consisting of names and forms is nothing but *Brahman*, is ascertained as *yoga*.

That this world is comprised of names and forms is one of the basic stands of Vedānta. The Guru, in his *Advaita Dīpikā* (Lamp of Non-Duality), revisualizes this concept in a slightly different and more modern way. There he says, "Countless names, countless concepts and countless objects of knowledge together constitute this world."

Now let us take the case of "form" or *rūpa*. What do we mean by the word? We, in the normal course, think only things seen with our eyes have definite forms. But the "form" understood here is not to be taken in that limited sense. Every object perceived with all our sense organs has its own form. Even ideas conceived in our mind have forms. That means, every experience has its own form, and these forms are thought of as the essential content of the object perceived. But the fact is that the form each of us is familiar with is only as we experience it. Is the experience we have of an object an exact replica of the object existing outside? We are not sure, and we do not possess any means to check it out either. Do two people perceiving the same object have exactly the same experience within them? We do not have any foolproof method to ascertain this either.

Let us take the case of the experience of seeing something, for example a green leaf. The greenness of the leaf perceived depends on many factors like our eyesight, the intensity of sunlight and the like. My eyesight need not necessarily be the same as yours. If colour-blind, I'll not be seeing the same colours as the normally sighted person sees. The greenness-experience I have, therefore, has to be different from the greenness-experience you have. Still both of us give the same name "green" to the colour each perceives, even when remaining incapable of ascertaining the degree of sameness of experience each of us has within. It is only for formality's sake we say, "I saw the same green colour that you saw." This is true with regard to perceiving the world as a whole as well. The experience I have of the world cannot be the same as any other person has. One question then arises: which is the real form of the world, the one experienced by me, or the one seen by you? We have no definite answer. The only possible answer is this: I think the form of the world I see is the real one, and you think the form of the world you see is the true one. The true world for each of us is the one each of us perceives or experiences in our own consciousness.

Who then sees the real world? No one does. We thus come to the conclusion that even the existence of the gross and external world is as the manifest form of our functional consciousness (*bhāna-vṛtti*) as was seen in Chapter 5, *Bhāna Darśanam*. In short, all forms, essentially, are experiences, and all experiences happen and have their being in consciousness as its functional manifestations. Form or *rūpa*, thus, has no being other than as functional modes of consciousness.

Forms attain specificity as part of the process of knowing. Along with knowing arises an inner urge to let others know what is thus known. Communicating one's knowledge or feeling to another requires the help of a medium agreeable and known to both, one that has become part of their being through the life-long process of educating themselves. It is through this medium that the knowledge or feeling is transmitted between individuals.

This process is there in the life of all living species, each instinctively having its own medium or language. Only in the case of humans has this medium grown to be highly complex and creative of imaginary worlds. Whether done orally or in writing, communicating ideas is acccomplished by inventing words capable of being charged with what is known or felt as their meaning-content. Such words are what we mean by "name" (*nāma*) here.

Every entity that forms part of the world, every idea formulated in our mind, is given a name devised by our mind, and this name is called "noun" in grammar. Every action that takes place in nature is signified by another type of words called "verbs." All this, taken inclusively, is what is meant by the word *"nāma"* here. All languages, with the help of such words, become capable of describing anything that happens anywhere in nature. The world of words (*nāma*), thus, is as extensive and complex as the world of forms (*rūpa*).

As part of experiencing the world, forms, one after another, get formulated in the mind, and with every such form there emerges or is devised a corresponding word or *nāma*. Conversely, the recalling of every word arouses the image or form of some corresponding thing or idea in our mind. In short, without form no name can exist, and without name no form can exist.

Names, thus, are as legion as are forms, and both get formulated in the mind. Names (*nāmas*), in other words, are the linguistic symbols devised by the mind to convey to someone else the knowledge and feelings that arise within.

In short, forms' being is in Consciousness, as in the case of names. Consciousness means *cidātmā* which is none other than *Brahman*. It thus becomes apparent that all the worlds we experience, comprised of names and forms, have no existence apart from *cidātmā* or *Brahman*. It is the being of *Brahman* that appears as the being of the world of names and forms and of ourselves.

Where do all the experiences have their being? In our mind, in our consciousness. What is mind (*manas*)? The mind mentioned in this verse, which is to be merged in *Brahman*, is a notion very familiar to the traditional *yoga* philosophy. Mental functions, particularly in the context of knowing, are conceived as having four factors involved, called *manas* (the questioning mind), *buddhi* (the intellect that reasons), *citta* (the memorizing mind) and *ahaṁkāra* (the evaluating I-sense). These four together are called *antaḥkaraṇas* (inner faculties), and their functions are known as *antaḥkaraṇa-vṛttis*, *vṛtti* meaning "function."

But the mind (*manas*) understood here is not the first of these four; it rather is the functional consciousness inclusive of all these four, a notion more akin to the concept of "mind" in modern Western psychology. While the above-mentioned four divisions take into account only the knowing function of consciousness, the possibilities of consciousness functioning are endless in variety. For example, love, hatred, anger, envy, ego, competition, attachment are all various functional modes of our own mind. The mind understood here, therefore, could better be taken as meaning "any specifiable and conditioned mode of the function of consciousness which otherwise is unspecifiable and unconditioned. Put otherwise, it is any particular functional mode of *cidātmā* become conditioned as an individuated consciousness. Mind, thus, has no being other than as a functional mode of *cidātmā*.

The world comprised of names and forms also has no being except as the functional modes (*bhāna-vṛtti*s) of *cidātmā* or *Brahman*, as we have seen earlier. What will the seeking mind think of the world and of itself, on becoming enlightened as to all this? It will realize: "The being of this world of endless names and forms is in one *Brahman* that is *cidātmā*; my being is also in the very same *cidātmā* or *Brahman*."

What really happens in each event of knowing a worldly object? The worldly object gives up the conditioning factor that makes it a worldly object, and the knowing mind gives up the conditioning factor that makes it the mind, and both realize their essential oneness in *cidātmā*, as *cidātmā*. For formality's sake and due to our ignorance, we simply call it a worldly experience. One who is enlightened on this *yoga*-secret hidden in all worldly experiences perceives all such only as new facets of realizing one's remaining merged in the being of *Brahman*. Life, for such a one, is simply a ceaseless flow of this experience of actualizing one's oneness with *cidātmā*. This ceaselessness of *yoga*-awareness is underscored in the definition of *yoga* given in the next verse.

Verse 4

चित्तस्य तैलधारावद्वृत्त्याऽविच्छिन्नयाऽत्मनि ।
निरन्तरं रम्यते यत्स योगो योगिभिः स्मृतः ॥४॥

cittasya taila-dhārāvad vṛttyā 'vicchinnayā 'tmani ।
nirantaraṁ ramyate yat sa yogo yogībhiḥ smṛtaḥ ॥4॥

> The state of incessant rejoicing in *Ātmā* that is, in oneself with a mental function that is unbroken like a streak of oil — that is thought of as *yoga* by the *yoga*-knowers.

Oil, when slowly poured out from one container to another, flows in an unbroken streak. A similar experience in which our mind ceaselessly finds its rest in *Ātmā* or the Self, is represented here as *yoga*.

Cittam is the word the Guru uses here to signify mind. What does he really mean by the word? It is not to be presupposed that various *ṛṣi*s of various systems of thought, when using the same word, do mean the same. Nuances of what they mean can vary with the nature of the system of thought. *Yoga* is defined by Patañjali thus: *yogaś citta-vṛtti-nirodhaḥ* (*Yoga* is comprised of restraining the functions of *citta*). Commentators on the *Yoga-Sūtras* of Patañjali are at variance in respect of the denotation of the word *"citta."*

The word, we feel, could best be understood as denoting all the mental functions together. Such functions are not to be let loose unguided by an ultimate goal. *Citta-vṛtti-nirodha*, thus, is a double-faced discipline — restraining the mind from its instinctive tendency to aimlessly stray away, and directing its functions so as to be conducive to the attainment of the final goal of life, as could be surmised from the other works of the Guru. Patañjali's definition gives more stress to the former aspect. This aspect, in practice, is to be supplemented with the latter, by attuning oneself with something of the highest value. If the former could be thought of as the negative side of the *yoga*-discipline, then the latter is its positive side. What Narayana Guru does in the present verse is to supplement what Patañjali said about *yoga* with its own positive aspect.

Does the Guru mean by the word *"cittam,"* the same as what Patañjali did? This question is difficult to answer definitely. The Guru points out the main function of *cittam* as rejoicing (*ramyate*). This could well be considered as a pointer to what he means by *cittam*. Common with everyone is the ceaseless desire to rejoice. So two things guide human activities: ensuring the chance for rejoicing and trying to avoid all that becomes obstructive to such gains. This dual process goes on unbroken like the flow of oil forming a streak. It could thus be presumed that what the Guru means by *cittam* is the state of mind filled with the desire for rejoicing.

Resorting to sense pleasures is the means people usually rely on to be happy in life, but a *yogī*'s rejoicing is not in such pleasures. A *yogī* finds happiness in his or her own being. *Cittam*, the functional mind filled with the desire for happiness, is nothing but a particular functional mode of our own consciousness, the essential content of *Ātmā*.

The longing for happiness is perceivedby the *yogī* as *Ātmā* itself manifesting in the form of that state, that means, as a minute element of the Self-Reality (*Ātma-kalā*). What then is the pleasurable object? It too is the same *Ātmā* manifesting in a different way. A *yogī*, in short, perceives only *Ātmā* functionally existing both in the pleasure-seeking mind and the pleasure-giving object. Rejoicing doubtlessly is an event that takes place in consciousness or *ātmā*. Thus, all the three factors involved in the situation — the rejoicing mind, the rejoiceable object, the act of rejoicing — have their being only in the one *Ātmā*, pure and unconditioned Consciousness in essence.

The rejoicing experience, a *yogī* of this vision has incessantly in his life, is nothing other than the Blissfulness of realizing the real content of *Ātmā*. He experiences it not merely at a particular time in which he practices meditation, but even when engaged in worldly activities. The meditation practised at a chosen time helps him only to stabilize this constant *yoga*-experience. The actual *yoga*-experience, thus, is something that runs all through life like the flowing of a streak of oil.

Verse 5

यतो यतो मनो याति सदाऽत्मनि ततस्ततः ।
नियम्य योजयेदेतद्योगोऽयं युज्यतामिह ॥५॥

yato yato mano yāti sadā 'tmani tatas tataḥ ।
niyamya yojayed etad yogo 'yaṁ yujyatām iha ॥5॥

Whichever object it goes after, restraining from it then and there, the mind should be united with *ātmā*/with oneself. This constitutes *yoga*. One should remain united to this *yoga*.

Mind, by nature, when conscious, always remains interested in something or other. Life for many is a flow of mind fixing its interest on one thing after another. Really it is one *Ātmā* alone that appears both as mind and the object of its interest. Those who have this insight see only *Ātmā* existing and functioning in the form of the mind and its functions. They naturally become more interested in the Reality that appears in the form of the mind and pleasurable objects than in the objects as such.

This unitive vision may impel one to make itself stable by practising certain disciplines such as *śauca* (cleanliness), to be content (*santoṣa*), austerity (*tapas*), self-learning (*svādhyāya*) and adoring God (*īśvara-praṇidhāna*). In the traditional *yoga* system these taken together are called *niyama* (restraint). Directing the mind, thus, to habitually seeing one alone in the many, and withdrawing it from the habit of seeing the many as real, are two essential opposite facets of the discipline called *yoga*. These two facets, like two sides of one coin, find their unity in the real *yoga*, and the genuine seeker has to attune himself to such a unitive *yoga*-situation. Only such a seeker becomes a real *yogī*. Others may see such a one engaged in worldly activities as everyone else, but he or she would be seeing all such activities merely as forming part of the beginningless and endless flow of actions (*karma*s) taking place in one *Ātmā*. This intuitive vision and one's own uniting oneself with it, together makes the *yoga* complete, and makes one a real *yogī*.

Mind becoming attached to pleasurable objects and not seeing the Reality that has assumed the form of itself and of the objects, is not an error that happens merely at any particular time. It rather takes place all through life. Therefore the above-mentioned yogic restraint of mind also has to go on throughout one's life. The mind thus has to be brought back each time it goes astray, and this has to be a constant practice as the Guru suggests in this verse which has much similarity with the following verse of the *Bhagavad-Gītā*:

yato yato niścarati manaś cañcalam asthiram
tatas tato niyamyaitad ātmany eva vaśaṁ nayet ||
—VI. 26

Whatever causes the changeful, unsteady mind to go out (again and again), from each such, restraining (it again and again) it should ever be led to the side of the Self.

Verses 6-7

सर्वानर्थकरः पुंसां सङ्कल्पः कल्पितैः सह ।
उन्मूल्य वासनाजालैर्येनाऽत्मनि निरुध्यते ॥६॥

दृश्यस्य न दृशोऽस्तित्वं अतो दृश्यं दृगात्मकम् ।
इति युञ्जीत दृग्रूपे यः स योगविदां वरः ॥७॥

sarvānarthakaraḥ puṁsāṁ saṁkalpaḥ kalpitaiḥ saha |
unmūlya vāsanā-jālair yenā 'tmani nirudhyate ||6 ||

dṛśyasya na dṛśo 'stitvaṁ ato dṛśyaṁ dṛg-ātmakam ।
iti yuñjīta dṛg-rūpe yaḥ sa yogavidāṁ varaḥ ॥7 ॥

> One who uproots all wilful activities of mind (*saṁkalpa*) — the cause of all disasters in human life — along with all that the mind wills as well as the inborn impressions and tendencies that arouse such wilfulness, and then restrains the mind in the *ātmā*/in oneself;
>
> And one who finds oneself one with the subjective consciousness, with the awareness that the perceived objects have no existence of their own, that the perceiving consciousness alone does really exist, and that all the perceived objects thus really are subjective consciousness in essential content, is the best among the *yoga*-knowers.

Suppose a lady visits a jewellery shop intending to buy a necklace. In the shop she gets struck by the attractiveness of a particular necklace and she chooses it, not caring for any other. The jeweller simply weighs it and fixes the price, not caring for its design, and she buys it. What attracted the lady is the beauty of the necklace, which, in her perception, no other necklace displayed there has. In her mind the lady already had some concept of a beautiful necklace, and she was attracted by the one that agreed with it. The same is the case with all of us. Each of us has in us many preconceived notions, for example, of good and evil.

How did such preconceived notions become well-rooted in our mind? The experiences we have had all through life, since our birth, leave some impressions, in our mind, helping us to differentiate and evaluate everything we come across. New impressions get formulated in us with every new experience we have. These are called *saṁskāra*s. The inborn impressions and tendencies with which we enter this world and which make up a part of our own being are called *vāsanā*s.

All such *vāsanā*s and *saṁskāra*s together are signified by the term *vāsanā* (inborn impressions and tendencies) by the Guru here.

It is these *vāsanā*s that cause the arising of wilful imaginations and ideations in the mind, either favourable and convincing (*saṁkalpa*) or unfavourable and confusing (*vikalpa*). Both *saṁkalpa* and *vikalpa* are covered here by the term *saṁkalpa* (wilful activities of mind).

Life is felt to be unbearably miserable mostly when such wilful imaginations and wishes remain unfulfilled, and what is unwilled happens in an unfavourable way. Liberation from such miseries is possible only through uprooting the wilful imaginations (*saṁkalpa*) and their root-cause the *vāsanā*s.

How is this to be accomplished? By restraining the mind (*nirudhyate*) and bringing oneself back to one's own self-content (*ātmani*).

Like becoming infatuated with the external appearance of the necklace, one may become attracted by the pleasure-giving qualities of the visible world and the things in it, inattentive to the gold-like Substance that underlies the being of all the visibles. That Substance is what we call *Ātmā*, and on perceiving It, mind becomes naturally withdrawn from the visible forms and moves towards what is Real in them. Then alone one realizes that what was thought of as *saṁkalpa*s and their root-cause *vāsanā*s, all have their being only in *Ātmā*. Then one no longer becomes tempted by the attractiveness of external appearances.

What is this *Ātmā* in its essential content? The substance or *ātmā* in the being of an ornament is gold. The ornament-forms are visible to the eyes, but the gold-substance as such remains invisible, for the reason that it has no form of its own. Similar is the Substance in the being of everything in all the worlds; it is not only invisible to the eyes, it is inaccessible to any of the senses as well. Its existence is simply known to us, and thus it is knowledge or consciousness in its essential content. This consciousness naturally is conscious of everything that happens within itself, and hence is the perceiver (*dṛk*) of everything. Whatever is perceived is known as *dṛśya*. It is the same consciousness that assumes the form of this *dṛśya*, and then perceives it. It is therefore said here *ato dṛśyam dṛgātmakam* (all the perceived objects thus really are subjective consciousness in essential content). Just as an ornament has no being separate from the gold, nothing in the visible world has being apart from the perceiving consciousness or *ātmā*.

Each of us is in the place of a distinct piece of ornament. We become attracted towards other objects or others who essentially are not different from us. Suppose an ornament thinks of itself, "I am gold," instead of treating itself as "I am an ornament." Similarly, let us think "I am *ātmā*" instead of considering oneself as "I am so and so." The "I" as an individual then merges in the being of the one all-underlying *Ātmā*. I then see not only myself as *Ātmā*, but I see this one *Ātmā* alone as existing in the form of everything. The best of *yoga*-knowers, thus, is the one who experiences this *yoga* state, or the state of merger of all the visible objects and of oneself in the being of one *Ātmā*, the all-perceiving Consciousness.

Verse 8

यदा पिबन् मनोभृङ्गः स्वानन्दमधुमाधुरीम् ।
न स्पन्दति वशीकृत्य योजितो योगवायुना ॥८॥

yadā piban mano-bhṛṅgaḥ svānanda madhu mādhurīm ।
na spandati vaśīkṛtya yojito yoga-vāyunā ॥8॥

> When the bumble-bee-like mind, having become charmed by the *yoga*-breeze and found oneness (with *Ātmā*), drinks rejoicingly, with no pulsation whatsoever, the honey-like sweetness of the *Ātman*'s *ānanda*-content, then it is real *yoga*.

Bumble bee is a creature that flies fluttering in the air, and often its direction of flight is controlled by the blowing wind. Mind is a sort of bumble bee. It moves in the direction to which the wind of *vāsanā*s and *saṁkalpa*s blows. This happens with only those who are fully ignorant about the nature and content of mind, its role in human life, and how life is to be guided with its help, and who live fully controlled by fleeting temptations. They feel life to be meaningless and purposeless.

Yet there are a few who wish to live life with a clear understanding of its meaning and the Reality that appears in the form of the mind and the life it controls. They perceive the mind simply as a momentary fluttering of the bee called *Ātman*, in the form of the function of doubting, imagining and willing. The same fluttering is seen by them in everything that happens in life every moment. The breeze that pushes life and mind on, with them, is that of *yoga*, and hence it could be named *yoga-vāyu*, the *yoga*-breeze. To elucidate: with them it is the state of remaining fully identified with *Ātmā*, it is the awareness that *Ātmā* alone unfolds itself as mind, as life, as the world, that pushes life on like a favourable wind.

When they start relishing honey from flowers, the wings of the bees that were till then fluttering, become motionless. Similar is the state of the mind that is guided by the *yoga-vāyu* towards *Ātmā* to enjoy its honey-like *ānanda*-content. The mind, on realizing, "The *ānanda* I enjoy is the essential content of *Ātmā*," "Myself is *Ātmā* in essence," "My fluttering also is part of the function of *Ātmā*," ceases to be mind, i.e. it forgets to remain as mind and also to flutter. What remains then is only the blissfulness of simply being *Ātmā*. That state of the mind remaining pulsationless in the being of *Ātmā* is to be called real *yoga*.

Verse 9

ध्यानमन्तर्भ्रुवोर्दृष्टिर्जिह्वाग्रं लम्बिकोर्ध्वतः ।
यदा स्यात्खेचरी मुद्रा निद्रालस्यादिनाशिनी ॥९॥

dhyānam antar bhruvor dr̥ṣtir jihvāgraṁ lambikordhvataḥ ।
yadā syāt khecarī mudrā nidrālasyādi nāśinī ॥9॥

When meditation and gaze together are fixed in between the eyebrows, along with the tip of the tongue touching above the uvula, then it is *khecarī-mudrā*, a dispeller of drowsiness, fatigue and the like.

The *yoga* so far presented by the Guru in the *Yoga-Darśanam* is conceived as aspects of the mystical-cum-philosophical experience of non-duality (*advaita*), familiar to Vedānta. The traditional *yoga* system is of a different nature. Instead of serving as a buttress to the philosophy of non-dualism, it is a sort of vision supplementary to the philosophy of the Sāṁkhya school of dualism.

Patañjali is the *r̥ṣi* who codified *yoga* into a perfect system of thought-cum-discipline. The Sāṁkhya school considers *puruṣa* (person or individual consciousness) and *prakr̥ti* (nature) as two basic realities, the former always constrained to remain under the restrictions of the latter. Liberating *puruṣa* from the clutches of *prakr̥ti* and enabling it to attain its original purity and freedom, is the goal of the yogic disciplines. The Sāṁkhya school conceives of a process of evolution (*pariṇāma*) happening in *prakr̥ti*, causing it to evolve as the world, all witnessed by *puruṣa*. Reversing this process of evolution through certain self-imposed disciplines, and helping the *puruṣa* attain back its pure state of freedom is what the Patañjali's system conceives as *yoga*, and for this reason, this process of reversal is sometimes named *prati-prasava* (giving-birth-reversed). *Yama* (abstention), *niyama* (observances), *āsana* (postures), *prāṇāyāma* (breath control), *pratyāhāra* (withdrawing the senses), *dhāraṇā* (concentration), *dhyānam* (meditation) and *samādhi* (final absorption) are the eight stages of discipline enjoined by Patañjali, and therefore, the system is also known as *aṣṭāṅga-yoga* (the eight-limbed *yoga*).

A system of purely physical *yoga* practice, giving more stress to the *āsana* and *prāṇāyāma* part of it, named *Haṭha Yoga*, meaning "the forced *yoga*," developed later. Patañjali's *yoga* is also known as *Rāja Yoga* (the kingly *yoga*), and the proponents of *Haṭha Yoga* often popularize it, particularly in modern times, as if it is *Rāja Yoga* itself.

Haṭhayoga-Pradīpikā and *Gheraṇḍa Saṁhitā* are the basic texts of *Haṭha Yoga*. And one of the most advanced disciplines taught in these is known as *mudrā*s, literally "marks." Of all the *mudrā*s, the most difficult and one meant to be practised strictly under the supervision of a proper *guru*, is *Khecarī-mudrā*. It is called thus because, as is claimed, it results in the experience of oneself moving about in the sky, *khe* meaning, "in the sky" and *carī*, "moving about." The Guru must have gone through such practices while being a student of *yoga* under Thaikkattu Ayyāvu.

Although such a way of *yoga* does not find a respectable place in the royal highway of his philosophy proper, references can be found here and there indicative of his familiarity with such, one being the present verse. The Guru, concluding this chapter on *yoga*, also states very clearly in the next verse that all the existing *yoga* systems could very well be brought under two classes, namely, *jñāna-yoga* and *karma-yoga*. When contemplating upon giving a definite shape to this chapter, as is evident from the present verse, the Guru must have thought it appropriate to make clear his opinion about such forced physical *yoga* disciplines. Above all, the Guru in those days was adored by many of his lay followers as a saint of unworldly yogic attainments called *siddhi*s. As a correction to all such, he states here very clearly what is the essential content of *Khecarī-mudrā*, the most difficult part of *Haṭha Yoga*, and the extent of its benefit in human life.

Khecarī-mudrā is the practice of meditatively concentrating on the middle of the eyebrows along with bending the tongue upwards until its tip touches its own root and then closes the upward cavity there, by remaining united with uvula. Describing it, the Guru does not claim that any kind of wisdom-related attainment is gained by this practice. Instead, he gives it the credit merely of a dispeller of drowsiness, fatigue and the like (*nidrālasyādi nāśinī*). Admittedly, the absence of drowsiness and fatigue creates an atmosphere favourable for attaining wisdom.

It could also be claimed that the compound word *nidrālasyādi* (drowsiness, fatigue and the like) refers to the nine *citta-vikṣepa*s (distractions of the mind) and the five *upadrava*s (disturbances) well known in the *yoga* system. These fourteen items together are known as *antarāya*s (hindrances to the concentration of mind). Another well-known aspect is that the purity and clarity of our knowledge (*sattva-guṇa*) is disturbed by the predominance of *rajo-guṇa* (active modality of nature) and *tamo-guṇa* (dark and inert modality of nature). Our awareness of this defect could impel us to correct it by practising certain well-recognized disciplines including the *Khecarī-mudrā*. Perhaps this was also in the mind of the Guru when he penned this verse. Otherwise, the Guru was not in favour of making such physical *yoga* practices an unavoidable part of a seeker's search for Reality. The Guru opined himself once that such practices help easy removal of phlegm from the body.

Concentrating the mind at the mid-point between the eyebrows is a meditation practice well-accepted in Vedānta as well. All the realized *ṛṣi*s recommend this as one of the best means to withdraw the mind from external objects of interest to the essential content of one's own being. The *Bhagavad-Gītā* also does the same (VIII.10). Concentrating the mind between the eyebrows along with repeating the sacred syllable *AUṀ* is yet another spiritual practice popular in India. The Guru gives recognition to it here, though as part of the *Khecarī-mudrā*.

That practising this *mudrā* does not form part of the *yoga* proper conceived by the Guru, is evident from the next verse.

Verse 10

ज्ञानं कर्मेति लोकेऽस्मिन् द्विधा योगः समासतः।
अनयोर्योगविस्तारः सर्वः परिसमाप्यते ॥१०॥

jñānaṁ karmeti loke 'smin dvidhā yogaḥ samāsataḥ ।
anayor yogavistāraḥ sarvaḥ parisamāpyate ॥10॥

In this world *yoga* can be summarized as being of two kinds: *jñāna-yoga* and *karma-yoga*. The entire range of *yoga* is conclusively comprised within the fold of these two divisions.

Though a distinct school of Indian thought, *yoga* had its impact on almost all other schools implicitly or explicitly. This is particularly true in the case of Vedānta. *Yoga* is a word known to most of the modern lovers of Indian wisdom. The *yoga* concept has even seeped into such non-spiritual disciplines as music and dance.

This development caused the sprouting up and propagation of many brands of *yoga*. Even within the framework of Vedānta the concepts of fourfold *yoga*s, namely, *karma-yoga, jñāna-yoga, bhakti-yoga* and *rāja-yoga* are popular among certain adherents. Some other well-known *yoga* cults are *haṭha-yoga, mantra-yoga* (the *yoga* of sacred formulas), *laya-yoga* (the *yoga* of merger), *nāda-yoga* (the *yoga* of sound), *dhyāna-yoga* (the *yoga* of meditation), and the like. Numerous are the *yoga* cults that have emerged in modern times, especially in the wake of *yoga* getting more and more acceptance in the West.

As we know, "to unite," or "to become united" is the key point in the *yoga*-concept. The nature of *yoga* conceived by each school or cult could vary according to the nature of what are thought of as being brought into union and how. In this verse the Guru proclaims that the entire wide range of *yoga* (*yoga-vistāra*) can easily fit into two general classes, namely *jñāna-yoga* and *karma-yoga*. The *Bhagavad-Gītā* also takes the same stand when it says:

> *loke 'smin dvividhā niṣṭhā purā proktā mayānagha*
> *jñānayogena sāṁkhyānāṁ karmayogena yoginām* ॥ — III.3

> There are two kinds of disciplines in this world as declared in ancient times by Me, O sinless one (Arjuna): the unitive way of wisdom (*jñāna-yoga*) of the Sāṁkhyas and the unitive way of action (*karma-yoga*) of the *yogin*s.

What *karma-yoga* means was made sufficiently clear in Chapter III of the *Gītā* as well as in Chapter 6 of the *Darśanamālā*. Its essential content could be summarized as follows:

All the *karma*s (actions) take place in the being of *Ātmā* or *Brahman*, because of Its own mysterious creative urge called *māyā*. That Reality, when active thus, is called *prakṛti* (nature). This *prakṛti* is in a process of constant rolling on like a giant wheel. The emerging and merger of individual entities happen in it as part of this process. Being part of the *prakṛti* that is active, we individuals too remain active, both physically and mentally, all through our life. The actions we happen to perform thus really do not belong to us individuals, but to the total *prakṛti*.

For the one who performs all the *karma*s in life with this awareness, the very same *karma* becomes a helpful means for realizing one's identity with the total *prakṛti*, the total Reality. Realizing one's oneness (*yoga*) with the total thus, with performing *karma*s as a means, makes one a *karma-yogin*. The same basic stand is proclaimed by the Guru in the *Darśanamālā* (6.1) when he says:

> *ātmaiva māyayā karma karoti bahu-rūpa-dhṛk* ॥
>
> (*Ātmā* alone perfoms all the *karma*s by assuming various forms).

The Guru elucidates it well in the rest of the chapter as we have already seen. All physical *yoga* practices could in a limited sense be also brought under the category of *karma-yoga*.

Jñāna-yoga, on the other hand, is a discipline that gives primacy to knowing, a discipline more interiorized than *karma-yoga*. "Knowing" here means knowing the ultimate Reality or *Brahman* as oneself in essence, or oneself as *Brahman* in essence. The *Bhagavad-Gītā* puts the essential content of this knowledge or *jñāna* into a nutshell as follows:

> *yena bhūtāny aśeṣeṇa drakṣasy ātmany atho mayi* ॥
>
> That knowledge by which all beings without exception will be seen in yourself and then in Me. — IV. 35

That means, perceiving the Reality that underlies the being of all the beings in the being of oneself, and then to see oneself in *Brahman*, is the essential content of wisdom or *jñāna*. Put otherwise, seeing the known world, the knowing self and the absolute Reality, as different perceptual facets of the one and only non-dual Reality is what *jñāna* means in Vedānta. The Guru himself gives vent to this perception in his Universal Prayer called *Daivadaśakam* (Ten Verses on God) as follows addressing God.

> Counting all the countables one by one, when everything is reckoned finished with, they disappear and continue to exist in the seeing mind. In the like manner, let this mind attain to rest pulsationless in You. — (Verse 2)

An individual being's existence is as part of the existence of the whole world. Therefore, what is real in one's own being is the imperishable Reality in the total being of the world. This state of one becoming enlightened as to one's own being in full identity with *Brahman*, the absolute Reality, is called *jñāna* or wisdom. One experientially living as one with the whole, as a wave's inseparability from the ocean, is a *jñāna-yogin*. This self-identity with *Brahman* is conceived by the Guru himself as *para-jñāna* (Transcendental knowledge) at the end of the *Jñāna-Darśanam* (see Verse 7.10 earlier).

Though divisible so into two for formality's sake, in principle and content, the two types of *yoga* are inseparable. One is meaningless without the other, and one who attains the one attains the other as well, as is explicitly stated in the *Gītā* in its Chapter V and as testified by actual life of saints like Narayana Guru himself. What is important is attaining the *yoga* state, whether resorting to the way of *karma* or of *jñāna*. This cosmic system has a structural coherence and perfection of its own, in which all the constituent elements, both subtle and gross, both mental and physical, appear as if discernible in a synthetic whole. Human beings also form an essential element of it. The real *yoga* they can experience in life is that of uniting themselves with the structural perfection of the whole.

10

Nirvāṇa Darśanam
(Vision by Emancipation)

THE five visions or *darśanas* presented in the second half of this work show in a graded fashion, five different facets of how an individual can actualize in life his or her oneness with the Absolute. The series began with seeing this oneness at the gross level of apparent activities (*karmas*), and then passing on through subtler and more interiorized realms of knowledge (*jñāna*), contemplative adoration (*bhakti*) and *yoga*.

Now we reach the stage of *nirvāṇa* or emancipation. *Nirvāṇa* literally means "becoming burned out" suggesting here the individual feeling as though oneself is becoming extinguished. The life of every living being, from birth to death, is a process comparable to a fire burning, death marking its final burning out. Into where does this fire of life disappear? It disappears into the source Reality from where it emerged. This source Reality was called *Parameśvara* (the Supreme God) in the first chapter. It was defined as *saccidānanda* in Chapter 2. The same was thought of in Chapter 3 as the Substance, like the stone in a *śivaliṅga*, that underlies the appearance of the world. In Chapter 4 the same was conceived as that which is to be attained by negating *māyā* and its effects. It was presented as the one unconditioned *sat* (existence) in Chapter 5.

The problem of the hereafter, as far as those who are familiar with the philosophical visions presented in this

Darśanamālā is concerned, does not arise at all. Birth, life and death are merely the emerging, rolling on and the merging back of individual waves in the ocean of *sat* or *Ātman*, referred to variously in the first five chapters. Nothing new is born when a wave emerges in the ocean, and nothing dies when it merges in the ocean. Waves are merely specific forms that emerge in the ocean owing to the intrinsic creative urge in it. Similar is the creative urge in *Ātman* or *Brahman* that causes the appearance and disappearance of specific forms. The *nirvāṇa* understood in this concluding chapter is comparable to the disappearance of waves in the being of the ocean. We, the waves, merely merge back into the ocean-like *Brahman*.

Most Vedānta textbooks end with a chapter on *mokṣa* or the Final Liberation. The *nirvāṇa* discussed here is synonymous with this concept of *mokṣa*, as *nirvāṇa* is the state in which all the sufferings of life become extinguished. The Guru cannot therefore be accused of transgressing the customary way of Vedānta in spite of the fact that *nirvāṇa* is a term that is popular in Buddhist canons.

Nirvāṇa, *parinirvāṇa* (final extinction of the individual), *mahā-parinirvāṇa* (the great extinction) are all popular terms in Buddhism. *Parinirvāṇa* is almost equivalent to the *videha mukti* concept of Vedānta. The death of Buddha, the enlightened one, alone is referred to as *mahā-parinirvāṇa*. *Nirvāṇa*, according to Buddhism, is something that happens at death, but it is conceived here as not related to death at all. On the other hand, it is an experience of oneself merging in the Absolute while living.

The Upaniṣads refer to this experiential state as *amṛtatva* (immortality), *śreyas* (final beautitude), *bhūmā* (the great) and the like. *Nirvṛti* (full contentment), *nirvṛtti* (accomplishment), *nivṛtti* (complete withdrawal), *parama-gati* (supreme goal), *parama-pada* (supreme state), *kaivalya* (absolute aloneness), *mukti* (liberation), *apavarga* (completion), *brahma-bhūyas* (absolute identity with *Brahman*), *brahmatva* (the state of being *Brahman*), *brahma-sāyujya* (becoming merged in *Brahman*), *brahma-saṁsparśa* (to be in touch with *Brahman*), *brahma-nirvāṇa* (to become lost in *Brahman*) are some other terms well known generally in the context of Indian philosophy relating to the attainment of the final goal of life. It could well be acknowledged that, in analysing or rather classifying the *nirvāṇa* states, the Guru bases himself on the notion of *jīvan-mukta* (to become liberated while living) of both Śaṅkara and *Yoga-Vāśiṣṭha*, for no reference to death finds place here. Nor is there any need to differentiate the philosophical death attained while living from actual death. The actual death of every being, philosophically speaking, is a sort of burning out process. Yet, it is thought of as so only by a very few, the enlightened. Such ones need not wait till death to enjoy the absolute contentment of *nirvāṇa*. For them every moment of life is an actualization of the *nirvāṇa*-experience.

Verse 1

निर्वाणं द्विविधं शुद्धमशुद्धं चेति तत्र यत्।
शुद्धं निर्वासनं तद्वदशुद्धं वासनान्वितम् ॥१॥

nirvāṇam dvividhaṁ śuddhaṁ aśuddhaṁ ceti tatra yat ।
śuddhaṁ nirvāsanaṁ tadvad aśuddhaṁ vāsanānvitam ॥1 ॥

Nirvāṇa is of two kinds: the pure and the impure. Of these, the pure *nirvāṇa* is devoid of all *vāsanā*s (incipient memory factors); and the impure, likewise, is accompanied by *vāsanā*s.

Nirvāṇa is the state in which an individual finds himself or herself completely extinguished in the being of the Total. One individual, by nature, is different from another, both physically and mentally. The way one burns out, therefore, has also to be different from that of another. We are quite familiar with the phenomenon of firewood becoming burned out. The way each piece of firewood burns is different, some discharging dark smoke, some emitting red flames, some flaming without sparks, some emitting sparks with sounds, and so on. Whichever the kind of firewood, its nature of burning and emitting smoke depends to a great extent on the moisture content in it. Almost similar is the *nirvāṇa* of individuals, depending on the *vāsanā*-content in each. Still for the sake of clarity in our studies, just as firewood could be classified as dry and wet, *nirvāṇa* could well be classified as *nirvāsanam* (devoid of *vāsanās*) and *vāsanānvitam* (accompanied by *vāsanās*). The former again is divided into two: *śuddham* (pure) and *aśuddham* (impure). We have already examined in detail what *vāsanā* signifies (see comments on Verse 9.2 earlier).

The *nirvāṇa* understood here could either be what one experiences while living, or be the total extinction, called death, of the individual entity. The way one accomplishes the former would vary according to the personal traits of the individual concerned. Some may have to undergo very severe and austere spiritual practices; some others attain it through some gentle means; and in the case of a very very few, it happens simply as if by nature with no enforced discipline at all. In spite of all these discernible differences, it remains a fact that what each experiences in the state of *nirvāṇa* is completely unknown to anyone else. It cannot even be guessed by another. Some in that state may be seen living as everyone does, forming part of the flow of the world, some others might live in complete forgetfulness of the world.

If the *nirvāṇa* is taken to mean the death of the individual, then a belief prevails in India that those who attain pure *nirvāṇa* are never reborn, but those who attain the impure *nirvāṇa* have to be reborn. A forceful breaker, upon hitting the shore and receding, influences the force of the wave that succeeds it. Similar is the case with humans. The *vāsanā*s of a person and his or her activities have their impact on those who are around him or her, and also genetically on the next generation. This scientifically-established fact, when conceived by the seers of India at a period of history when science was not so developed, assumed the form of the theory of reincarnation.

As the waves become less and less forceful, as they become no waves at all in effect, their capability to give rise to new waves also recedes, and finally vanishes. Comparable to it is the state of rebirthless pure *nirvāṇa*.

Verse 2

अतिशुद्धं शुद्धमिति शुद्धं च द्विविधं तथा ।
अशुद्धशुद्धञ्चाशुद्धमशुद्धाशुद्धमुच्यते ॥२॥

atiśuddhaṁ śuddham iti śuddhaṁ ca dvividhaṁ tathā ।
aśuddha-śuddhaṁ cāśuddhaṁ aśuddhāśuddhaṁ ucyate ॥1 ॥

The pure *nirvāṇa* also is of two kinds: the highly pure and the pure. The impure *nirvāṇa* as well is considered divisible likewise as the pure impure and the impure impure.

The classification of *nirvāṇa* or *mukti*, as conceived by the Guru in the present chapter, does not find place in any of the available traditional scriptures or classical textbooks on Vedānta. *Yoga-Vāśiṣṭha* makes reference to *sapta-bhūmikā*s (seven grades of *nirvāṇa*). The *brahmavit* (knower of *Brahman*), *brahmavid-vara* (the elect knower of *Brahman*), *brahmavid-varīyān* (the superior knower of *Brahman*) and *brahmavid-variṣṭha* (the most superior knower of *Brahman*), the last four grades given by the Guru here, appear in the *sapta-bhūmikā*-gradation also as the last four. But the overall scheme of gradation conceived by the Guru varies from that of the *Yoga-Vāśiṣṭha*.

The idea of various kinds of unworldly attainments (*siddhi*s) is already available in the collective psyche of India, based on the stories of many *siddha*s, seers, saints and *ācārya*s (masters). All such *siddhi*s must have been codified and graded by the Guru in such a way that they fit in with the *mukti* or *nirvāṇa* concept. Anyway, the present classification is to be seen as the Guru's own original idea.

What he calls *śuddha* (pure) *nirvāṇa* is again subdivided into *śuddha* (pure) and *atiśuddha* (highly pure). Likewise, the *aśuddha* (impure) *nirvāṇa* also is classified, possibly based on the intensity of *vāsanā*s present, into two: the *aśuddha-śuddha* (impure-pure) and *aśuddha-aśuddha* (impure-impure). *Aśuddha-śuddha* means that which is comparatively pure amongst the impure, and *aśuddha-aśuddha*, the most impure amongst the impure.

The Śaṅkara school of Advaita Vedānta classifies *mukti* as *jīvana-mukti* and *videha-mukti*, the former being the liberation one experiences while living, and the latter is the one a *jñānin* attains upon death. The *yoga* system calls the penultimate stage *samādhi* (the ultimate goal being pure aloneness, *kaivalya*), classified as *savikalpa samādhi* (*samādhi* conceivable) and *nirvikalpa-samādhi* (*samādhi* inconceivable). Within the *savikalpa* or conceivable *samādhi* itself are seen different grades. However, the scheme of classification conceived by the Guru here is entirely different from all these. All the Guru's subdivisions of *nirvāṇa* are defined in the verses to follow.

Verse 3

अतिशुद्धं त्रिधा पश्चाद्वरे चैकं वरीयसि ।
एकमेकं वरिष्ठेऽथ शुद्धं ब्रह्मविदि स्थितम् ॥३॥

atiśuddhaṁ tridhā paścād vare caikaṁ varīyasi ।
ekam ekaṁ variṣṭhe 'tha śuddhaṁ brahmavidi sthitam ॥3॥

Again the highly pure (*atiśuddha*) is of three grades: one is seen in *brahmavid-vara*, the next in *brahmavid-varīyān*, and the third in *brahmavid-variṣṭha*. And the pure *nirvāṇa* is seen well founded in *brahmavit*.

The *śuddha nirvāṇa* was first divided into *śuddha* (pure) and *atiśuddha* (highly pure) in the last verse. Of the two, the highly pure is seen here as having three grades found in *brahmavid-vara* (the elect knower of *Brahman*), *brahmavid-varīyān* (the superior knower of *Brahman*) and *brahmavid-variṣṭha* (the most superior knower of *Brahman*). The *śuddha nirvāṇa* is seen in a *brahmavit* (knower of *Brahman*), all these are to be defined later. Such a vertically ranging gradation of *brahmavit*, *brahmavid-vara*, *brahmavid-varīyān*, and *brahmavid-variṣṭha* is found in the *Yoga-Vāśiṣṭha* also. Yet they are to be defined by the Guru here in his own way.

Verse 4

अशुद्धशुद्धं विरजस्तमोऽन्यत्सरजस्तमः ।
मुमुक्षौ प्रथमं विद्यात् द्वितीयं सिद्धिकामिषु ॥४॥

aśuddha-śuddhaṁ virajas tamo 'nyat sarajas tamaḥ ।
mumukṣau prathamaṁ vidyāt dvitīyaṁ siddhi-kāmiṣu ॥4॥

The pure-impure *nirvāṇa* is devoid of *rajo-guṇa* and *tamo-guṇa*. These two *guṇas* are present in the impure-impure *nirvāṇa*. The former is found in the seekers of liberation, and the latter in those who are desirous of psychic powers.

This verse defines the *aśuddha-śuddha* (pure-impure) and the *aśuddha-aśuddha* (impure-impure) *nirvāṇa*s, and tells us in whom these *nirvāṇa*s can be found in actual life. According to Indian thinkers, the three *guṇa*s (modalities of nature) — *sattva* (pure and clear), *rajas* (affective-active) and *tamas* (dark and inert) — are inherent in each individual as part of nature. Winning over the domination of the latter two is a prerequisite for all seekers of liberation (*mumukṣu*s). Such a seeker, subduing the forcefulness of *rajas* and the inertness of *tamas*, strives for the attainment of one's final goal. Such a one exemplifies the *aśuddha-śuddha* (pure-impure or impure-pure) *nirvāṇa*. Still lower is the status of the *aśuddha-aśuddha* (impure-impure) *nirvāṇa*, to be found in those who are yet under the spell of *rajo-guṇa* and *tamo-guṇa*. They too strive for some attainment, and to that extent their effort also is to be classed under spiritual practices, though the most inferior, the impure amongst the impure. There is a type of spiritual aspirant who yearns for certain unworldly psychic powers or attainments, called *siddhi*s. The *nirvāṇa* they experience could be classed under the impure-impure type. Considering such unworldly powers as marking spiritual attainments and treating those who have such *siddhi*s as godlike, is a common practice all over the world among laymen and even among religious scholars. The Guru considers here the desire for such attainments as only the lowest grade of spiritual aspiration. Patañjali's *yoga* system also acknowledges such attainments as possible, but he himself admits that these really are obstacles to the real spiritual goal of *samādhi* or *kaivalya*. The Guru degrading such attainments as the most impure amongst the impure suggests all this, as if it is a warning.

Verse 5

दग्ध्वा ज्ञानाग्निना सर्वमुद्दिश्य जगतां हितम् ।
करोति विधिवत्कर्म ब्रह्मविद्ब्रह्मणि स्थितः ॥५॥

dagdhvā jñānāgninā sarvam uddiśya jagatāṁ hitam I
karoti vidhivat karma brahmavid brahmaṇi sthitaḥ II5 II

Brahmavit (the knower of the Absolute) is the one who, having burned down everything in the fire of wisdom, finds himself in *Brahman*. He performs actions in conformity with prescribed rules of conduct aiming at the good of the world.

The present verse describes the *nirvāṇa* experienced by a *brahmavit* in his state of *śuddha* (pure) type of *nirvāṇa*. He is a *jñānin*, a man of wisdom. A person becomes a *jñānin* when he or she is capable of perceiving intuitively the inseparable oneness of the one absolute Reality or *Brahman* and the multifarious evanescent worldly apperances. In all that appears as many, he or she perceives one *Brahman* alone as creatively existing. No other reality is seen as existing by such a *jñānin*. The "many" thus becomes burned down in the fire of wisdom (*jñānāgni*). One of such a perception is to be called a *brahmavit* or knower of *Brahman*. Such a one sees oneself as a fleeting speck of the existence of *Brahman*.

Brahman unfolding itself as this world, has a coherent structural system of its own. No one can tamper with it. The *Brahman*-knower is no exception. Each individual, forming part of the whole, has a specific role to play in maintaining this structural coherence. With this awareness, the *Brahman*-knower ceaselessly engages in activities natural to him or her. As these actions come to pass as part of the eternal flux of nature, there is no sense of attachment towards the actions he or she happens to perform. Such is the way of life of a *brahmavit* (knower of *Brahman*). This is the ideal life-pattern recommended in the *Bhagavad-Gītā*.

Verse 6

संन्यस्य सर्वकर्माणि सततं ब्रह्मनिष्ठया ।
यश्चरत्यवनौ देहयात्रायै ब्रह्मविद्वरः ॥६॥

saṁnyasya sarva-karmāṇi satataṁ brahmaniṣṭhayā ।
yaś caraty avanau deha-yātrāyai brahmavid-varaḥ ॥6॥

One who moves about the world simply for the sake of bodily existence, finding oneself fully established in *Brahman*, with all *karma*s having been properly renounced, is the *brahmavid-vara* (the elect knower of *Brahman*).

Verse 7

अन्येन वेदितो वेत्ति न वेत्ति स्वयमेव यः ।
स वरीयान् सदा ब्रह्मनिर्वाणमयमश्नुते ॥७॥

anyena vedito vetti na vetti svayam eva yaḥ ।
sa varīyān sadā brahma-nirvāṇam ayam aśnute ॥7॥

He who becomes conscious of something only when informed by others, but does not do so by himself, is the *brahmavid-varīyān* (the superior knower of *Brahman*). He always is in the state of enjoying absorption in *Brahman*.

Verse 8

स्वयं न वेत्ति किञ्चिन्न वेदितोऽपि तथैव यः ।
स वरिष्ठः सदा वृत्तिशून्योऽयं ब्रह्म केवलम् ॥८॥

svayaṁ na vetti kiñcin na vedito 'pi tathaiva yaḥ ।
sa variṣṭhaḥ sadā vṛtti-śūnyo 'yaṁ brahma kevalam ॥8॥

He who does not become conscious of anything by himself, and remains so even when informed by others, such a one is the *brahmavid-variṣṭha* (the most superior knower of *Brahman*). Remaining functionless, he simply is *Brahman* itself.

The overall gradation of *nirvāṇa* conceived in this chapter could well be charted out as follows:

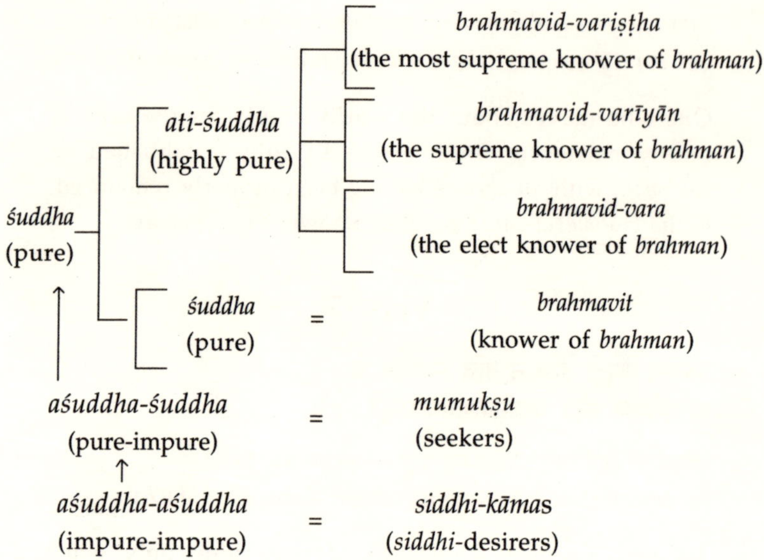

Verse 9

हेयोपादेयता नह्यस्याऽत्मा वा स्वप्रकाशकः ।
इति मत्वा निवर्तेत वृत्तिर्नावर्त्तते पुनः ॥९॥

heyopādeyatā na hy asyā 'tmā vā svaprakāśakaḥ ।
iti matvā nivarteta vṛttir nāvarttate punaḥ ॥9॥

Nothing of this world is worth giving up or worth accepting; and as to *Ātmā*, It always shines on its own. With this enlightenment attained one should withdraw from everything. No functioning repeats in such a one again.

With the definitions of all grades of *nirvāṇa* having been given, the Guru now proceeds to explicate the ideal *nirvāṇa*'s state of functionlessness. Along with it is pointed out the necessity of practising intentional withdrawal of oneself from all functions or activities in order to attain such a *nirvāṇa*.

One who finds oneself as well as all the worlds as the one *Ātmā* or Self manifesting itself variously, does not feel the need of possessing anything nor the need to give up anything in order to make oneself happier. Such a one always feels saturated with the contentment of remaining neutral towards everything. With the conviction that *Ātmā* alone exists, the desire to be engaged in wish-fulfilling activities, both physical and mental, subsides.

This natural tendency could well be nurtured with the intentional practice of withdrawing the external and internal faculties from their desire-motivated activities. Such self-withdrawal is known as *nivṛtti-mārga* in Vedāntic parlance. Thus, the conjoining of and the mutual compensation between, proper awareness and properly-directed self-withdrawal lead one to the *nirvāṇa* state one is competent for.

The passage *"vṛttir na āvartate punaḥ"* (no functioning repeats in such a person) is a varied version of the dictum *"na ca punar āvartate"* (he does not return hither any more) with which the *Chāndogya Upaniṣad* ends. This Upaniṣadic passage is often interpreted as meaning, "The *jīvanamukta*, after death, is not reborn again in this world." But one who has realized the oneness of *Ātmā* does not see oneself as an individual who was born once and destined to die one day. On the other hand, in one's own perception, one simply forms part of the everlasting self-unfoldment of the one birthless and deathless *Ātmā*. He or she simply is one with the immortal *Ātmā*. Having realized one's own immortality, one is no longer worried about the after-death.

It will be found on closely examining the above Upaniṣadic passage, that it does not deal with the state after death. A person, when thinking of himself or herself as an individual entity existing on its own, then he or she will have his or her own functions and activities. But, on the individual's attaining *nirvāṇa* in the self-effulgent *Ātmā*, all the functions and activities are of the *Ātmā*; the individual's functions and activities thus cease to be. This is the intuitive perception the Upaniṣadic passage denotes. The Guru's words here *"vṛttiḥ na āvartate punaḥ"* also signify the same. A liberated person becomes free of the notions that certain things are to be given up in life and certain other things are to be accepted. A liberated person does not return to the world where such notions are meaningful.

Verse 10

एकमेवाऽद्वितीयं ब्रह्मास्ति नान्यन्न संशयः ।
इति विद्वान्निवर्त्तेत द्वैतान्नावर्तते पुनः ॥१० ॥

ekam evā 'dvitīyaṁ brahmāsti nānyan na saṁśayaḥ ।
iti vidvān nivartteta dvaitān nāvartate punaḥ ॥10 ॥

> The one and non-dual *Brahman* alone exists. Nothing else does exist; no doubt is there. This enlightenment having been attained, the wise one should liberate himself from duality. Henceforth no turning back occurs.

This chapter on *nirvāṇa* concludes by pointing out the nature of the state of absorption of the individual into the being of *Brahman*, as a blissful non-dual experience. Those who yearn for such an ecstatic state of self-absorption have to first become fully convinced of the non-duality of the Real, and then should extricate themselves from all situations of duality such as birth and death, pain and pleasure, good and evil, internal and external, cause and effect, knower and known. The aspirant has to accomplish this on one's own guided by the speculations made so far. Once thus withdrawn, one returns no more to the world of duality. In other words, the blissfulness of *nirvāṇa*, in essence, is one becoming merged experientially in the being of the self-effulgent, non-dual *Atman* or *saccidānanda*, where duality of any kind is of no relevance. The words *"ekam eva advitīyam"* (the one and non-dual), again, is a reiteration of a passage from the *Chāndogya Upaniṣad* (VI.2.1).

The range of philosophical visions that constitute this "garland" began with examining the nature of what we call the "creation of the world," basing itself on the Upaniṣadic stand. It ends here, again following the Upaniṣadic lines, depicting how an individual who forms a part of the created world, becomes experientially absorbed in the being of the non-dual *Brahman*.

A seeker's tying both ends together and wearing it on oneself is where the value of this "garland" becomes realized as non-dual *ānanda*.

ॐ तत् सत्

AUṀ TAT SAT

Glossary

Abhāva: Non-existence. The opposite of *bhāva*. Non-existence has two main divisions:

(1) The absence of one entity in another (*saṁsarga-bhāva*) which is of three kinds:

(a) Prior non-existence (*prāg-abhāva*)

(b) Annihilative non-existence (*pradhvaṁsa-abhāva*)

(c) Absolute non-existence (*atyanta-abhāva*)

(2) One object not being another (*anyonya-abhāva*) or reciprocal non-existence.

Ābhāsa-caitanya: Pure Consciousness (*caitanya*) that appears to have a form that is unreal (*ābhāsa*). For example, the mother-of-pearl appearing to be silver, gold appearing as ornaments.

Adharma: That which is against *dharma* (see).

Adhidaivatam: *Adhi* stands for *adhiṣṭhāna* (basis) and *daivata* means residing deity, suggesting the universal aspect of what is being dealt with. *Adhidaivatam* thus indicates, perceiving some aspect of reality from its universal point of view as against the particular *adhyātmam* (see).

Adhyāsa: Superimposition; false attribution; illusion.

Adhyātmam: (*adhi* + *ātmā*) *Adhi* stands for *adhiṣṭhāna*, basis, *ātmā* means oneself or the self. The word is used in

Upaniṣads to indicate perceiving some aspect of reality as related to one's own being or the particular as against to universal or *adhidaivatam* (see).

Advaita: Non-duality. The vision that one Reality alone really has existence.

Ahaṁkāra: The I-sense each individual has.

Ahantā: I-sense denoting the subjective aspect of a knowledge situation, the object-aspect being known as *idantā* (this-sense) (see).

Ajāta-vāda: The theory that no creation takes place, only what already exists gets transformed into new forms.

Ajñāna: Ignorance. The mistaken notion concerning oneself and the world, that what appears manifestly is real, completely oblivious of the one all-underlying Reality called *Brahman* or *Ātman*.

Akṣara: The imperishable. Refers to the Ultimate Reality, *Brahman*.

Amanībhāva: The state in which the searching mind (*manas*) becomes merged and lost in what it searches for, i.e. *Brahman* or the Absolute.

Ānanda (*Ānandam*): Bliss. To be understood in the context of the Good in Western philosophy as a supreme value. *Sat*, *cit*, and *ānanda* are terms conjointly used to describe the Absolute (*Brahman*) in Vedānta. As related to an individual being, it is to be understood as the value-consciousness that enables one to evaluate one's own experience either as pleasant or unpleasant.

Anātmā: (*Anātman*): Non-self.

Antaḥkaraṇas: The common name for the four mental faculties involved in the process of knowing: namely, *manas* (questioning), *buddhi* (reasoning), *citta* (memorizing and recalling) and *ahaṁkāra* (relating what is known in terms of one's value-experience).

Anumiti-jñāna: Knowledge attained through inference.

Anusandhāna: Close enquiry or investigation. It, in the Vedāntic context, means persistent attempt of the mind to contemplatively perceive the substance that assumes the form of the very same mind.

Antarāyas: Literally means that which comes in-between. In the context of the Yoga System, it denotes the obstructions, that occur in the spiritual pursuit of a seeker.

Anvaya: Stating the positive reason for an inference, e.g. there is fire where there is smoke (see *vyatireka*).

Anyā: The functional aspect of consciousness in which reality is seen as many.

Aparā: Relativistic, conditional.

Apara-Brahman: Lower *Brahman* as opposed to *Para-Brahman* (Supreme *Brahman*). The causal Reality conceived as appearing as all the effects. Also called *kārya-Brahman* (see).

Aparā-vidyā: Worldly knowledge, aimed at worldly gains.

Aparokṣa-jñāna: Non-indirect knowledge, as against direct knowledge (*pratyakṣa-jñāna*) and indirect knowledge (*parokṣa-jñāna*) (see). Self-knowledge alone in the example of *aparokṣa-jñāna*. Narayana Guru, by defining *pratyakṣa-jñāna* in a different way, equates it with *aparokṣa-jñāna*.

Apavāda: *Apa* meaning "negatively" and *vāda* "to argue." *Apavāda* thus meaning "to argue out" or to affirm the real through negating the unreal. The word in literature means, "exception to a rule."

Ārya-satyas: The four noble truths that form the foundation of the philosophy of Buddhism.

Aṟivu: The Malayalam and Tamil word denoting consciousness as the pure and unconditioned Reality as well as any specific knowledge. The philosophical poem by Narayana Guru, laying bare the ultimate Reality conceived by Vedānta as Consciousness in essence, is named *Aṟivu*. The Guru often uses the word as a synonym for *ātmā*.

Asambhava: Contradiction — one of the logical fallacies.

Āsana: Bodily posture; the third stage in the eightfold spiritual discipline according to Yoga.

Asat: The unreal; that which does not exist.

Asatya: the unreal, untruth. That which has phenomenal appearance only, and no substantial existence.

Aṣṭāṅga-yoga: The Yoga discipline, having eight stages, conceived by Patañjali in his *Yoga-Sūtras*.

Āstika-darśanas: Six orthodox schools of thought in India: Nyāya, Vaiśeṣika, Sāṁkhya, Yoga, Pūrva-Mīmāṁsā, Uttara-Mīmāṁsā. These are qualified as *āstika* because they acknowledge the authority of the Vedas. The schools that do not accept the Vedas are known as *nāstika-darśanas* (see).

Asti-bhāti-priya: Existence, functional modes of consciousness, experience of pleasure or pain. The essence of *sat-cit-ānanda* as experienced by an individual.

Ātmā (*Ātman*): The self (from the root *āt*, meaning "to pervade"). The invisible reality or stuff that pervades any visible form. Often confused with *jīva*, the soul.

Used in slightly altered senses according to contexts. The simplest meaning of the word is "I" or "oneself."

Ātmāśraya: Tautology, one of the logical fallacies.

Ātma-jñāna: The knowledge of the self, self-knowledge, to know oneself.

Ātma-vidyā: Self-knowledge; the science of the self.

AUṀ: Pronounced *oṁ*. The most sacred and potential of all words in Indian scriptures. Some consider it even as an object of worship. In Vedic rituals, it is known as *anujñākṣara*, and in the wisdom context of Vedānta it is the verbal symbol representing *Brahman*, the Absolute. One Upaniṣad, namely *Māṇḍūkya*, is solely meant to show how this mono-syllable is so sublime in its meaningfulness.

Āvaraṇa: When a piece of rope is mistaken for a snake, the real (rope) is as if veiled by something and something unreal (snake) is projected on it. The veiling factor is called *āvaraṇa* and the projecting of the unreal is termed *vikṣepa* by Śaṅkara. Narayana Guru calls both together as *āvaraṇa*.

Avidyā: Nescience or ignorance. That because of which the unreal is taken as the real, and the real as the unreal. The root cause of illusions and sufferings.

Avyākṛta: Literally, "that which is not specifically shaped." The gold-substance in an ornament has no specific form; then it is *avyākṛta*. When given a specific shape it is called *vyākṛta*.

Ayathārtha-jñāna: The opposite of *yathārtha-jñāna* (see).

Bāla: Literally "a child." In the wisdom context, the ignorant are often called *bāla*s, because their thinking is not mature.

Bhagavān: The word denoting God, used in the context of devotion (*bhakti*). Literally, one in possession of brilliant qualities (*bhaga*s).

Bhakti: Devotion. Contemplative perception.

Bhāna: Any apparent manifest form of consciousness. Literally, "lustrous appearance."

Bhānāśraya: The basis of *bhāna* (see).

Bhāva: Any transient form the eternal Reality (*sat*) assumes. Without *bhāva, sat* never exists, neither can *bhāva*s be there without *sat* existing.

Bhāvanā: Imagination, conception, thought. A *vāsanā* finding specific apparent form.

Brahmā: The Creator.

Brahman: The Absolute. Derived from the verb root *bṛh*, "to grow constantly." Literally, "that which grows constantly."

Brahmātmaikyam: The oneness of *Brahman* and *ātman* — the ultimate goal of Vedāntic search.

Caitanya: *Cit* in its functional state.

Cidābhāsa: *Cit* (consciousness) in its fallacious appearance (*ābhāsa*); same as *ābhāsa-caitanya* (see).

Cidātmā: (*cit* + *ātmā*) *Ātmā* (the self) pure consciousness in essence.

Cid-vastu: (*cit* + *vastu*): *Cit* means pure unconditioned Consciousness, and *vastu*, substance. The one all-underlying Reality is Consciousness in essence and thus is *cid-vastu.*

Cit: Literally, "consciousness." The essential content of the imperishable Reality pervading all the perishable and visible forms is pure Consciousness. Hence, *Brahman* is designed as *cit*. (See *sat* and *ānanda* also.)

Cittam: The memorizing and recalling faculty of consciousness.

Darśana: Literally, '"vision." The Indian equivalent to "philosophy." Vision of Reality as seen from the point of view of a given system of philosophy. Nyāya, Vaiśeṣika, Sāṁkhya, Yoga, Pūrva-Mīmāṁsā and Uttara-Mīmāṁsā are the six such systems of Indian Philosophy. Narayana Guru, in his *Darśanamālā*, uses this word to mean any particular point of view of the non-dual Reality. He presents ten such visions strung together systematically into a garland.

Darśana-sampradāyas: Schools of philosophy.

Devas: Gods. Inhabitants of Vedic heaven.

Dharma: Derived from the root *dhṛ* "to support." The universal functional system that sustains the world and life. Righteous way of life fully in harmony with the functional system of the universe.

Dhyānam: Meditation. The seventh stage in the *aṣṭāṅga-yoga* (see).

Dṛk: Eye. The viewing person, the knowing personal consciousness.

Dṛśya: That which is visible; the visible, objective world; any object of knowledge.

Dvaita: Duality or dualism. The popular name of Madhva's philosophy. This name is given deridingly to the Madhva system by other schools. He calls his philosophy *tattva-vāda* (the doctrine of the ultimate principle).

Guṇas: Qualities or functional peculiarities inherent in the total nature and in individual beings. They are three: *sattva*, *rajas* and *tamas*.

Hetu: Reason. The middle term is formal logic.

Idantā: This-sense, referring to the sense of objectivity as against subjectivity (*ahantā*) (see).

Indriya-jñāna: Sense perception. Narayana Guru defines it as the knowledge by which "this" and "that" are known.

Iṣṭa-aniṣṭa-udāsīna: Desirable, undesirable, indifferent. The three value senses we feel towards anything we happen to know.

Jagat: The world. Literally, that which is always on the move.

Jagatpatiḥ: The Lord (*patiḥ*) of the world (*jagat*).

Jīva-jñāna: Narayana Guru defines *jīva-jñāna* as the knowledge by which one becomes aware of "I" and "mine."

Jīvan-mukti: Liberation while living.

Jñāna: Wisdom. In the Vedāntic contex, the wisdom of the non-difference of oneself from the universal Reality. The way of *jñāna* (*jñāna-mārga*) is contrasted with that of rituals and actions (*karma-mārga*).

Jñānī (*jñānin*): One who possesses Wisdom.

Jñātā (*jñātṛ*): The knower, thẹ subject as against object (*jñeya*).

Jñāna-yoga: The *yoga* state attained through *jñāna* (see). The state of experiencing one's own oneness with the all-underlying Reality with wisdom (*jñāna*) as a means.

Kāraṇa: Cause. Gold is cause and ornament is the effect. What really exists in all ornament-forms is gold alone. Similarly, what really exists in the world-appearance is *Brahman* alone, which is its cause. This way of thinking is called *sat-kāraṇa-vāda* (theory giving primacy to cause). Indians distinguish two kinds of causes, viz. *upādāna-kāraṇa* (material cause) like clay for pots, and *nimitta-kāraṇa* (efficient cause) like the potter and his tools.

Kāraṇa-bhāna: Specially used by Narayana Guru to denote that specific mode of consciousness at deep-sleep in which one is ignorant of everything.

Kāraṇa-brahman: *Brahman* or the Absolute understood as the causal substance for everything apparent. Also known as *nirguṇa-Brahman* and *para-Brahman.*

Karma: All actions in general. Philosophically, the creative urge inherent in the imperishable Reality, causing the emergence of all manifest forms from Itself. In the Vedic context, the ritual of burnt-sacrifices enjoined by the Vedas. As a religious belief of the Hindus, the incipient memory factors clinging to the souls as a residue of their past deeds. All are bound to enjoy or suffer the fruits of their deeds, and will have to reincarnate for this purpose. One might be accumulating more *karma*s in the new birth. This vicious chain of *karma*s goes on till one attains final release. Such *karma*s are divided into three categories — *sañcita karma*s (the actions accumulated in all the previous births), *āgāmī karma*s (fresh actions done in the present lifetime) and *prārabdha karma*s (actions already initiated but eating of its fruits is not finished with).

Karma-vāsanā: The propensities in an individual as a result of the *karma*s inherent in one (see *karma*s).

Karma-yoga: The *yoga* of action. Realizing one's oneness with the total existence by performing deeds with the awareness that all actions belong to total nature, not to any individual being.

Karma-yogin: One who lives with the perception of sublimating all one's actions as *karma-yoga* (see).

Kartṛtva: The state of being the doer of actions.

Kārya: Effect. Clay is cause and pot an effect.

Kārya-Brahman: Brahman or the Absolute perceived in the form all effects, having apparent specific forms. Also called *saguṇa-Brahman* and *apara-Brahman.*

Khyāti-vāda: The explanation given by different schools of Indian thought for illusory appearance.

Kośa: Sheath. In the Śāṅkara School of Vedānta, the five sheaths that supposedly overcovers *ātmā* making it imperceptible. *Annamaya* (of the essence of food), *prāṇamaya* (of the essence of vital breaths), *manomaya* (of the essence of mind), *vijñānamaya* (of the essence of the knowledge) and *ānandamaya* (of the essence of the happiness) are the five such sheaths. Pealing these sheaths one by one makes the *ātmā* within visible.

Karma-sṛṣṭi-vāda: The theory that the creation of the world happened as a gradual process of unfoldment. For example, according to the *Taittirīya Upaniṣad,* in the beginning there was the Self (*ātmā*); from this Self space came into being; from space air came into being; from air, fire; from fire, water; from water, the earth; from the earth, herbs; from herbs, food; from food, man.

Kūṭastha: Fully stable like a rock. Referring to *Brahman* or *Ātman.*

Laya: Dissolution; final dissolution on of the world; complete absorption of the mind.

Loka: The world. Literally, "that which is perceptible."

*Mahā-vākya*s: The great dicta that concisely state the essential teaching of Vedānta.

Mamatā: The "mine-sense" one feels towards anything one likes.

Manas: Mind. That which is constituted of *manas* is called *manomaya. Manas* consists of the questioning and imagining faculties of consciousness.

Mānasa-pratyakṣa: Mental perception.

Manonirodham: Restraining the mind.

Māyā: The mysterious urge inherent in the Absolute (*Brahman* or *ātman*) to unfold itself as all the worlds and the phenomenon of life. The very appearing of the world caused thus ends up in becoming a sort of veil put over the Absolute, hiding its vision from our view and making the illusory that the apparent world is the real.

Māyāvin: The wielder of *māyā*, an epithet of God.

Mudrās: Names of certain positions of fingers and the like, practised in worship and *yoga*.

Nāma: Name. *Nāma* along with *rūpa* (form) distinguishes every individual entity in this world.

Nāstika-darśanas: The six heterodox schools of Indian thought — Cārvāka, Jaina, the four schools of Buddhism (Sautrāntika, Yogācāra, Vaibhāṣika, Mādhyamika). These schools are considered heterodox just because they do not recognize the Vedas as authoritative.

Nimitta-kāraṇa: Efficient cause.

Nirguṇa-Brahman: *Brahman* understood as having no qualities. (See *kāraṇa-Brahman*.)

Nirupādhika-jñāna: Unconditioned knowledge. Knowledge not conditioned by subject and object. Knowledge so conditioned is called *sopādhika-jñāna* (see).

Nirvāṇa: Literally, "burning out" as of fire. The Buddhist term for final extinction of the individual being. Narayana Guru uses the word in the *Darśanamālā* to cover all kinds of goals of spiritual enquiry.

Nivṛtti-mārga: The way of withdrawal, followed by those who are interested in wisdom. (See *pravṛtti-mārga*.)

Niyama: Self-restraint. The second of the eight principal steps for final attainment according to the Yoga school. It consists of cleanliness (*śauca*), contentment (*santoṣa*), austerity (*tapas*), self-learning (*syādhyāya*) and meditation on God (*Īśvara pranidhāna*).

Oṁ tat sat: Auṁ — That alone exists.

Pañca-bhūtas: The five (*pañca*) basic elements (*bhūtas*) that constitute the world — space (*ākāśa*), air (*vāyu*), fire (*agni* or *tejas*), water (*ap*) and earth (*pṛthvī*).

Pañcendriyas: The five sense-organs.

Parā: Beyond; pertaining to the ultimate or supreme as opposed to the immanent here and now aspect of reality which is *aparā*. It could mean the transcendental.

Para-Brahman: The higher *Brahman*. Śaṅkara conceives of two aspects of *Brahman*. The lower *Brahman* (*apara-Brahman*) is the ultimate Reality having the form of the world for its attributes. The higher *Brahman* is attributeless, and hence is inconceivable. Also called *kāraṇa-Brahman* (see).

Paramātmā: The Supreme or Transcendental Self.

Parameśvara: The supreme (*param*) controller (*īśvara*). The ultimate Reality theologically conceived.

Parā-vidyā: Transcendental knowledge. The supreme wisdom represented by the Upaniṣads.

Pariṇāma: Evolution.

Pariṇāma-vāda: Theory of evolution. The theory that the world emerged as a result of evolution. The same as *karma-sṛṣṭi-vāda* (see).

Parokṣa-jñāna: Indirect knowledge, knowledge we gain other than through direct perception.

Pradhāna: That aspect of *māyā*, according to Narayana Guru, because of which the potential for the unfoldment of the world is contained in *Brahman*, just as a tree in a seed.

Prajñā: Consciousness.

Prājña: Name of the consciousness at the sleeping state.

Prakṛti: Nature. Literally, "that which is always in an active state." This activeness is inherent in the ultimate Reality or *Brahman*. *Brahman* in its active state is called *prakṛti*.

Pramāṇas: Any valid means of certitude (*pramā*). Six of them are recognized by Vedāntins, and their validity is only in worldly knowledge. They are *pratyakṣa* (perception), *anumāna* (inference), *upamāna* (analogy), *śabda* or *śruti* (scriptural testimony), *arthāpatti* (presumption), and *anupalabdhi* (non-apprehension).

Prapatti: The form of devotion, in which one surrenders oneself fully to the will of God.

Prasthāna-trayī: The three basic source books of Vedānta, namely, the Upaniṣads, *Bhagavad-Gītā* and *Brahma-Sūtras*.

Pratijñā: The statement of the proposition to be proved; the first member of the five-membered Indian syllogism.

Pratibhāsa: Phenomenal appearance.

Pratīti: Clear and distinct knowledge. In Vedānta, the term means illusory appearance.

Pratyakṣa-jñāna: Perceptual knowledge.

Purāṇas: Literally, "the ancient." The collection of legends of antiquity, meant mainly for teaching the common man the philosophy of the Upaniṣads with the help of numerous tales.

Puruṣa: Literally, "person." The word is used both in universal and particular senses. In the universal sense, He is the cosmic person who has the entire cosmos for His body. In this sense, He is often called *virāṭ-puruṣa.*

Rāga: Passionate affection one feels towards pleasurable objects.

Rūpa: Form, along with *nāma* (name), distinguishes every individual entity in this world. Hence the world is often spoken of as constituted of *nāma*s and *rūpa*s.

Śabda: Literally, any sound or word. In the philosophical context, and scriptural utterance, one of the *pramāṇa*s (see). The only means that leads to transcendental knowledge. Also called *āgama* and *śruti.*

Saccidānanda (*sat* + *cit* + *ānanda*): Existence-Consciousness-Value experience, the only positive definition of *Brahman.* (See *sat*, *cit* and *ānanda.*)

*Ṣaḍ-bhāva*s: The six (*ṣaḍ*) stage in the life of a being, namely, *asti* (existence), *janma* (birth), *vṛddhi* (growth), *pariṇāma* (evolution), *apakṣaya* (degeneration) and *vināśa* (destruction).

*Ṣaḍ-darśana*s: The six schools of Indian philosophy, namely, Nyāya, Vaiśeṣika, Sāṁkhya, Yoga, Pūrva-Mīmāṁsā, Uttara-Mīmāṁsā.

Sādhanā: Spiritual discipline undergone for the attainment of a particular goal (*sidhhi*).

Sādhya: That which is possible. The goal to be attained through some *sādhanā* (see).

Sad-vastu: The existential substance.

Saguṇa-Brahman: *Brahman* or the Absolute conceived as having qualities (*guṇa*s), the same as *kārya-Brahman* and *apara-Brahman* (see).

Sākṣin (*sākṣī*): Witness; witnessing consciousness.

Śakti: Literally vital power. The consort of Śiva. She is the daughter of the Himalayas and is also a huntress, and known under various aspects in mythology and iconography.

Sama: One of the two modes of the knowing function human consciousness, in which one Reality alone is perceived in all multiple apparent forms against *anyā* (see).

Samādhi: Finding one's own proper (*samyak*) abode (*ādhi*) and becoming stabilized in it.

Samāna-adhikaraṇa: The common (*samāna*) substratum, (*adhikaraṇa*). *Ātmā* is the one substratum that underlies all the appearances, both subjective and objective.

Sāmānya: The generic.

Saṁkalpa: Mind's wilful imagining. Positively-oriented wilful function of mind, as against *vikalpa* (see).

Saṅga: The attachment one feels towards pleasurable objects.

Sarjana: The emergence of new forms from some already existing substance.

Śarīra: Literally, "that which perishes." The physical body or the visible and perishable aspects of existence.

Sat: That which exists always. The subsisting Reality in all the transitory forms of the visible world, even as gold is the subsisting reality in all ornaments. *Brahman,* as this subsisting Reality, is designated as *sat.* (See *ānanda* and *cit* also.)

Sat-kāraṇa-vāda: The theory that cause alone is Real and all effects are superimpositions projected on to *sat,* and thus unreal. This is the theory of Śāṅkara.

Siddhi: Unworldly attainments; attainment of one's final goal.

Śiva: Literally, "the auspicious." The ancient hero-god of prehistorical times, associated with radical virility and renunciation. He is an unconventional god like Dionysius, wearing skins and dancing in ecstasy, drunk with cosmic consciousness. He is the most ancient and the most important figure of the Indian Pantheon, and occupies his seat in Banaras in the plains, and Kailāsa in the Himalayas.

Śivaliṅga: The phallus symbol signifying Śiva.

Sopādhika-jñāna: Knowledge conditioned by subject-object duality, as against *nirupādhika-jñāna* (see).

Śruti: That which is heared. Another name of *śabda* (see) as a valid means of knowledge (*pramāṇa*) (see).

Sthūla: That which is gross.

Sthūla-bhāna: The concretized manifestation of consciousness, the Reality, resulting in the experience of the gross (*sthūla*) world.

Sūkṣma-bhāna: That functional mode of consciousness because of which the subtle factors such as mind and sense-organs, their objects and vital functions, emerge.

Śūnya: Empty; empty of content; vacuum.

Śūnya-vāda: Nihilism of Buddhism.

Taijasa: Name of the state of consciousness in the dreaming state.

Tanmātra: From *tat* (that) and *mātra* (mere). The thing in itself.

Tat-tvam-asi: That thou art, one of the *mahā-vākya*s (see).

Tattva: The state of "that" pure and simple; basic principle; basic Reality.

Triguṇas: The triple modalities of nature, originally conceived by Kapila in the *Sāṁkhya-Pravacana-Sūtras*: *sattva* (pure), *rajas* (active), *tamas* (dark-inert).

Tripuṭi: The factors involved in the event of knowing something, namely, the knower, the known and the act of knowing. Literally, the three-petalled one.

Turīya: Literally, the fourth. The transcendental state of consciousness in which the *tripuṭi* (see) merges in the all engulfing Self-radiance. Narayana Guru defines it as, "to know that which is bottomless and topless, from top to bottom."

Upādāna-kāraṇa: Material cause.

Upādhi: Conditioning factors that make the indistinct Reality appear in distinct forms, or indistinct consciousness appears as distinct knowledges.

Upamiti-jñāna: Knowledge acquired through inference.

Upāsanā: Literally, "to sit at the side of something, particularly a deity, as a mark of submission and respect." This could attain sublimity as meditative adoration.

Vairāgya: Sense of detachment towards everything transient and of no intrinsic value.

Vaiśvānara: The name given to the state of the individuated self, in which one is conscious of the external objects in the waking state. Literally, "the universal man."

Vāsanā: Incipient memory factors or propensities that are inborn in individuals. Such unconscious factors decide to a great extent how one behaves in life.

Vedānta: Literally, the end (*anta*) of knowledge (*veda*). When the Vedic teachings had been revalued in philosophical terms by later *ṛṣis* (sages), a body of literature called

"Vedānta" arose in the history of Indian thought. These often go contrary to the Vedic tendencies of rituals and obligations, announcing freedom and stressing Self-realization. Later came Śaṅkara, Rāmānuja and Madhva, referred to as three typical Vedāntic philosophers, who expounded its teachings, although the *gurus* of the Vedāntic line (*paramparā*) are many.

Vidyā: Science or knowledge. That function of consciousness because of which one understands the Real as the real and unreal as the unreal.

Vikalpa: The opposite of *saṁkalpa*. It denotes many mental functions such as variant imagination (*vibhinna-kalpanā*), various imaginations (*vividha-kalpanā*), attributing proximity (*saṁsargāropaḥ*) arriving at a conclusion taking to account only one side of the context (*pakṣataḥ-prāpti*). *Vikalpa* could be of two kinds: that occurs unwillingly (*vyavasthitam*) and that happens opted by oneself or someone else (*aicchikam*). Eight different possibilities of *vikalpa* misleading us have been distinguished, the reason why the wise ones always forewarn us that *vikalpa* causes suffering.

Vikr̥tis: Anything that evolves from *prakr̥ti*.

Vikṣepa: See *āvaraṇa*.

Virāṭ-puruṣa: See *puruṣa*.

Viṣaya: Any object of knowledge.

Viṣaya-caitanyas: Consciousness transformed into the form of the object to be known.

Viṣaya-jñāna: Objective knowledge.

Viśva-vīrya: Cosmic creative urge. Equivalent to the *elan vital*.

Vivarta-vāda: The theory that what seems to be creation is only the appearance of forms, effecting no intrinsic change in the causal Reality, the one Pure Consciousness or *Brahman*. Creations thus are mere illusory appearances.

Vyākṛta: Reality having assumed a specific form (see *avyākṛta*).

Vyatireka: Stating the negative reason for an inference, e.g. there will be no smoke where there is no fire. An inference becomes fully valid only when both *anvaya* (see) and *vyatireka* conditions agree.

Yama: To restrain. The first step of the spiritual practice according to Patañjali's Yoga system; it consists of *ahiṁsā* (non-hurting), *satyam* (speaking truth), *asteya* (not stealing), *brahmacarya* (continence), *aparigraha* (non-acquisitiveness), all body-based disciplines.

Yathārtha-jñāna: Knowing things as they really are, as when a piece of rope is seen really as rope. This kind of knowledge, in traditional Vedānta, is known as *paramārtha-jñāna.*

Yoga: (From the root *yuj*). Each finding one's inseparable oneness with the one causal Reality, just as an ornament finds its oneness with gold. As a contemplative method of self-enquiry, the way of expressing an inexpressible reality by pointing out its two opposite sides and leaving the unitive meaning to be understood by the reader or seeker on his own. For example, attaining immortality and crossing over death are two expressions meaning the same. But these two expressions are opposite in nature. They have in between them a meaning that cannot be expressed as it is. Different systems of *yoga* have been developed in India, each giving emphasis to some particular pair conjoined. Patañjali's system is known also as *Rāja-*

yoga. *Haṭha-yoga*, *Jñāna-yoga*, *Bhakti-yoga*, *Mantra-yoga*, *Kuṇḍalinī-yoga*, are some other popular *yoga* systems. Each of the eighteen chapters of the *Bhagavad-Gītā* is also named a *yoga*. The *Bhagavad-Gītā* itself claims to be a *Yoga-Śāstra* (a textbook the science of *yoga*).

Yogī (*Yogin*): One who is an adept in *yoga*.

Yugapat-sṛṣṭi: Instantaneous creation. The concept that the world is created instantaneously, as when the world appears to be when one wakes up from deep sleep.

Index